Democracy in Times of Crises

Emmanouil M.L. Economou •
Nicholas C. Kyriazis • Athanasios Platias
Editors

Democracy in Times of Crises

Challenges, Problems and Policy Proposals

 Springer

Editors
Emmanouil M.L. Economou
Department of Economics
University of Thessaly
Volos, Greece

Nicholas C. Kyriazis
Department of Economics
University of Thessaly
Volos, Greece

Athanasios Platias
Department of International
and European Studies
University of Piraeus
Piraeus, Greece

ISBN 978-3-030-97297-4   ISBN 978-3-030-97295-0 (eBook)
https://doi.org/10.1007/978-3-030-97295-0

© The Editor(s) (if applicable) and The Author(s), under exclusive license to Springer Nature Switzerland AG 2022

This work is subject to copyright. All rights are solely and exclusively licensed by the Publisher, whether the whole or part of the material is concerned, specifically the rights of translation, reprinting, reuse of illustrations, recitation, broadcasting, reproduction on microfilms or in any other physical way, and transmission or information storage and retrieval, electronic adaptation, computer software, or by similar or dissimilar methodology now known or hereafter developed.

The use of general descriptive names, registered names, trademarks, service marks, etc. in this publication does not imply, even in the absence of a specific statement, that such names are exempt from the relevant protective laws and regulations and therefore free for general use.

The publisher, the authors and the editors are safe to assume that the advice and information in this book are believed to be true and accurate at the date of publication. Neither the publisher nor the authors or the editors give a warranty, expressed or implied, with respect to the material contained herein or for any errors or omissions that may have been made. The publisher remains neutral with regard to jurisdictional claims in published maps and institutional affiliations.

This Springer imprint is published by the registered company Springer Nature Switzerland AG
The registered company address is: Gewerbestrasse 11, 6330 Cham, Switzerland

*To the freedom fighters of the
Battle of Salamis, who fought and died
for the salvation of Hellas and the
savior of democracy
And to all those who have fought or died
throughout the world over time, for
freedom, justice, and democracy.*

Acknowledgments

We would like to begin by thanking H.E. the President of the Hellenic Republic Mrs. Katerina Sakellaropoulou. The conference was held under her auspices.

We feel the need to express further our many thanks to those who contributed to the success of our *Salamis and Democracy: 2500 Years After* conference, a direct product of which is the book in hand.

We wish to thank all of our conference participants for providing us with their splendid speeches and papers, as well as the rest of the members of our Organizing Committee, our colleague Professor Dr. Michail Pikramenos (Vice President at the Greek Council of State and Aristotle University of Thessaloniki), and Zafeirios Rossidis, Media Counselor, who is also currently the Head of Public Diplomacy Office at the Permanent Mission of Greece at the United Nations in Geneva.

Our many thanks should be also given to Guy Feaux de la Croix (former Ambassador of Germany in Greece) for his encouragement.

The conference was organized in cooperation with five institutions: (1) the Department of International and European Studies at the University of Piraeus, (2) the Department of Economics at the University of Thessaly, (3) the Delphi Economic Forum, (4) the Council for International Relations-Greece, and (5) the Kostas and Artemis Kyriazis Foundation. We are grateful to all these institutions.

We also need to thank Professor Aggelos Kotios (Rector, University of Piraeus) and Professor Christos Kollias (Dean, University of Thessaly) for their inspiring inaugural speeches. We also wish to thank our chairpersons, who provided us with superb coordinative assistance in each of the conference's sessions. These included Professors Constantine Arvanitopoulos (Tufts University), Eirini Cheila (University of Piraeus), Christos Hadjiemmanuil (University of Piraeus), Charalampos Papasotiriou (Panteion University), Ioannis A. Tassopoulos (University of Athens), Aristotle Tziampiris (University of Piraeus), and Associate Professor Dr. Konstantina Botsiou (University of Peloponnese).

Special thanks should also be given to Symeon G. Tsomokos, Founder and President of the Delphi Economic Forum (Greece), who provided us with technical assistance and support so as to efficiently conduct the conference through online means.

Our thanks also go to the Tsakos Group of companies for providing to our conference a grant that covered the running expenses of the event.

We also wish to sincerely thank our colleagues Manfred J. Holler (University of Hamburg), Christopher Achen (Princeton University), and Paul Cartledge (Cambridge University) for their assistance during our contacts with the publishers concerning the publication of both books.

We also wish to thank our colleague Professor Emeritus Dr. George C. Bitros (Athens University of Economics and Business) for his continued encouragement and advice on various organizational and academic issues regarding the preparation and successful outcome of the conference and this book.

We also wish to thank Elias Kastritis for his editorial assistance with this chapter and Maria-Alexia Platia for her contribution regarding the design illustration on the cover of the two books.

Our final thanks go to our editors at Springer, Niko Chtouris and Dr. Johannes Glaeser and Harini Devi, as well as their colleagues Yvonne Schwark-Reiber and Parthiban Gujilan Kannan, who all handled the publication and ensured the high quality of both collective volumes that are related to the *Salamis and Democracy: 2500 Years After* conference. They provided us with superb coordinative and editorial services.

Volos, Greece	Emmanouil M.L. Economou
Volos, Greece	Nicholas C. Kyriazis
Piraeus, Greece	Athanasios Platias
December 31, 2021	

Contents

Introduction: Democracy in Times of Crises 1
Emmanouil M. L. Economou, Nicholas C. Kyriazis, and Athanasios Platias

Part I Challenges, Crises and Threats to Democracy

The Crisis of Democracy: A Self-Inflicted Wound 21
Christopher H. Achen

Democracy Erodes from the Top: Public Opinion and Democratic "Backsliding" in Europe 41
Larry M. Bartels

Part II Defining the Limits of Democratic Governance

On the Limits of Democracy 71
Geoffrey M. Hodgson

The Battle of Salamis and the Future of Democracy 93
George C. Bitros

Part III Policies Towards Improving the Quality of Democratic Governance

Policy Making by Randomly Selected Citizens: The Perspective of Elected Politicians 117
George Tridimas

Legislature by Lot: A Way Out of the Problems of Modern Democracy or Just Another Unrealistic Approach? 137
Spyridon Vlachopoulos

Asymmetric Information, Social Choices, and Democracy 147
Emmanouil M. L. Economou and Nicholas C. Kyriazis

Part IV Intertemporal Aspects of Democracy Regarding Ancient and Modern Greece and the World

Democracy in Ancient and Modern Times: About the Relevancy of the Ancient Greek Experience for Our Own Societies 165
Guy Féaux de la Croix

Europe in Modern Greece: The Constant Navarino 193
Kevin Featherstone

Part V Modern Aspects of Law in Relation to the Present-Day Democratic Institutions

Democracy and Social Rights 205
Joaquim de Sousa Ribeiro

Public Confidence and the Judiciary in a Democratic Society 213
Michail N. Pikramenos

Index 225

Contributors

Christopher H. Achen Department of Politics, Princeton University, Princeton, NJ, USA

Larry M. Bartels Department of Political Science, Vanderbilt University, Nashville, TN, USA

George C. Bitros Athens University of Economics and Business, Athens, Greece

Guy Féaux de la Croix University of Thessaly, Department of Economics, Volos, Greece
Cologne Chamber of Lawyers, Cologne, Germany

Joaquim de Sousa Ribeiro Law Faculty, Court, University of Coimbra, Coimbra, Portugal

Emmanouil M.L. Economou Department of Economics, University of Thessaly, Volos, Greece

Kevin Featherstone Eleftherios Venizelos Professor of Contemporary Greek Studies and Professor of European Politics, London School of Economics and Political Science (LSE), London, UK
Hellenic Observatory, LSE, London, UK

Geoffrey M. Hodgson Institute for International Management, Loughborough University London, London, UK

Nicholas C. Kyriazis Department of Economics, University of Thessaly, Volos, Greece

Michail N. Pikramenos Supreme Administrative Court (Council of State), Thessaloniki, Greece
Law School of Aristotle University of Thessaloniki, Thessaloniki, Greece

Athanasios Platias University of Piraeus, Department of International and European Studies, Piraeus, Greece

George Tridimas Ulster Business School, School of Accounting, Finance and Economics, Newtownabbey, Co, Antrim, UK

Spyridon Vlachopoulos School of Law, National and Kapodistrian University of Athens, Athens, Greece

Introduction: Democracy in Times of Crises

Emmanouil M. L. Economou, Nicholas C. Kyriazis, and Athanasios Platias

Abstract This collective volume comes as a sequel to an international academic conference entitled *Salamis and Democracy: 2500 Years After* that occurred between October 3 and 5, 2020, on the occasion of the 2500th anniversary of the great historical event of the Battle of Salamis which saved Greek culture and the newly founded democratic regimes throughout the Hellenic world during the Classical period (508–323 BCE). According to renowned historians, Salamis changed the course of world history and, especially, that of the West. The Introduction explains the purpose of the book and describes in brief the chapters as provided by well-renowned scholars from around the globe, who discuss various topics that are related to democracy, such as Brexit, Euroscepticism and the rise of populism. The authors further analyze various aspects of democracy, as well as various types of democratic regimes, such as mixed government, direct democracy, and cases of quasi democracies. This discussion is related to the pivotal question of how the quality of democracy today can be improved at the global level.

Keywords Democracy · Democratic regimes · Problems · Crisis · Quality of democracy · Policy proposals

This collective volume comes as a sequel to an international academic conference entitled *Salamis and Democracy: 2500 Years After* that occurred between October 3 and 5, 2020, on the occasion of the 2500th anniversary of the great historical event of the Battle of Salamis, which saved Greek culture and the newly founded democratic regimes throughout the Hellenic world during the Classical period (508–323 BCE). According to renowned historians, Salamis changed the course of world

---

E. M. L. Economou (✉) · N. C. Kyriazis
Department of Economics, University of Thessaly, Volos, Greece
e-mail: emmoikon@uth.gr; nkyr@uth.gr

A. Platias
University of Piraeus, Department of International and European Studies, Piraeus, Greece
e-mail: platias@unipi.gr

© The Author(s), under exclusive license to Springer Nature Switzerland AG 2022
E. M. L. Economou et al. (eds.), *Democracy in Times of Crises*,
https://doi.org/10.1007/978-3-030-97295-0_1

history and, especially, that of the West (Strauss, 2005; Hanson, 2006; Holland, 2007).

The conference took place under the auspices of H.E. the President of the Hellenic Republic Mrs. Katerina Sakellaropoulou. This celebration year also coincides with another important event for Greece (and not only): the Greek Revolution of 1821 and the Greek War of Independence, starting in March 1821, that led to the creation of the modern Greek state and intensified the gradual collapse of the once mighty Ottoman Empire. In fact, the Battle of Salamis should not be considered only as a Greek victory. It should be further considered as a victory and as the heritage of all those citizens, scholars, philosophers, and political thinkers who are inspired by democratic values and the democratic ethos.

But what was of great importance to us, the organizers, was to celebrate this monumental event not only by focusing on analyses that are related to history and classical studies but also to examine and contemplate the messages and values that inspired the victors of the Battle of Salamis and then to determine if these messages could be applied usefully in the modern day, useful for confronting various problems that plague democracies nowadays. We take this approach because the Battle of Salamis is directly related to democracy, in the sense that the decisive role for the Greek victory should be attributed to the mighty Athenian fleet which comprised two-thirds of the Hellenic navy at the time (Thucydides, *Histories* 1.74). The role of the Athenians in securing the Greek victory was instrumental, since the majority of the crews were singularly inspired by the democratic values for which they fought.

Democracy as a political system is related to government by choice. In democracies, citizens choose, through their votes, their government, president, prime minister, and political parties. Citizens go on to express, even if in an incomplete way, their social preferences by choosing a particular political program proposed by one among many other programs of the other political parties. In countries where elements of *direct* or *participatory* democracy are applied, such as in contemporary Switzerland, citizens participate directly in law-making through initiatives and referenda.

In 483 BCE, such a referendum occurred in ancient Athens. At that time, Athens and the Greek city-states faced an existential threat posed by the mighty Persian Empire. King Xerxes planned a renewed invasion of Greece, after the failure of the first one by his father, Darius, who was repulsed by the Athenians and Plataeans at the Battle of Marathon in 490 BCE.

The leading Athenian statesman of that time was Themistocles. He understood clearly that a successful Greek defense again the impending Persian invasion had to consist of two elements: a combination of land and sea power. But Athens and the other Greek city-states did not even possess enough ships to face the Persian fleet, a vast armada manned by the subjected peoples of the Persian Empire such as Phoenicians, Egyptians, and Greeks from the Greek city-states of Asia Minor. Themistocles had to convince the Athenian Assembly of citizens to devote the proceeds of the Laurion silver mines to finance a great shipbuilding program of 100 plus 100 *trireme* warships during two consecutive years instead of (as an alternative proposal) dividing it equally among all citizens, to the amount of 10 drachmae each (equivalent to half a month's wage for a skilled workman).

The Athenians listened to the arguments of both proposals, an early example of listening to the experts before voting, which thereafter became the norm in the Athenian democracy. In the end, they were persuaded by Themistocles and voted for his program, which became what is commonly known now as the Themistocles' Naval Law (Bitros et al., 2020).

After the Greco-Persian Wars (490 and 480/479 BCE), democracy became widespread throughout the known Greek world. Robinson (2003, 2011), based on ancient literary authors and epigraphic evidence, provides a detailed analysis of the multitude of city-states that were subsequently governed by democratic regimes during the Classical period. After the defeat of the Persians, Athens became a leader of a grand alliance of city-states on both sides of the Aegean Sea, known as the Athenian Alliance or as the Delian League (Thucydides, *Histories* 1.96). It is essential to note that Athens was not only the military leader of the Alliance due to its naval supremacy but also the most powerful state in economic and political terms (Kallet-Marx, 1993). Athens "exported" to her allies its model of governance (democracy), its economic system, one based on a prototype version of a free market economy with innovative and sophisticated economic institutions, and its cultural and ethical codes of behavior, norms, and social values. In fact, a network of economic, military, geopolitical, and cultural cooperation was created among Athens and its allies (Economou et al., 2021a, 2021b; Halkos et al., 2021).

Thus, after defeating the Persians and ascending as the savior of Hellas and Europe, Athens gradually became the focal point of
the various cultural developments throughout Greece. The tendencies and tastes that prevailed in Athens significantly influenced the corresponding societies and cultures throughout the rest of the Greek world of the Classical period and after, just like how the American way of life was "extracted" and adopted, to a greater or lesser extent, by the Western allies of the USA during the Cold War and later on. The great tragedians and comedians such as Sophocles, Euripides, Aeschylus, and Aristophanes performed their immortal plays in the Athenian theaters, influencing all of the known Greek world in their respective times, to a greater or lesser extent, just like how Hollywood and the gargantuan American music and entertainment industry spread throughout the world during the Cold War era and even more acutely nowadays.

Furthermore, just like today where the US dollar is the most internationally recognized and accepted form of money, the Athenian *drachma* became the main unit of currency for performing international transactions due to its purity regarding its silver content, which was backed up by the prestige of the mighty Athenian economy.[1]

---

[1] There is a vast recent bibliography in the last 30 years which refutes the older beliefs (of basically Marxist oriented historians such as Finley (1973, 1983)) regarding the primitive character of the ancient Greek economy. By contrast, now we know that the Athenian economy was characterized

During this period, democracy as a construct was not static, instead evolving in its constitutional nature in various ways. The Athenian "constitutional" paradigm was the landmark which inspired democrats throughout the known Greek world. But not every democracy necessarily pursued exactly the same political institutions as those of Athens (Robinson, 2003, 2011). There were also particular variations among the democratic city-states in the same logic as nowadays. For example, today we observe variations between the constitutions of modern Switzerland and Germany, but of course both Switzerland and Germany are democracies. Through the passage of time, democracies further evolved into becoming the first organized federal states in history. A detailed analysis regarding ancient Greek federalism is provided, among others, by J.A.O. Larsen, culminating in his seminal book, *Greek Federal States*, published in 1968. For more recent evidence, one can read, among others, Mackil (2013), the collective volume with the title *Federalism in Greek Antiquity*, edited by Beck and Funke (2015), and Economou et al. (2015), Economou and Kyriazis (2016), and Economou (2020).

Of course, after the Roman conquest and subjugation of Greece, democracy was abolished throughout Europe. It was "re-invented" sometime during the Late Medieval European period, with the case of the Old Swiss Confederacy starting in 1291 and with the cases of certain autonomous cities such as Augsburg in Bavaria, Germany, and Florence in Italy, two cities which were not necessarily unified state entities but which nevertheless began to practice some form of democracy. Other important historical points regarding the re-emergence of democracy include, among others, the *Magna Carta* royal charter of rights issued in 1215; the rise of the maritime commercial states such as England and the United Provinces (Dutch Republic); the *Glorious Revolutions of 1688* which established the English Parliament as the most important regulator of political developments, in collaboration with the British Crown; the American Revolution of 1776; and the French Revolution of 1789, which espoused ideas such as the abolition of slavery, universal suffrage, liberty, toleration, constitutional government, and the separation of church and state. These developments in France inspired further revolts in later centuries, such as the 1917 Russian Revolution.

Approximately 80 years later, the famous *Gettysburg Address* was delivered by US President Abraham Lincoln at the Soldiers' National Cemetery in Gettysburg, Pennsylvania, on the afternoon of November 19, 1863. Numerous scholars such as Stow (2007) have argued that President Lincoln, one of the greatest and most prestigious American Presidents ever, was greatly inspired (2294 years after) by the *Funeral Oration* delivered by Pericles at the end of the first year of the Peloponnesian War (431–404 BCE). In his particular speech, President Lincoln defined the very essence of democratic governance with the famous motto:

---

by free market economic principles, even if of a primitive stage of development. See among others on this, Cohen (1992), Figueira (1998), Amemiya (2007), Ober (2008, 2015), Lyttkens (2013), Bresson (2016), Harris et al. (2016), Economou and Kyriazis (2019), Bitros et al. (2020), Economou (2020), Economou et al. (2021a, 2021b), and Halkos et al. (2021).

Government of the people, by the people, for the people, shall not perish from the earth.

In fact, such a motto captures the very essence of *direct* or *participatory* democracy like the ancient Greek ones, as described in the writings of political philosophers such as Aristotle, Thucydides, and Polybius. The nucleus of this democratic system is found in the power of citizens.

2500 years after the Battle of Salamis, democracy in all of its various forms faces new threats and challenges globally, such as the partial loss of public confidence in democratic institutions, the precarious rise of populism and extremism, and the persistent problem of human rights violations (Aatola, 2021). The intractable crisis of the ongoing COVID-19 pandemic has only amplified these threats.

These current trends have direct relation to the very essence of the main purpose of the successful *Salamis and Democracy: 2500 Years After* conference, the purpose being to collect the proceedings and publish two books as collective volumes, consisting of the papers of our colleagues and participants. One of these books, *Democracy and Salamis: 2500 Years After the Battle that Saved Greece and the Western World*, deals with the historical aspects of the Battle of Salamis. The other book, *Democracy in Times of Crises. Challenges, Problems and Policy Proposals for Today's and Future Societies*, which is the book in hand, discusses various problems and dysfunctions that modern democracies face nowadays. In assembling this latter book, we were inspired by the democratic origins of the Greek naval victory at Salamis, and we sought to publish a collective volume which deals with current problems of democracy, ultimately seeking answers for a brighter future for our modern societies.

In the present volume, the authors examine these problems from various standpoints which do not necessarily coincide. Nevertheless, their arguments and perspectives promote the ongoing discussion on democracy and enrich our theoretical and practical knowledge of it. And more fundamentally, since, as mentioned above, democracy has everything to do with choice, the reader, after considering the contributions of these various experts, will be able to decide for him or herself which viewpoints and arguments are the most convincing.

Part I (Chapters 2 and 3) is titled "Challenges, Crises and Threats to Democracy," and it investigates the core challenges and threats that modern democracy faces. It also considers the importance of mixed government, surveying the various existing forms of democratic governance and focusing in particular on developments within the USA and the EU.

In the first contribution "The Crisis of Democracy and the Importance of Mixed Government," Christopher Achen analyzes Brexit in Europe and the election of Donald Trump in the USA as exemplars of problems facing modern democracies. Taking a somewhat pessimistic view of the median voter's capacity for correct decision-making, he points to the sinister rise of populism, where people vote according to their individual or group identities. Since voters generally lack an understanding of constitutional principles and do not necessarily possess a zealous care for the protection of human rights, one cannot readily rely upon popular opinion and elections to protect those democratic norms against abuses from within.

Analyzing the US electorate, Christopher Achen concludes that both of the mainstream American political parties now use nominating systems that are as badly tilted toward populism as they were once tilted toward party insiders. He then proceeds to a brief presentation of the history of *mixed governments*, followed by a discussion of the new trend toward a "folk theory of democracy" and the results of *initiatives*, *referenda*, and *primaries*, which were often negative. He concludes by arguing in favor of mixed government with broad representation of all groups, separation of powers, and checks and balances.

In "Democracy Erodes from the Top," Larry M. Bartels discusses the issue of a crisis (or not) of faith in democracy within the context of a global wave of populism. His main finding is that the contemporary wisdom pointing to a crisis of democracy in contemporary Europe is strikingly at odds with data from public opinion surveys. He argues that, if there even is such a crisis in some countries, then it is due to the governing elites and not to the citizen's majority. Using data from the *European Social Survey*, he summarizes the broad trends in European public opinion from 2001 to 2019, reflecting the attitudes toward antipathy to immigration, European integration, distrust of political elites, ideological polarization, and dissatisfaction with the workings of democracy.

Bartels finds that popular opinions have actually remained largely unchanged since the turn of the century. In particular, ordinary Europeans became significantly more sanguine about immigration over this period, support for further EU integration was neither particularly low nor declining, and there is little evidence of an increase in extremism and polarization in European politics. He also finds that, while there are certainly "many citizens" who are dissatisfied with the workings of democracy, there is no evidence that European support for democracy as a system of government has weakened over the first two decades of the twenty-first century. He then analyzes political issues in Hungary and Poland, finding that identification with ruling parties was positively related to trust in politicians and parliament. Voters in Hungary and Poland did not choose authoritarians at the ballot box, but rather they chose the only readily available alternatives to an unsatisfactory incumbent government, only to have their votes rather transparently trumped up by the winners, who expanded the powers of the ruling party at the expense of the courts, the media, and other political actors.

As to the question of why there is no widespread opposition in Hungary and Poland, Bartels concludes that according to every one of the available indicators, the quality of life in Hungary under Victor Orban and in Poland under Jarosław Kaczynski has continued to improve. This raises a disturbing but realistic issue, known from at least Roman imperial times (*panem et circenses*, "bread and games") as the prevalence, in the preferences of ordinary citizens, of material prosperity over democratic values such as freedom of speech.

Bartels concludes, somewhat pessimistically too, that when citizens experience peace, security, and prosperity, they will mostly be content to let the people in charge carry on, even toward the erosion of democracy.

Part II of the book (Chapters 4 and 5) is titled "Defining the Limits of Democratic Governance," and it discusses various considerations regarding the limits of democracy. It also examines directly the question of the feasibility (or not) of implementation of direct democracy procedures in decision-making.

This means that Part II presents also the different views of two eminent scholars on whether direct democracy is possible (or not) nowadays, and leaves the reader him or herself to decide on which viewpoints to accept or not.

In "On the Limits of Democracy," Geoffrey M. Hodgson argues that while representative democracy is vital, a direct and participative democracy is not necessarily the panacea that some people uphold. There are dangers in "hyper-democracy" just as there are dangers in anti-democracy. Pushing democracy too far, without due attention to practical details of implementation and possible adverse outcomes, is a danger to democracy itself.

He then outlines some problems, practical and ethical, that may arise out of "hyper-democracy," such as the abuse of minority groups. A further problem of democracy in general and of "hyper-democracy" in particular is the high cost of obtaining information as weighed against its low benefits. For example, as the author argues, citizens' assemblies involve large information costs for participants, which are greater when issues become highly complex. This is followed by a discussion of the literature. Among Hodgson's conclusions is that democracy involves exploitation and testing of what is feasible and desirable in society; but he also concludes that democracy is not a delegatory machine for automatically enacting the popular will.

Hodgson then discusses some aspects of *deliberative* democracy and the participation of workers in decision-making, a kind of democracy that is relatively successful. He then raises several arguments as to why *representative* democracy is vital for the following phenomena: (1) legitimization of government, (2) acceptance of its outcomes, (3) government turnover, (4) incentives for politicians to be responsive to citizens, (5) constraint on bad behavior of government, (6) protection of human rights, (7) toleration of opposition, and (8) development of a civic culture.

According to Hodgson, a major constitutional reform is required in many democratic countries, including the USA and the UK, to ensure that democracy improves and does not regress into an elective dictatorship. Much remains to be done to improve modern democracy, but it must be evidence-based.

In "The Battle of Salamis and the Future of Democracy," George C. Bitros, agreeing with the views of previous authors that US democracy has major flaws, follows a different approach in his analysis. First, he briefly highlights the importance of Salamis, since what triumphed there was Athenian democracy in the mode of self-government, under a *direct* democracy. Then, he poses the pertinent question of what would happen today if a Salamis-like challenge were posed to the USA, such as from a likely adversary like China. Does the US elite apply adequate prudence and accurate foresight in viewing China's rising power, as did Themistocles 3 years before the Battle of Salamis?

The answer depends upon economic factors, such as the risk of ever-growing US deficits and the political dysfunction surrounding them, and directly political factors, such as the quality of democracy at home. Unsound and unprincipled economic policies have led to huge financial deficits, and by analogy, democracy itself has accrued substantial political deficits. For example, well-organized minority and interest groups have captured many institutions of democracy, with the consequence that the latter have stopped catering to the interests of the many.

Bitros further raises and analyzes two core issues that are related to weaknesses in the current democratic system of governance: (i) can citizens delegate their choices over policies in a consistent way during an election, and (ii) can citizens hold politicians accountable for their implementation? The answer to both questions is negative for a variety of reasons. First, a collective ordering of preferences is outright impossible (the well-known Arrow's *Impossibility Theorem*). Second, due to the well-established and well-studied *principal-agent* problem, a politician (the agent of the principal, the people) will give precedence to short-term party and personal interests over the long-term ones of his or her constituents. Third, the *informational asymmetry* problem confers several advantages to political parties because the management of politics through parties simply means management through interest groups. The political parties controlling the government limit political competition.

Further problems of governance arise because governments generally lack the insights and agility of contemporary management science and further lack automatic mechanisms to coordinate information offered across many ministries and state agencies, information that is essential to confronting problems of national importance.

Bitros then proposes novel reforms, but nonetheless inspired by the Athenian institutional setup, via the framework of modern *digital direct* democracy. The advantages of such a reform would be as follows: first, voting by unbundling issues in favor of case-by-case decisions would result in a consistent ordering of the preferences of citizens; second, policies would be implemented promptly and effectively; third, the overall system is more flexible; fourth, the system would be based upon merit and fairness, rather than ideology or cronyism because such a system assured that (a) all qualified and interested citizens had an equal chance of holding public office, (b) factionalism was minimized, since there was no point making promises to win over key supporters, and (c) clientelism in the form of distributing state benefits to particular groups of voters so as to get re-elected was absent; and fifth, the active participation of voters and their reverence for listening to the experts (who they were arguing in the assembly of citizens on certain important issues concerning state policies) would diminish information asymmetries. Lastly, such a system would hold the administration accountable, solving partly the principal-agent problem.

Bitros of course recognizes pragmatically that given today's polarized political climate, one where elite corporate interests exert outsized influence and sometimes outright control on most Western governments, the prospects for implementing any radical changes for the purposes of serving popular interests are very slim. Thus, he emphasizes the necessity of inculcating a democratic ethos into children during their formative years as a means to increase the quality of democracy in the long run.

Part III (Chapters 6–8) is titled "Policies Towards Improving the Quality of Democratic Governance," and it relates directly to Part II since it discusses methods of democratic governance that could be useful to increasing the quality of governance in contemporary democracies.

In his "Policy Making by Randomly Selected Citizens. The Perspective of Elected Politicians," George Tridimas examines recent experiments in decision-making by assemblies of randomly selected citizens. His methodology is inspired by the idea that the deliberation of an assembly that is a miniature of the population increases the fidelity of popular representation and the quality of decision-making *after* hearing the opinion of experts, a decision-making paradigm inspired by the Classical Athenian citizens' Assembly.

A major issue previously given scant scholarly attention is whether elected politicians will accept reforms to allow policy-making by assemblies in the face of having to relinquish their own decision-making powers. The conditions for politicians to accept this change, elaborated upon in a formal model, are as follows: they make a cost-benefit analysis for their own utility, and if the benefits are higher than the costs of an election, then they will be in favor of the change.

George Tridimas proceeds with some historical and modern examples of sortition and continues with a review of the theory. In a properly made model accompanied by mathematical analysis, he presents two alternatives for the policy-makers: elections vs. assemblies. The decision to choose a policy by assemblies instead of by elections for representatives depends upon setting a higher payoff in the case of assemblies. In particular, if the probability and expected payoff of winning the election contest is *smaller* than the probability and expected payoff of his ideal policy implemented by an assembly, plus the expected cost savings from not campaigning, adjusted for the expected loss incurred from the uncertainty about how far the decision of the assembly deviates from his ideal point, then an elected politician may be willing to grant policy-making powers to a randomly drawn assembly of citizens. Tridimas summarizes neatly the different choice combinations in a table display, according to probability ranges for two representative politicians.

In "Legislation by Lot: A Way Out of the Problem of Modern Democracy or Just Another Unrealistic Approach?", Spyridon Vlachopoulos examines the connection between *sortition parliaments* and modern democracy. A sortition parliament is a legislative body the members of which are randomly selected among the citizens by lot, as happened in ancient Greek democracies. This nullifies the privilege of wealth, eloquence, or charisma and does not allow for favoritism.

Vlachopoulos then presents some examples of modern usages of sortition, namely, Ireland in 2012 and in 2017–2018 when citizens were chosen by lot from the electoral register to be members of the Constitutional Convention to draft the new constitution.

He continues with a discussion of the advantages and disadvantages of sortition parliaments. The advantages are manifold: sortition parliaments introduce a new element—randomness—into the state's organization, one which will strengthen the peoples' democratic consciousness. Such systems offer equal opportunity to all citizens of becoming parliamentarians. Furthermore, they increase the diversity and representativeness of the legislative body and are thus more probable to think and act "outside the box," that is, less traditionally, thereby finding new solutions for old problems. Such systems are moreover not limited by political cost considerations; since they have no affiliations to any political parties, they are freer from party allegiance to decide on policy. Sortition also guarantees equality of male and female representation.

The disadvantages of such a system are in turn themselves numerous: most obvious is the lack of accountability in contrast to elected representatives who are accountable to their voters by virtue of being consciously chosen. Additionally, it is quite probable that the sortition parliament would be composed of citizens who do not possess the necessary skills in order to perform their duties. It may actually decrease the interest of the people for political life, since the probability for any given citizen to be selected by lot is nowadays vanishingly small due to the size of the population. Somewhat paradoxically, political parties, by uniting people with the same ideology or interests, strengthen political homogeneity, a feature which is absent in a sortition parliament where political parties do not exist. Sortition parliaments may thus be chaotic, leading to instability of democratic governments and the political system. In a sortition parliament, the will of the people does not truly rule, since membership in it depends solely on luck.

Recognizing these steep disadvantages, Vlachopoulos concludes that we could combine the advantages of traditional representative democracy with "small and gradual" doses of alternative models, for example, with a second legislative body the members of which are chosen by lot and who will have advisory competencies.

In "Asymmetric Information, Social Choices and Democracy," Emmanouil M. L. Economou and Nicholas C. Kyriazis analyze the issue of *asymmetric information* in representative democracy and compare it to ancient direct democracy. Asymmetric information in today's representative democracy leads to fake news, virulent populism, anti-intellectualism, and outright wrong decisions.

The authors discuss the process of determining the common good in a democracy, offering a brief review of the literature. Next, they discuss how the common good was defined under Athenian direct democracy, converged upon by voting separately on each issue but only after listening and being guided by experts. The experts themselves had a strong incentive to offer legitimate and sound advice in order to build public trust and good reputation in their person. Otherwise, they would be discredited and even punished by fines. Economou and Kyriazis analyze the issue (s) of choice and decision-making under direct democracy through the example of Themistocles' Naval Decree of 483/2 BCE, the order that led to the building of the Athenian fleet that fought at Salamis.

They then proceed to present a theoretical model of determining the common good as a social welfare function under a direct democracy. Crucial here is the institutional setup of voting in the assembly, namely, the disaggregation of issues and voting case-by-case. Thus, each voter-citizen revealed his preference case-by-case, listening to the experts, thereby also revealing his personal welfare function. Winning proposals were established for each case through majority voting. Summarily, the integration of the winning choices of each case into a single welfare function reflected the common good as perceived by the majority of citizens.

There are further advantages to *direct democracy*: the social welfare function is "open," in the sense that it can be enriched at any time through the introduction of new proposals. Moreover, in the Athenian case, the discussion of each issue in front of the assembly generated common knowledge which diminished information asymmetry, creating common norms, values, common purpose, and a sense of belonging. Thus, direct democracy transformed taking decisions on various state policies into a coordination and cooperation game.

The authors end by discussing modern forms of democracy, initiatives, referenda, and the *recall* procedure, concluding that direct democracy provides its people with the dignity to decide for themselves on issues that concern them.

Part IV (Chapters 9 and 10) is titled "Intertemporal Aspects of Democracy Regarding Ancient and Modern Greece and the World," and it concerns various issues of democracy that are specifically related to Greece's path throughout history while also addressing more global issues.

In "Democracy in Times Ancient and Modern," Guy Feaux de la Croix writes that Salamis was a victory for freedom, paving the way for democracy to evolve in Classical times. De la Croix directly addresses the question of its relevancy for our own times. He reviews the literature of relevancy studies and builds toward a normative interpretation of Athenian democracy, delivered by analyzing the following core issues:

- How *Greek* is our democratic identity?
- We are not fettered to who we are, but rather who we want to be, and ancient democracy is an inspiration to that ideal.
- As to our democratic origins—why in Greece? De la Croix points to shaping factors such as geography and the related rise of a city-state culture.
- Freedom and democracy, hen and egg. In the beginning arose freedom, which the Greeks discovered. The great achievement of the ancient Greeks was to recognize the intrinsic ethical quality of freedom, building their institutional system directly upon it.
- Freedom and equality, again the proverbial hen and egg. In the historical beginnings of democracy, it is not the freedom of the individual but rather the quest for equality that comes to the fore.

Casting present-day democratic worries in the light of ancient experiences, modern democracies show increasing inequality and a degeneration of formal democracy toward de facto oligarchy. Elites are discredited.

In addition to the above, de la Croix raises the following issues: (i) the lack of political competence of citizens necessary for participation, (ii) a democracy of populism and of group interests rather than one of democratic values, (iii) the effectiveness of democracy in securing a sustainable future for its people, and (iv) quintessential problems that plague modern democracies, such as a lack of strong political education, which could prove to be the Achilles heel of our democracies.

Having understood the supreme importance of proper education for the good functioning of democracy, Athens, a cultural democracy, introduced the *Theorika*, that is, a payment by the state to the poorer citizens in order to enable them to follow the 4-day-long theatrical contests. The challenge facing us today is thus about a culture of democracy grounded in a much broader basis, a basis that should include historical knowledge as well as knowledge of other cultures, and a minimum of ethical convictions.[2]

De la Croix further reviews the safeguards of Classical Athens in defense of its democracy and compares them to modern Germany, finding the latter deficient. He is pessimistic about today's widespread application of digital communication because, in his view, it has proven time and time again to derail the honest and transparent processes of democratic politics. Compared to Athens, modern democracies are awash with scientific and political doubts about their future competence, due to the short-term nature of democratic interest politics.

De la Croix concludes that democracy still has value in itself and that more philosophizing is needed, issuing a serious commandment to think clearly and act virtuously. Truly, if we took at least some of the lessons to be learned from classical experience more seriously, then they might very well help us make our modern world a better place.

In his "Europe in Modern Greece: The Constant Navarino," Kevin Featherstone examines Greece's relationship with Europe in the modern period in order to see what Europe has given Greece. He argues that today's relationships have links that date back to the Battle of Navarino (20 October 1827), the important naval battle of the combined British, French, and Russian fleets against the Ottoman-Egyptian fleet that played a decisive role in Greece's independence after the revolution of 1821.

After 1827 and Greece's independence, Greece had a strongly normative desire to emulate the kind of modernity exemplified by the great European powers of its time, but it was stymied by its strategic incapacity to do so. In an echo of the past, modern Greece defines the EU's incompleteness, the limits of the EU's capacity to act effectively. Featherstone then summarizes the relations between Greece and Britain and France during the Greek Revolution, with an emphasis on the financial loans granted to Greece and the subsequent interference of these two countries in Greece's economic affairs. He concludes that the early loans and the meddling of the two great powers hindered Greece's independent economic development and little was done to foster domestic capacity. Which of these themes does not resonate today is Featherstone's great rhetorical historical question. He then briefly reviews Greece's participation in the EU (2021 being the landmark of 40 years of membership), finding a parallel of Palmerstone's attitude to 1843 Greece with Schauble's 2010 doubts regarding Greece's bailout and ability to repay its debts. Featherstone argues that due to conditions that are particular to Greek society and politics, the liberal-inspired measures imposed by the Troika after 2010 were bound to fail, for example, because Greek state institutions are caught in a social trap. Those in charge create and serve the expectations of key groups of voters.

---

[2] In Ancient Greece and Classical Athens in particular, education was not related only to a technical process of technical knowledge aggregation. It was further related to *paideia*, which consisted of a parallel process of building into the character of youth the required ethos that would enable them to become worthy of themselves and of their fellow citizens. On this Bitros and Karayiannis (2011), Kyriazis and Economou (2015), and Bitros et al. (2020, pp. 113–116).

Thus, the provisions and conditions attached to the rounds of bailouts were often misconceived, and they deepened the Greek recession more than was necessary, ultimately foreclosing the opportunity for more meaningful reforms. If the EU repeats in the future the mistakes of the Greek bailout, then it will face deeper existential challenges that directly confront the EU's values and purposes. And of course, these values and purposes are directly conceived from the overall democratic ethos and principles upon which the EU was formed.

Part V (Chapters 11 and 12) is titled "Modern Aspects of Law in Relation to the Present-Day Democratic Institutions," and it examines various aspects that relate issues of law to democratic governance. In "Democracy and Social Rights," Joaquim de Souza Ribeiro argues that linking democracy and social rights puts together two fields of the constitutional order normally seen as separate and mutually disjointed. But a successful approach to the democratic ideal presupposes that those social rights must be guaranteed.

According to the author, democracy and political equality go hand in hand but cannot be limited to elections. Citizens must be involved in public decisions, thereby enhancing their sense of identity and responsibility, qualities that are essential for the smooth and proper functioning of the democratic system. This level of involvement is further necessary to satisfy the underlying principle of popular sovereignty, a lesson to be drawn from Classical Athens. This again raises the issue of social protection, through guarantees incorporated in the constitution and accepted as established codes of behavior by the state authorities. Some states, like Portugal, enshrine such guarantees in their constitution.

Freedom, linked to the normative idea of dignity, is performed through the exercise of personal autonomy and the free development of individual personality. However, this exercise of freedom presupposes and involves access to goals and opportunities as well as the possession of capacities and the availability of real, material resources for the satisfaction of vital interests.

Democracy needs freedom and freedom needs material conditions. And binding the state to social rights is the most solid and consequential legal-constitutional way of ensuring those rights. Social rights ensure the minimum requirements for active citizenship. Economic inequality inhibits de facto political equality. Thus, social rights must compensate and remove the situations of impoverishment and severe want that violate human dignity, instead giving their holders the feeling that they count as persons that they have value. Feelings of true inclusiveness bring about constitutive belonging and social cohesion as well as reinforce community ties that are favorable to a broader democratization in the economic, social, and political fields.

In "Public Confidence and the Judiciary in a Democratic Society," Michail N. Pikramenos analyzes various aspects of the judicial system in relation to the general public, with a view toward building and strengthening trust and public confidence of citizens toward the judicial system.

He reviews the situation and the involvement of various international bodies in this regard. The judicial group on *Strengthening Judicial Integrity* (Vienna 2000) recognized the need for a code according to which the conduct of judges may be measured. This need resulted in the so-called *Bangalore Principles* of judicial conduct, which established articulated standards for the ethical conduct of judges and was designed to convey clear guidance to judges while providing to the judiciary a framework for regulating judicial conduct. The principles for this conduct are impartiality, integrity, and propriety. These three principles help to reinforce citizens' confidence in the judicial system.

Judges must therefore accept limitations greater in number than those placed upon ordinary citizens, and judges do so freely and of their own choice. Furthermore, adequate public information and education about the scope, roles, and functions of the judiciary can effectively contribute toward an increased understanding of the courts as the cornerstone of democratic institutional systems. The Council of Europe, with its *Plan of Action on Strengthening Judicial Independence and Impartiality*, intends to build real trust in the judiciary throughout the EU by strengthening judicial independence and impartiality.

A fundamentally important issue is freedom of expression and possible limits to criticisms by the press of decisions made by courts. The press has an unofficial yet essential role of holding judges accountable to the people, verifying that judges indeed discharge their duties in conformity with their tasks. Similarly, the National Center for State Courts of the USA conducted public opinion surveys to identify the factor that most directly affects public confidence in the courts. They found that procedural fairness is the most important factor.

Michail N. Pikramenos argues that in order to promote trust, citizens must be properly informed of the nature of the judiciary and that the relation of the social media toward that end is important. A more informed citizenry may be achieved through the introduction of a judicial spokesman and the implementation of a set of press guidelines. The author concludes, however, that trust must be earned and ensured between the citizens of the EU and the system of justice throughout the EU. Trust, after all, is the bedrock of any successful operation, whether it be a private one or one by the state.

References

Aatola, M. (2021). *Democratic vulnerability and autocratic meddling. The "Thucydidean Bring" in regressive geopolitical competition*. Palgrave McMillan.
Amemiya, T. (2007). *Economy and economics in Ancient Greece*. Routledge.
Beck, H., & Funke, P. (2015). *Federalism in Greek antiquity*. Cambridge University Press.
Bitros, G. C., Economou, E. M. L., & Kyriazis, N. C. (2020). *Democracy and money: Lessons for today from Athens in Classical times*. Routledge.
Bitros, G. C., & Karayiannis, A. (2011). Character, knowledge and skills in ancient Greek *paideia*: Some lessons for today's policy makers. *Journal of Economic Asymmetries, 8*, 195–221.
Bresson, A. (2016). *The making of the ancient Greek economy: Institutions, markets, and growth in the city-states*. Princeton University Press.
Cohen, E. E. (1992). *Athenian economy and society: A banking perspective*. Princeton University Press.

Economou, E. M. L. (2020). *The Achaean federation in Ancient Greece. History, political and economic organization, warfare and strategy*. Springer Verlag.
Economou, E. M. L., & Kyriazis, N. (2019). *Democracy and economy: An inseparable relationship since ancient times to today*. Cambridge Scholars Publishing.
Economou, E. M. L., & Kyriazis, N. (2016). The emergence and the development of the Achaean federation. Lessons and institutional proposals for modern societies. *Evolutionary and Institutional Economics Review, 13*, 93–112.
Economou, E. M. L., Kyriazis, N., & Metaxas, T. (2015). The institutional and economic foundations of regional proto-federations. *Economics of Governance, 16*(3), 251–271.
Economou, E. M. L., Kyriazis, N. C., & Kyriazis, N. A. (2021a). Money decentralization under direct democracy procedures. The case of Classical Athens. *Journal of Risk and Financial Management, 14*(1), 30. https://doi.org/10.3390/jrfm14010030
Economou, E. M. L., Kyriazis, N. C., & Kyriazis, N. A. (2021b). Managing financial risk while performing international commercial transactions. Intertemporal lessons from Athens in Classical times. *Journal of Risk and Financial Management, 14*(11), 509. https://doi.org/10.3390/jrfm14110509
Figueira, T. J. (1998). *The power of money. Coinage and politics in the Athenian Empire*. University of Pennsylvania Press.
Finley, M. I. (1973). *The ancient economy*. University of California Press.
Finley, M. I. (1983). *Economy and society in Ancient Greece*. Penguin Non-Classics.
Halkos, G., Kyriazis, N. C., & Economou, E. M. L. (2021). Plato as a game theorist towards an international trade policy. *Journal of Risk and Financial Management, 14*, 115. https://doi.org/10.3390/jrfm14030115
Hanson, V. D. (2006). A stillborn West: Themistocles at Salamis, 480 BC. In P. E. Tetlock, R. N. Lebow, & G. Parker (Eds.), *Unmaking the west: "What if?" scenarios that rewrite world history* (pp. 47–89). University of Michigan.
Harris, E. M., Lewis, D. M., & Woolmer, M. (Eds.). (2016). *The ancient Greek economy: Markets, households and city states*. Cambridge University Press.
Holland, T. (2007). *Persian fire. The first world empire and the battle for the West*. Anchor Books.
Kallet-Marx, L. (1993). *Money, expense and naval power in Thucydides' History 1-5.24*. University of California Press.
Kyriazis, N., & Economou, E. M. L. (2015). Democracy and education: A history from ancient Athens. In J. Backhaus (Ed.), *The university according to Humboldt. History, policy, and future possibilities* (pp. 75–84). Springer Verlag.
Larsen, J. A. O. (1968). *Greek federal states: Their institutions and history*. Clarendon Press.
Lyttkens, C. H. (2013). *Economic analysis of institutional change in Ancient Greece. Politics, taxation and rational behaviour*. Routledge.
Mackil, E. (2013). *Creating a common polity: Religion, economy, and politics in the making of the Greek Koinon*. University of California Press.
Ober, J. (2008). *Democracy and knowledge. Innovation and learning in Classical Athens*. Princeton, Princeton University Press.
Ober, J. (2015). *The rise and the fall of Classical Greece*. Princeton University Press.
Robinson, E. W. (2003). *Ancient Greek democracy: Readings and sources*. Wiley-Blackwell.
Robinson, E. W. (2011). *Democracy beyond Athens: popular government in the Greek classical age*. Cambridge University Press.
Stow, S. (2007). Pericles at Gettysburg and ground zero: Tragedy, patriotism, and public mourning. *American Political Science Review, 101*(2), 195–208.
Strauss, B. (2005). *The Battle of Salamis: The naval encounter that saved Greece-and the Western civilization*. Simon & Schuster.
Thucydides. (1928). *Histories (The Peloponnesian War).*, Engl. Trnsl. C. F. Smith. Loeb Classical Library, Harvard University Press.

Emmanouil M. L. Economou is currently an Adjunct Assistant Professor at the Department of Economics, University of Thessaly (Greece). He is a member of the Laboratory of Economic Policy and Strategic Planning (L.E.P.S.PLAN) at the same. He is also a Member of the Laboratory of Intelligence and Cyber-Security, Department of International and European Studies, University of Piraeus (Greece). His research focuses on Economic History, Institutional Economics, International Political Economy, and Defense Economics. He is an author of eight books (three in English and five in Greek) published in acclaimed publishing houses such as Springer, Routledge, and Cambridge Scholars Publishing.

He has contributed to the international academic bibliography with 38 papers in peer review quality academic journals, such as the *Journal of Institutional Economics* (2); *Defence and Peace Economics* (2); *Sustainability, European Journal of Law and Economics*, and *Journal of Risk and Financial Management* (3); *Peace Economics, Peace Science and Public Policy* (2); *European Journal of Law and Economics, Economics of Governance, Evolutionary and Institutional Economics Review*, and *Homo Oeconomicus*; etc.

He has contributed to the international academic bibliography with 24 papers in English and Greek collective volumes. Furthermore, he has published 79 papers as Discussion Papers (64 in English, in the IDEAS RePec—Munich International Library and 15 as "ΚΟΙΔΑ" Discussion papers published by the Laboratory of Economic Policy and Strategic Planning (ERGOPOLIS) of the Department of Economics, University of Thessaly, in Greek). He has participated in 42 International and Greek conferences.

Nicholas C. Kyriazis combines academic and business experience. He took his diploma and Ph. D. in Economics in Bonn University in Germany in 1979 and has been a visiting Professor at Harvard University with a Fulbright grant and a visiting Professor at Trier University. He is Professor Emeritus at the Department of Economics, University of Thessaly, Greece, where he also served as a Dean during the 2013–2015 period. He has published 14 academic books in English or Greek language, 60 papers in international referred academic journals such as the *European Journal of Law and Economics* and the *Journal of Institutional Economics*, and 26 papers in book chapters (collective volumes).

In 2005, the President of the French Republic honored him with the France's highest decoration, the Knight of the Legion of Honor (*Chevalier de la Legion d' Honneur*), for his contribution to European integration and the preparation for the EMU as a member of the Delors-Moreau committee. He has also published many articles in journals for a wider audience and articles in the Greek press, for economic, political, and defense issues. Previous business positions he held include (among others) Directorate General for Research of the European Parliament, advisor to the government of the National Bank of Greece, advisor to the Minister of Finance, and advisor to the Minister of Defense, and he has contributed as one of the major consultants for the Greek Command, Control, Communications, Computers, and Military intelligence (C4I). He was also secretary of the National School for Public Administration. He is currently a Vice-Chairman of the Quality Assessment Committee of the Legislative Drafting Process of the Hellenic Parliament.

Athanasios Platias is Professor of Strategy at the University of Piraeus. He is also the Chairman of the Department of International and European Studies.

He received a degree in Public Law and Political Science (with excellence) from the Law Faculty of the University of Athens. He also received an M.A. and a Ph.D. degree in International Relations from the Department of Government at Cornell University.

He has been a Ford Foundation Fellow with the Center for Science and International Affairs at Harvard University, a Research Fellow with the Peace Studies Program at Cornell University, and a MacArthur Fellow in International Peace and Security at the Program for Science, Technology, and International Security at MIT and the Center for International Affairs at Harvard University.

Professor Platias held several senior policy advisory positions in various Greek Ministries during the last 35 years. He was also a member of the Supervisory Council of the University of

Piraeus (2012–2017) and Director of the graduate program in International and European studies (2008–2020).

Professor Platias is the author of numerous books and articles. He has written in five principal areas: (i) grand strategy and strategic theory, (ii) geopolitics and geoeconomics, (iii) international security, (iv) theory of international relations, and (v) Greek foreign and defense policy. His most recent books on strategy are *Thucydides on Strategy: Grand Strategies in the Peloponnesian War and Their Relevance Today*; *The Art of War*, an analysis of the ancient Chinese treatise Sun Tzu's Art of War; and the *The Art of Strategy*, an effort to develop a holistic theory on strategy.

Part I
Challenges, Crises and Threats to Democracy

The Crisis of Democracy: A Self-Inflicted Wound

Christopher H. Achen

> But do you want the people to govern?—*a security guard inspecting the author's checked-out books at a university library exit in the summer of 2019.*

Abstract One of the oldest propositions in political science is that a mixed government with checks and balances is superior to the alternatives. Once a commonplace among thoughtful observers, that proposition has come under critical attack in the last century from populists of many kinds, who have wanted to put more power into the hands of citizens to rule directly. As populist thinking has gained currency among theorists and politicians, its adherents in the United States and Britain have increasingly bent governmental structures to their will. The consequences of doing so, long predicted by mixed government theorists, have in fact occurred, resulting in bad policy decisions and bad leaders. Thus in the two oldest democracies, the "crisis of democracy" stems directly from misconceived democratic theories and their embodiment in current laws and institutional rules.

Keywords Trump · Brexit · Populism · Referendums · Primaries · Mixed government

---

C. H. Achen (✉)
Professor Emeritus, Department of Politics, Princeton University, Princeton, NJ, USA
e-mail: achen@Princeton.edu

1 Introduction[1]

In a democracy, citizens face two dangers. The first is that the government will not do what they want. The second is that it will. The second outcome is often the more frightening. The rise of populist governments in Europe and the United States has brought this topic widespread attention.[2]

Some of the concern about a "crisis of democracy" stems from democratic backsliding in relatively new or shallow-rooted democracies such as Hungary, Poland, Romania, and Turkey. Moreover, democratic failures in Latin America and elsewhere are familiar from twentieth-century history, so that the recent electoral authoritarianism of countries like Venezuela, Nicaragua, and the Philippines gets little attention. What have been more disturbing to many observers were the new and dramatic successes of populist forces in two of the oldest and most stable democracies—the 2016 referendum vote in the United Kingdom to exit the European Union, followed by the victory of Donald Trump in the 2016 US presidential election. This paper concentrates on the issues raised by those two events.[3]

David Cameron, the British prime minister at the time, initiated the EU referendum as fulfillment of a campaign promise. He believed that the "remain" vote would win easily and thus silence his within-party critics on the issue (Clarke et al., 2017, p. 2). He misjudged, and "leave" won by just under four percentage points. Difficult negotiations about how to manage the eventual "Brexit" (Britain's withdrawal) dragged on. Economic uncertainty and political dislocations continue as this paper is written.

Trump's presidential campaign may have begun as a kind of advertising stunt for his often-struggling businesses. He used one national television appearance to promote his brand of steaks. Almost no one in the Republican Party took him seriously: No one so politically inexperienced and obviously unqualified had ever been elected president. However, he won most GOP primaries and got the nomination on the first ballot. Even then, only one of the five living former GOP presidential nominees endorsed him, and most Republican intellectuals fled his cause. Some suburban Republican voters defected from the ticket in November, too, though not many. Trump lost the popular vote by just over two percentage points, a gap large enough to ensure defeat in the Electoral College in every American presidential election since 1824. In the end, though, Trump picked up just enough white lower middle-class and working-class voters in Wisconsin, Michigan, and Pennsylvania to

---

[1] I thank Jonathan Prenner, Philip Pettit, and Melissa Lane for their assistance in the preparation of this paper. Helene Landemore, David Froomkin, Steve Macedo, Chuck Beitz, Arlene Saxonhouse, and Larry Bartels read a preliminary draft; their criticisms and suggestions improved the final version considerably. Responsibility for remaining errors remains with me.

[2] Throughout this paper, "populist" and "populism" will refer to people and doctrines favoring direct rule by citizens. Both terms have often embraced a more elaborate set of meanings, depending on the country and the time period (see, e. g., Müller, 2016).

[3] Events along the Danube and to its east also appear to illustrate the thesis of this paper, but for reasons of space and the author's limited expertise, they are omitted from the discussion here.

win all three states by a total margin of fewer than 78,000 votes. That and his other state victories made him president.

How did Brexit and Trump's victory occur? Much has been written about neoliberal economics, the loss of factory jobs, and growing economic inequality. These have been blamed for growing white working class alienation from major political parties and from government generally. Undoubtedly, some of those forces were at work in both Britain and the United States. However, most careful empirical studies have come to quite different conclusions. "Leave" voters and Trump voters were somewhat less educated than average, but not dramatically so, and they were not particularly anxious economically. Economic explanations have fared poorly in statistical tests. What actually mattered were issues of identity, including race and immigration (Hobolt, 2016; Clarke et al., 2017, esp. Chap. 7; Sides et al., 2018, especially Chap. 8; Hooghe & Dassoneville, 2018; Mutz, 2018).

None of this should be a surprise. Observers at least since Graham Wallas (1908) have known that voters have a difficult time sorting out the policy implications of their choices and rarely vote on that basis. Thus, referendums make sense only when the topic poses a straightforward choice that almost anyone can understand. On more complex questions, people will vote their identities, not necessarily in alignment with the relevant policy considerations. One Northern Ireland woman said that her understanding was that "Prods" (Protestants) should vote "leave" and Catholics should vote "remain." Only months later did she understand that her voting rule had been mistaken: "We were not clear what Brexit was about."[4] Stories of that kind proliferate after every important referendum or election.

Thus, holding a referendum on an issue as complex as EU membership was a profound misjudgment. Cameron's decision was particularly distressing in light of his Conservative Party's long-standing devotion to parliamentary supremacy and opposition to plebiscitarianism (Beer, 1966, chap. 1). Indeed, British constitutional principles remain founded on parliamentary supremacy, as Britain's Supreme Court ruled in its review of the Brexit vote. It required that parliament vote to uphold the result of the referendum. Members of parliament did so, though most knew that the decision would have disastrous consequences. The legitimacy of plebiscitarianism in the popular mind was too strong to resist. The voters acted like troubled teenagers bent on self-harm and shouting, "I get to decide about my life." Parliament handed them a knife.

Similarly, the sources of Trump's election were not policy-based. His isolationist and anti-immigrant stance does not imply that the voters had become more enthusiastic about isolationism or less accepting of immigrants, which they have not (Sides et al., 2018, pp. 210–215; for parallel results in the European Union, see Bartels, 2022). Like referendums, elections turn primarily on group loyalties like race, religion, or partisanship, along with the state of the economy; they are not policy or constitutional judgments. Trump primed threats to white identity,

---

[4] https://www.washingtonpost.com/world/europe/could-brexit-bring-new-troubles-to-northern-ire land/2018/11/06/31adbb9e-d7a5-11e8-8384-bcc5492fef49_story.html?utm_term=.5327803a920f.

especially those coming from immigration. Voters with that identity disproportionately backed him (Jardina, 2019). He was their hero and savior.

In the presidential primaries, Trump attracted a passionate following, but he never reached 50% of the Republican primary vote in any state until late in the primary season, when his nomination was assured. By the general election, however, when the opponent was a Democrat, another identity came into play-partisanship. Most Republicans fell into line. Fully 90% of them supported Trump, almost exactly the same fraction that had supported the two previous GOP nominees, Mitt Romney and John McCain (Achen & Bartels, 2017, pp. 338–339). To most voters, Trump was in the end just another Republican candidate, and they voted accordingly. His lack of qualifications for the job, along with his crude violations of political, constitutional, and ethical norms, escaped their notice or made no difference.

Many observers were shocked by the voters' disregard of Trump's threat to democracy. However, it has long been known that the voters generally lack an understanding of constitutional principles and protections for human rights (Graham & Svolik, 2020; McClosky, 1964; Prothro & Grigg, 1960). Thus, one cannot rely on popular opinion and elections to protect those democratic norms against abuse. A wealth of survey research over the past half century has established these points beyond reasonable doubt (see Achen & Bartels, 2017, chap. 2).

The parties themselves have the responsibility to vet candidates for competence and adherence to democratic norms. If they fail to do so, the voters generally cannot grasp the depth of the threat. Demagogues' political parties and ideological fellow travelers often surrender their consciences to the leader, too, as most Republican officials did in the wake of the 2020 presidential election. Only the American judiciary prevented Trump's attempt to override the vote and declare himself the winner.

American parties have substantially abandoned their historic responsibility to help the voters decide in a responsible manner. Party control of nominations has changed dramatically since the early days of the American republic. Since Andrew Jackson's third candidacy in 1832, presidential nominations have been awarded in party nominating conventions (Merriam, 1921). From the early twentieth century through the 1968 presidential election, the delegates to those conventions were chosen by a mix of presidential primaries in a few states and party-controlled state conventions in the others. The system was tilted heavily toward party insiders, so that it relied on their responsiveness to strong popular opinions in years of political upheaval. The year 1968 was such a year, with anti-war candidates Eugene McCarthy and Robert Kennedy sweeping all the primaries, while the incumbent vice president, Hubert Humphrey, stayed out. Favorite son candidates who ran as pro-war Humphrey stand-ins were soundly rejected at the polls. The 1968 Democratic Party convention in Chicago nevertheless nominated Humphrey, while Chicago police beat demonstrators outside the convention hall. Humphrey went on to narrowly lose the general election to his weak Republican opponent, Richard Nixon, who had lost both the 1960 presidential race and the 1962 California gubernatorial election. The imbalanced nomination system, which put too much weight on party insiders and not enough on popular judgment, was exposed as faulty.

In the wake of that electoral disaster, the Democrats established the McGovern-Fraser Commission, named for Senator George McGovern of South Dakota and Representative Donald Fraser of Minnesota. The commission endorsed a series of reforms that made party nominations more dependent on winning primary elections. Subsequent modifications have created the current system, by which nearly all delegates are popularly elected in either primaries or caucuses open to all registered party members and in some states, to independents as well, or even to registered members of the opposing party.[5] (The history is traced in Ranney (1975), Shafer (1983), and Kamarck (2016).) In the wake of the disastrous George McGovern candidacy in 1972 and the failed presidency of Jimmy Carter from 1977 to 1981, the Democrats injected additional experienced judgment into their nominating convention in the form of party officials and elected politicians ("superdelegates"). In practice, however, those insider delegates have simply endorsed the candidate with the delegate plurality from the primaries, whether they agreed with the choice or not.

Republicans have followed suit with a similar set of changes, so that both American parties now use nominating systems that are just as badly tilted toward populism as they were once tilted toward party insiders. Thus, the fact that Republican officials and officeholders overwhelmingly favored anyone but Trump made no difference. He was nominated in spite of being thought incompetent to be president by the vast majority of those who knew him personally or had dealt with him professionally. The voters, judging him only from television, the Internet, and social media, had a different opinion, and their views prevailed. (See Bartels (1988) for an analytically and normatively sophisticated treatment of how momentum and voter uncertainty can combine to create unlikely presidential nominees; Polsby (1983) is a searing critique of the presidential primary process.)

2 Democracy, Demagoguery, and Mixed Government

The irresponsible rhetoric by Donald Trump and by some advocates of "leave" in the British EU campaign is by no means unique to the current era. The 1930s Louisiana governor and senator, Huey Long, was a classic demagogue, as was the red-baiting Joseph McCarthy, the Wisconsin Republican Senator from the early 1950s. American southern racist candidates have a very long history. In Britain, politicians inflaming anti-immigrant sentiments date at least to Enoch Powell in the 1960s. Anti-Catholic rhetoric has an even longer history, and not only in Northern Ireland. In every democracy, demagoguery is a common feature of elections. There are always a good many voters easily taken in. From time to time, they form a majority.

---

[5]Some states do not have party registration, so that their primaries are necessarily open to all registered voters. In those states, a party's nominees may be chosen by voters who oppose that party principles, either by happenstance or by deliberate sabotage.

This feature of popular opinion was well-known to the ancient Greeks (Finley, 1962).[6] Due to the many city states of that period and their frequent changes of governmental form, political thinkers then had far more experience of alternate forms of governance than most moderns. Not spending their entire lives in a single structure, they perhaps had less incentive to apologize for any single alternative and to romanticize its workings. In any event, the political limitations of ordinary people were seen clearly. So were those of kings and aristocrats.

The classic cure for the ills of each sector of the population was to mix their influence. "No part of ancient political theory has had a greater influence on political theory and practice in modern times than the theory of the mixed constitution" (von Fritz, 1954, p. v). Although Aristotle's *Politics* is often cited informally as the standard reference, the idea long predates him (Blythe, 1992, p. 3). Writing in the previous century, Thucydides (VIII, 97, 2) referred to the concept as if it were well-known. Even Plato, best known for his theory in *The Republic* that a specially trained elite should rule, came in his later years to recognize in *The Laws* that, in practice, a mixed system was the best that could be attained (Plato 2016, book 3, pp. 691–693). Aristotle (2013), too, was not entirely consistent. While he endorsed mixed government, he also suggested in other passages of *The Politics* that an enlightened ruler would be best or that rule by the middle class would be the key to stability and moderation. (See Balot, 2015 for detailed discussion.) Polybius (2010), writing in the mid-second century BCE, was perhaps the first to set out a detailed and unqualified case for mixed government.[7]

Classical authors often cited Lycurgus's Sparta as an example of mixed government. Polybius (book 6, 48) regarded Lycurgus's intelligence as "superhuman." Polybius thought that the Roman republic also embodied his mixed-government ideals, and it was that system to which he devoted most of his attention. These and other mixed governments known to the Greeks gave separate offices to different people and groups, perhaps to a king, an aristocracy, or the people. Their powers often seemed to overlap: There was no separation of powers in the modern sense. The point was instead that different orders of society each had power and that power served to counterbalance the characteristic excesses of the other two orders. This was a system that combined two different ideas—pluralist representation and "checks and balances"—though not in the American constitutional sense of achieving limits on each branch of government by separating their powers.[8] The resulting political system was thought more likely to be stable (Blythe, 1992, chap. 1).

---

[6]Lane (2012) argues that the word "demagogue" was used rarely in Greece and did not mean to the Greeks what it does to us. On the dangers of reading modern political notions back into the Greek experience, see Saxonhouse (1996).

[7]Blythe (1992) traces the history of the theory before Polybius was rediscovered in the sixteenth century.

[8]Though often combined in both theory and practice, pluralist representation and checks and balances are distinct notions. The Committee of Public Safety in the wake of the French Revolution had at least some mixture of social class backgrounds among its members, but it functioned essentially without checks during the Terror (Palmer, 1989, chap. 1 and p. 225).

This idea enjoyed remarkable longevity, and it eventually incorporated the notion that mixed government provided, not just stability, but better decisions. In the medieval and early modern era, that argument was advanced in debates by conciliarists over the polity of the Church and then by subsequent generations as a critique of royal absolutism (Blythe, 1992; Sigmund, 1963; Tierney, 1955). Montesquieu ([1748] 1989, book 11, chap. 6) proposed mixed government as his vision of the workings of the British system of his time. His American readers were well informed not only about his work but also about the endorsement of mixed government by his classical predecessors (Richard, 1994). John Adams was a particular devotee of that tradition (Ryerson, 2016, pp. 295–296).

Famously, the Founders in the late eighteenth century wrote a version of Montesquieu's model into the federal constitution, where the presidency, the Senate, and the House of Representatives were meant to be analogs adapted to American conditions of the British king, House of Lords, and House of Commons. Instead of mixing popular views with those of kings and nobility, the American system was meant to combine public opinion as reflected by a directly elected body (the House of Representatives) with indirectly elected officials (the Senate and the president), who were expected to take longer, more statesmanlike views. Popular views, representative but sometimes unwise, were to be balanced by insider judgments, sometimes biased but often better informed. It is this modern version of mixed government that is the focus of this paper. In the contemporary world, kings and nobility are (mostly) gone, but the problem of balancing popular preferences with the judgment of elected officials and political professionals remains very much with us.

The American Founders were well aware of the fractious and incoherent politics of the colony of Rhode Island, where unbridled democracy was having just the effects that the classical theorists had foreseen (e.g., *Federalist* 51 in Hamilton et al., 1961). Thus, the Constitution was strongly republican rather than populist, and it was deliberately designed to make change by narrow majorities difficult. This constitutional structure continues to exert a powerful influence on the workings of American democracy, though, as noted earlier, populist reformers have enjoyed some success in altering the balance. What are the modern sources of their thought?

3 The Progressive Revolt and Its Consequences

Unforeseen by the American Founders, political parties arose quickly after the constitution was adopted. By the end of the nineteenth century, in an era of heavy immigration, political machines run by a political party came to dominate many large cities and to exert powerful influence on the politics of their states. The machines dealt in favors and patronage. They were interested in winning elections, not in battling large businesses, whose accommodation and largess they often sought. They also had no interest in scrupulous adherence to the law. They typically favored the poor and the immigrants; the middle class were often locked out (Banfield, 1961; Banfield & Wilson, 1966, chap. 9; Rakove, 1979; Trounstine,

2009; Golway, 2014). The machines' lawlessness and corruption gave their enemies powerful talking points.

Middle-class reformers sought institutional reforms that would reduce the power of machines. Under the banner of the Progressive movement, they promoted a variety of anti-party tools, including the use of primaries for selecting candidates and of initiatives and referendums at the state level. In these efforts, Progressives had the conceptual support of the liberal tradition, in which sovereignty resides with the people, whom the Progressives conceived of as open-minded, unprejudiced, thoughtful observers of politics. Citizens might fail in their judgments occasionally, but with enough information and deliberation, they were likely to come to sound judgments most of the time. "Without such assumptions the entire movement for such reforms as the initiative, the referendum, and recall is unintelligible" (Hofstadter, 1955, p. 261).

Idealization of ordinary people is long dead among empirical researchers and even longer among practical politicians, who deal regularly with actual voters. However, it persists in much political theorizing, where the political behavior of the highly educated and engaged is too often taken as representative:

> Isn't it possible that in a different institutionalization of the democratic ideal, citizens could be as informed, rational, engaged, and generous with their time as they can be when they shop smartly, contribute to Wikipedia, participate in citizens' assemblies or deliberative polls, or spend hours marching against a president they do not like? (Landemore, 2020, p. 45)

Alas, as empirical research has repeatedly demonstrated, the vast majority of people spend almost no time on civic activities like these, and they have successfully resisted a long list of "different institutionalizations" and exhortations meant to change them. (Recent treatments include Hibbing & Theiss-Morse, 2002 for the United States; Whiteley, 2012 for Britain). In the many states influenced by the Progressives, however, the honorific self-image of the educated middle class won out, so that now, much everyday American political commentary is based on the "folk theory of democracy," the Progressive view that Hofstadter skewered more than half a century ago (Achen & Bartels, 2017, chap. 2).

Ordinary citizens do have the advantage, relative to party elites, that, for good or ill, they are representative of the population at large. To the Progressives, that consideration dominated all others. It seemed to follow that having the voters make political decisions themselves was "more democratic." With time, that view has become embodied in American political culture and practice. In consequence, initiatives and referendums play an important role in many states, and primaries have been adopted almost universally. The next two sections take up these two Progressive reforms in turn.

4 Initiatives and Referendums

In about half of American states, disproportionately those in the western United States, citizens can gather signatures and put a proposition on the ballot to be voted up or down by the population, with no intervention by politicians ("initiatives"). Most of those states permit citizen-initiated constitutional amendments as well, although only California and a handful of others are foolish enough to make the process relatively easy. Legislatures can also lay propositions before the voters ("referendums").

Initiatives and referendums are said to be more democratic than legislative enactments because a representative group of citizens decides them. But here again, the theory is distant from the reality. Even the voters who get to the polls, already an unrepresentative group, routinely ignore the propositions on the ballot. In the United States, this "roll off" effect often means that a third or more of those who cast a ballot simply ignore the referendums (Achen & Bartels, 2017, pp. 69–73). Hence, intense, narrowly self-interested, or prejudiced minorities can sometimes determine the outcome.[9] Dreamy invocations of "the people" in referendums often bear little resemblance to the facts.

Worse yet, interest groups have learned to master these processes, since it frequently lets them bamboozle the population without having to deal with experienced legislators whom they cannot fool. Those with substantial bankrolls play an outsized role. The result is a great deal of bad policy. (Broder, 2000 gives a brief overview; the literature is enormous.) Half a century ago, in 1964 in California, for example, the realtors association used the initiative to repeal a fair housing (anti-racial discrimination) ordinance passed by the legislature. This well-known early example has been followed by a lengthy string of victories-by-initiative for prejudice against racial, ethnic, and sexual orientation groups. The list would be even longer if national initiatives were constitutionally permissible. Thus far, however, proposals to amend the US national constitution to permit initiatives and referendums have gone nowhere.

5 Primaries

The Progressives also favored popular control of party nominations. Though this policy took longer to be fully adopted than did initiatives and referendums, it, too, is now standard in American politics, so that with rare exceptions, the only way to become a party nominee at any level of government is to win a primary. Again, the argument is that choosing nominees by popular election is "more democratic" than

---

[9] Echoing John Stuart Mill's (1861, chap. 3) claim about the benefits of political participation, Smith and Tolbert (2004) argued that the initiative process itself helps educate the voters. Dyck and Lascher (2019) show that the evidence for such an effect is mixed at best.

having them chosen by the parties ("party bosses"), who are unrepresentative of the people as a whole.

The theoretical advantage of primaries in achieving equal representation routinely disappears in practice, even when the presidency is the office at stake. In passionate political years like 2016 and 2020, few American primaries reached 40% turnout, and most fell considerably lower. Presidential caucuses, which may require several hours of the voters' time, fared even worse, with turnouts generally below 10%. The 2016 North Dakota caucus had a turnout of less than 1% (http://www.electproject.org/2016P; http://www.electproject.org/2020p). The poor are usually underrepresented, as was noticed soon after presidential primaries became widespread (Shafer, 1983, p.) and the less educated even more so. Thus, the notion that primaries and caucuses are "more democratic" because their voters "mirror the population" is sheer myth.

6 What About Europe?

Most criticisms of primaries and plebiscites focus on the United States, since that is the large country with the most experience of them. But what about elsewhere? It would be helpful to enthusiasts for direct democracy if the customary failures of primaries and referendums were an exclusive feature of "the profoundly flawed American system" (Landemore, 2020, p. 47).

Alas, movement toward American Progressive ideas is now well along in other countries as well. For example, the British Labour Party recently changed its rules in order to choose its leader in a more populist fashion, resulting in a man who was far from being the first choice of those public figures who know him best, his fellow Labour Members of Parliament. In the sources of his party leadership, Jeremy Corbyn was a kind of left-wing Trump. Nor is Britain alone in this endeavor. In recent years, the use of primaries to choose party nominees for national leadership has grown in Italy, France, Taiwan, and elsewhere. More frequent demagogic nominees will be forthcoming.

European experience with referendums is more limited, less extensively researched, and thus less familiar. In Ireland, popular votes are required to validate constitutional changes, including EU treaties. Many other countries have used referendums to approve or disapprove accession to the EU and, less commonly, to agree to treaties deepening the EU. But for the most part, doctrines of parliamentary supremacy still reign in Europe, and referendums there are far less frequent than in American states. David Cameron's decision to reject that tradition and his party's constitutional theory in favor of a gamble with his country's economic livelihood is an exception.

Hobolt (2009) argues that national referendums on EU treaties can work when the campaign is sufficiently intense and elite guidance is clear, but as she notes, many observers are skeptical. The fact that Denmark rejected the Maastricht Treaty in 1992 and Ireland the Nice Treaty in 2001, in both cases against the near-unanimous judgment of the political parties and media, suggests that the voters often struggle. In both cases, a second referendum was called a year later with more publicity and a reversed verdict, as Hobolt notes, but it is hard to regard those desperate salvaging events as an endorsement of referendums. Moreover, as the Brexit vote demonstrates, the voters can flounder even more helplessly when the issues are complex, elites are divided, and voters' identities and prejudices seem to provide simple, powerful alternate cues.

In Europe, only Switzerland uses national and cantonal referendums on a regular basis. As in the United States, the questions on the ballot are sometimes merely technical or consensual, with the voters approving legislative or constitutional proposals by their government in accordance with the Swiss constitution. It is fair to say that many Swiss initiatives and referendums over the past 125 years have resulted in sensible outcomes. But troubling proposals regularly appear as well. From the beginning, Swiss voters have often fallen victim to their prejudices or to bad advice from self-interested parties. Lowell (1895a, p. 53) provides the following examples from the earliest years of Swiss experimentation with plebiscitary decision-making:

1. In 1870, the Zurich legislature proposed limiting hours of work to 12 per day and forbidding the employment of school-age children. The people voted it down. In 1881, the same legislature proposed that employers provide compulsory insurance against worker sickness and be legally responsible for workplace accidents. The voters said no.
2. In 1878, the Zurich legislature proposed that daughters inherit equally with sons. The people rejected it. Free textbooks for children were rejected in 1887 and 1888.
3. In 1892, a national initiative proposed banning the production of kosher meat for Jews. The federal legislature opposed it, but the voters approved it enthusiastically, with 60% in favor.

Lowell (1895a, 56, 62) summarizes early Swiss experience with the initiative and referendum: "The confederation has made a short and, so far, not an altogether happy experiment with this institution." He adds:

> It may be noticed, moreover, that, of the few laws it [the initiative] has produced in Switzerland, not one, so far as I know, has been passed in the interest of labor....If there is any one class in the community to which the Referendum and Initiative would be an advantage, it would not appear to be the working-class.

Voter prejudice has persisted in Swiss referendums. A few prominent examples since Lowell's time:

- In 1959, 40 years after most of Europe and North America had enfranchised women, the Swiss federal government endorsed female suffrage and put the matter to a vote. The proposal was beaten 2-1.
- In 2004, a proposal to grant citizenship automatically to *third-generation* foreigners living in Switzerland was defeated at the polls.

- In 2009, an initiative to ban minarets on mosques was proposed by right-wing Swiss politicians. Opposed by the Swiss government, it passed with 58% of the vote.
- Most recently, Hainmueller and Hangartner (2013) studied Swiss municipalities that vote on citizenship for individual immigrants. The voters receive in advance a summary of each applicant's characteristics. Hainmueller and Hangartner found that even for otherwise identical applicants, those from Turkey and the former Yugoslavia drew 40% more "no" votes. National origin was the largest single variable influencing the vote.

Devotees of popular participation often cite Switzerland as a shining example. Again, Landemore (2020, p. 47) is illustrative. She asks, "How about, again, Switzerland, where popular participation is deeply entrenched and is usually acknowledged to serve the common good?" However, once one looks past abstract theory to examine closely the full history and actual workings of Swiss popular participation, the record is frequently morally troubling. In particular, Swiss voters have exhibited a notable tendency to discriminate against minorities and the weak, just as voters do everywhere else.[10] "More democratic" has frequently meant "more abusive of minorities." Blindness to those evils is not a good foundation for democratic theorizing.[11]

Thus, the available referendum results from Europe are just as depressing as in the American case. National referendums, carried out even though parliaments are perfectly able to act responsibly, fly in the face of all we know about how voters make decisions. David Cameron ignored that history, and his error serves as one more example of the abuse of referendums.

7 Human Beings and Their Limitations

Referendums and initiatives sometimes accomplish good legislation that legislatures have blocked. Primaries sometimes choose excellent nominees that parties have overlooked or rejected. The point here is not that legislatures and parties are always right. It is instead that both leaders and populace routinely go astray. Hence both need constraints and balance. Neither can be trusted to always choose wisely and morally.

---

[10] For a variety of positive and negative views about the Swiss experience with referendums, along with proposals to improve them by making them either more deliberative or more susceptible to elite restrictions on their negative aspects, see the issue of *The Swiss Political Science Review* 24, 3, October, 2018.

[11] Some political theorists have argued that the ills of referendums might be ameliorated by preceding them with citizen assemblies that would advise the citizenry how to vote. Experiments of this kind are often mentioned reverently. Alas, real-world experience has been disappointing (e.g., de Jongh, 2013).

Yet, reading the current academic literature on plebiscitary and participatory democracy, one finds few references to those facts of human experience. The powers of xenophobia, racism, sexism, and other prejudices are largely underestimated, when they are not missing entirely from the discussion. Instead, we have taken from some French Enlightenment thinkers and their successors a stylized version of their reaction against the *ancien regime*. In consequence, we are too often anxious to believe that for all but a tiny recalcitrant minority, human error and bloody-mindedness may be overcome. Proper education, freedom of thought, and patient deliberation will lead to sound judgments. Of course, no thoughtful person literally believes that. But we routinely proceed as if we did. The voters are fundamentally good people; we say, they try their best; and we would all be better off in their hands than under the control of dubious and devious minorities, like party officials or elected representatives. We may not believe in an official popular "Cult of Reason," as the French Revolution sought to establish, but its low-church version remains very much alive.

The largest problem with populist democratic theory of all varieties, then, is not its limited engagement with the scientific evidence and with the everyday realities of politics. It is rather that these theories ignore the ancient wisdom about mixed government, a central part of the political theory tradition. In the modern era, the defining feature of mixed government is a compromise between popular opinion and the narrower but often more knowledgeable judgment of insiders. That is how the term has been used throughout this paper. By contrast, plebiscitary and populist doctrines go to one extreme. Only popular wishes count. Hence demagogues and demagoguery have free play, as long experience has demonstrated and as the events of 2016 reaffirmed.

8 Prospects for Change

The biggest obstacle to restoring mixed government in all aspects of British and American political life is that the populist genie is out of the bottle. More than 80 years ago, Francis Wilson (1934. 24, fn. 31) wrote:

> It may be noted, however, that the rise of the idea of popular sovereignty and national sovereignty assisted in the rejection of the mixed constitution. The separation of powers may be reconciled easily with the idea of the ultimate and unitary power of the people, while the mixed constitution can recognize the power of the people only in a limited sense.

Hence when political failures occur, as they did in the Democratic Party's presidential nominations in 1968, critics quickly revert to John Dewey's (1927, p. 146) remark that "the cure for the ills of democracy is more democracy." Indeed, that statement was explicitly cited in the McGovern-Fraser Report as a justification of greater use of primaries in presidential nominations (Commission on Party Structure and Delegate Selection 1970, p. 14).

Presidential candidates should be chosen by a mixed system of popular preference and the informed judgment of party officials who know them well. Neither group will always judge wisely, but a compromise between them will generally be better than either acting alone. We let people choose their doctors, but we do not let doctors treat patients unless they pass an examination set by their peers and are licensed by a state (Kamarck, 2018, p. 709). We let people choose their airline and their flight time, but we do not let airline pilots fly passengers unless they are licensed by fellow pilots working as government officials. After all, we think, without proper qualifications, doctors and pilots might kill several hundred people. But for the presidency, a position that controls the American nuclear arsenal that might kill a hundred million people or more, unqualified amateurs unapproved by their peers are welcome to apply and may be elected.[12]

The political problem with giving party insiders a stronger role in presidential nominations, however much they might add, is that Americans have long been anti-party. It is all too easy to appeal to those sentiments in attacking any role for knowledgeable insiders. In consequence, "superdelegates" have struggled to attain legitimacy. Every insurgent candidate with no appeal to the experienced professionals who know him or her personally wants superdelegate influence reduced and argues for "more democracy." As part of the deal that Hillary Clinton cut with Bernie Sanders to gain his support in 2016, the Democrats again reduced superdelegate powers in their 2020 presidential nominating convention. Thus, strengthening the role of insiders or otherwise achieving a nomination procedure that takes sensible account of the voters' limitations and balances those against a less representative but better informed group of insiders—all that seems very difficult to achieve in the current climate.

Reforming initiatives and referendums will be equally challenging. Progressive Era mechanisms for direct democracy have value when elected officials fail egregiously to tackle some important policy issue. The American originators of initiatives and referendums saw them in that light—a tool to be used only rarely (Ford, 1912). Clear issues of national identity may also qualify, as when Quebec voted on independence in 1980 and 1995 or when Scotland did in 2014. Perhaps "conscience legislation," such as abortion policy or gay marriage, also fit the criterion. In each case, however, parliaments need to specify clearly what the vote means and how it would be implemented. That injects at least a bit of mixed government into the referendum process. Vague, complex, or reprehensible proposals have no place on the ballot, nor do those with highly uncertain consequences.

---

[12] In spite of their inherent plebiscitarianism, presidential primaries incorporate elements of mixed government in one respect. Before voting starts, an "invisible primary" takes place, in which party insiders, donors, and influential opinion-makers assess potential candidates. When that group settles on a candidate, the resulting advantages in money, staff quality, and journalistic notice often suffice for nomination (Cohen et al., 2008). But when the person informally selected has substantial flaws as a candidate or when insiders are not well agreed (as Republicans were not in 2016), outsiders can win or come close to winning. Thus, the vetting process is highly imperfect.

In the United States at the state level, however, low thresholds on the number of signatures required and a legal option to pay signature collectors (upheld by the Supreme Court in *Meyer v. Grant* 486 U.S. 414, 1988) have helped initiatives proliferate as tools of interest groups and of disreputable, sometimes abhorrent popular factions. Legislators too often shirk their responsibility for hard decisions by passing the buck to the public via referendum or by capitulating in advance to what would be the inevitable result of a well-funded special interest initiative. In both the United States and Switzerland, the courts have sometimes intervened to overturn some of the worst abuses, but the "voice of the people" often intimidates jurists as well.

In sum, the voters currently have the power, and they are loathe to share it with those who may sometimes be more knowledgeable or more ethical than themselves. Thus, a better balance is resisted. Here, too, power corrupts.

9 Conclusion

Contemporary frailties of democracy have led to pessimism about its health, but the diagnosis of the illness has often been mistaken. Both the rise of Donald Trump and the outcome of the Brexit vote trace directly to an excessive reliance on popular opinion untempered by informed judgment. In both cases, the abandonment of mixed government is the source of the infection. Picking presidential nominees solely by primaries and deciding complex economic issues by plebiscite have enfeebled polities.

Recent Anglo-American democratic crises are due in large part to excessive popular control. Yet in the West, most of the criticism has come from those who want still more populist and participatory democracy. They resemble the eighteenth-century doctors who, faced with a patient sick from blood loss, called for more leeches to be applied. Recent events have brightly illuminated the dangers of that kind of approach to political reform. As Carl Friedrich (1937, p. 500) put it nearly a century ago:

> Direct popular action in its several forms serves to strengthen the democratic element of the mixture [in mixed government]. If the dose is too strong, it will destroy the balance. That it provides 'real democracy,' as the German propaganda minister would try to make us believe, is a Utopian dream or a sorry sham.

The frequent failures of Western liberal democracies have not gone unnoticed elsewhere. Fueled by the rise of China, threats to balanced government have also emerged from those who want *less* popular control. Dunn (2014) has written on "breaking democracy's spell" and has encouraged his readers to consider the merits (and demerits) of alternative governmental structures, including the Chinese form. Bell (2015) makes an explicit case for the superiority of "meritocratic government" with little democracy, and he fancies that the current Chinese government, while not perfect, is on its way to that goal. In his view, the China model consists of "democracy at the bottom, experimentation in the middle, and meritocracy at the top." He describes the model as "both a reality and an ideal" (Bell, 2015, p. 180).

Bell mentions some checks on governmental power in China, such as "the principle of collective leadership, term limits, and the introduction of a mandatory retirement age" (Bell, 2015, pp. 180, 116), but the weakness of those "parchment barriers" has become all too clear in the Xi Jinping era (cf. Madison in Hamilton et al., 1961, *Federalist* 48). Too much elite control is bad for the same reason that too much popular control is dangerous: No one group embodies all the wisdom in a society, and even virtuous rulers will be tempted to abuse their power. Hence, we need controls on the virtuous just as much as on the powerful (Montesquieu ([1748] Montesquieu, 1989, book 11, chap. 4; Chan, 2014, p. 195).

Within Western democratic thinking, too, an American strain of thought has embraced stronger elite rule via responsible party government (Committee on Political Parties 1950; Ranney, 1962). Faced with the constraints of checks and balances in the American constitutional structure, these scholars have thought to break through the roadblocks by uniting the president with legislative majorities in both houses of Congress and a sympathetic Supreme Court. The vehicle for carrying along all three branches of government is to be the political party. This is the standard theoretical model for parliamentarianism. However, like the literature on the Chinese model, this framework pays little attention to the case for mixed government. In particular, party government is quite different from giving political leaders and insiders a partial role, checked and balanced by popular preferences. By contrast, party government is meant to *overcome* checks and balances.

In spite of their profound differences, the "China model" and the "doctrine of responsible party government" have this in common, that they are open opponents of checks and balances in government. The China model has a veneer of popular sovereignty, and responsible party government is meant to be backed by a popular majority at the polls, but in each case, the central goal is to make party rule possible without too much popular interference. Plebiscitarianism, too, is a foe of checks and balances, but from the opposite pole. It embraces popular rule without restrictions from parties or other governmental institutions. The devotees of each of these points of view may make occasional gestures toward mixed government ideas. More often, they sweep past them in their haste to justify empowering the devotees of some partial perspective in the society, majority or minority, who will then be able to expeditiously enforce their will without much need to compromise. Ay, there's the rub.

A full version of mixed government, with broad representation of all groups, separation of powers, and checks and balances, will, in ordinary circumstances, generate a broadly acceptable compromise among participants. That will be better government than rule by self-interested and unrepresentative factions or by narrow and temporary majorities, even if that compromise takes a little longer to achieve. But in a polarized era under the spell of populism, with foolish politicians and even more foolish voters disinclined to listen to evidence or find common ground with those who disagree, factions and narrow majorities rule. The Brexit referendum has led British politics astray since its occurrence, and it will ultimately impose substantial costs on the British people. The presidential nomination process in the United States is currently irresponsible, even dangerous. In both cases, getting back to a sensible version of mixed government will prove an arduous quest. In the meantime, we run the risk of a further series of self-inflicted democratic crises.

References

Achen, C. H., & Bartels, L. M. (2017). *Democracy for realists*. Princeton University Press.
Aristotle. (2013). *Politics* (2nd ed. C. Lord, Trans.). University of Chicago Press.
Balot, R. (2015). The "mixed regime" in Aristotle's politics. In T. Lockwood & T. Samaras (Eds.), *Aristotle's politics: A critical guide* (pp. 103–122). Cambridge University Press.
Banfield, E. C. (1961). *Political influence: A new theory of urban politics*. Free Press.
Banfield, E. C., & Wilson, J. Q. (1966). *City politics*. Vintage.
Bartels, L. M. (1988). *Presidential primaries and the dynamics of Public Choice*. Princeton University Press.
Bartels, L. M. (2022). *Public opinion and the crisis of democracy in Europe*. Princeton University Press. Forthcoming.
Beer, S. H. (1966). *British politics in the collectivist age*. Knopf.
Bell, D. A. (2015). *The China model*. Princeton University Press.
Blythe, J. M. (1992). *Ideal government and the mixed constitution in the Middle Ages*. Princeton University Press.
Broder, D. S. (2000). *Democracy derailed: Initiative campaigns and the power of money*. Houghton Mifflin Harcourt.
Chan, J. (2014). *Confucian perfectionism*. Princeton University Press.
Clarke, H. D., Goodwin, M., & Whiteley, P. (2017). *Brexit*. Cambridge University Press.
Cohen, M., Karol, D., Noel, H., & Zaller, J. (2008). *The party decides: Presidential nominations before and after reform*. University of Chicago Press.
Commission on Party Structure and Delegate Selection. (1970). *Mandate for Reform*. Democratic National Committee.
Committee on Political Parties. (1950). *Toward a more responsible two-party system: A report of the Committee on political parties*. American Political Science Association/Rinehart & Company, Inc..
de Jongh, M. (2013). *Group dynamics in the citizens' assembly on electoral reform*. Doctoral dissertation. Aarhus University.
Dewey, J. (1927). *The public and its problems*. Henry Holt.
Dunn, J. (2014). *Breaking democracy's spell*. Yale University Press.
Dyck, J. J., & Lascher, E. L., Jr. (2019). *Initiatives without engagement*. University of Michigan Press.
Finley, M. I. (1962). Athenian demagogues. *Past & Present, 21*, 3–24.
Ford, H. J. (1912). Direct legislation and the recall. *Annals of the American Academy of Political and Social Science, 43*, 65–77.
Friedrich, C. (1937). *Constitutional government and politics*. Harper and Brothers.
Golway, T. (2014). *Machine made: Tammany Hall and the creation of modern American Politics*. Liveright.
Graham, M. H., & Svolik, M. W. (2020). Democracy in America? Partisanship, polarization, and the robustness of support for democracy in the United States. *American Political Science Review, 114*, 392–409.
Hainmueller, J., & Hangartner, D. (2013). Who gets a Swiss passport? *American Political Science Review, 107*(1), 159–187.

Hamilton, A., Madison, J., & Jay, J. (1961). In C. Rossiter (Ed.), *The federalist papers*. New American Library.
Hibbing, J. R., & Theiss-Morse, E. (2002). *Stealth democracy: Americans' beliefs about how government should work*. Cambridge University Press.
Hobolt, S. B. (2009). *Europe in question: Referendums on European integration*. Oxford University Press.
Hobolt, S. B. (2016). The Brexit vote: A divided nation, a divided continent. *Journal of European Public Policy, 23*(9), 1259–1277.
Hofstadter, R. (1955). *The age of reform*. Vintage.
Hooghe, M., & Dassoneville, R. (2018). Explaining the Trump vote: The effect of racist resentment and anti-immigrant sentiments. *PS Political Science and Politics, 51*(3), 528–534.
Jardina, A. (2019). *White identity politics*. Cambridge University Press.
Kamarck, E. C. (2016). *Primary politics*. Brookings.
Kamarck, E. C. (2018). Returning peer review to the American Presidential nomination process. *New York University Law Review, 93*, 709–727.
Landemore, H. (2020). *Open democracy*. Princeton University Press.
Lane, M. (2012a). The origins of the statesman—demagogue distinction in and after Ancient Athens. *Journal of the History of Ideas, 73*(2), 179–200.
Lane, M. (2012b). The origins of the statesman—demagogue distinction in and after Ancient Athens. *Journal of the History of Ideas, 73*(2), 179–200.
Lowell, A. L. (1895a). The referendum and initiative: Their relation to the interests of labor in Switzerland and in America. *International Journal of Ethics, 6*(1), 51–63.
von Fritz, K. (1954). *The theory of the mixed constitution in antiquity*. Columbia University Press.
Lowell, A. L. (1895b). The referendum and initiative: Their relation to the interests of labor in Switzerland and in America. *International Journal of Ethics, 6*(1), 51–63.
McClosky, H. (1964). Consensus and ideology in American politics. *American Political Science Review, 58*, 361–382.
Merriam, C. E. (1921). Nomination of presidential candidates. *American Bar Association Journal, 7*(2), 79–85.
Mill, J. S. (1861). *Considerations on representative government*. Parker, Son, and Bourn.
Montesquieu. ([1748] 1989). *The spirit of the laws*. Anne M. Cohler, Basia C. Miller, and Harold S. Stone eds. : Cambridge University Press.
Müller, J. W. (2016). *What is populism?* University of Pennsylvania Press.
Mutz, D. C. (2018). Status threat, not economic hardship, explains the 2016 Presidential vote. *Proceedings of the National Academy of the United States of America.* https://doi.org/10.1073/pnas.1718155115
Palmer, R. R. (1989). *Twelve who ruled*. Princeton University Press.
Plato. (2016). In M. Schofield (Ed.), *Laws*. Cambridge University Press.
Polsby, N. W. (1983). *The consequences of party reform*. Oxford University Press.
Polybius. (2010). *The histories*. (R. Waterfield, Trans.). Oxford University Press.
Prothro, J. W., & Grigg, C. M. (1960). Fundamental principles of democracy: Bases of agreement and disagreement. *Journal of Politics, 22*, 276–294.
Rakove, M. (1979). *We don't want nobody nobody sent*. Indiana University Press.
Ranney, A. (1962). *The doctrine of responsible party government*. University of Illinois Press.
Ranney, A. (1975). *Curing the mischiefs of faction*. University of California Press.
Richard, C. J. (1994). *The founders and the Classics*. Harvard University Press.
Ryerson, R. A. (2016). *John Adams's Republic: The one, the few, and the many*. Johns Hopkins University Press.
Saxonhouse, A. (1996). *Athenian democracy: Modern mythmakers and ancient theorists*. University of Notre Dame Press.
Shafer, B. E. (1983). *Quiet revolution*. Russell Sage.
Sides, J., Tesler, M., & Vavreck, L. (2018). *Identity crisis*. Princeton University Press.
Sigmund, P. E. (1963). *Nicholas of Cusa and medieval political thought*. Harvard University Press.

Smith, D. A., & Tolbert, C. J. (2004). *Educated by initiative*. University of Michigan Press.
Thucydides. (2013). *The war of the Peloponnesians and the Athenians*. (J. Mynott, Trans.). Cambridge University Press.
Tierney, B. (1955). *Foundations of the conciliar theory*. Cambridge University Press.
Trounstine, J. (2009). *Political monopolies in American cities*. University of Chicago Press.
Wallas, G. (1908). *Human nature in politics*. Archibald Constable.
Whiteley, P. (2012). *Political participation in Britain*. Palgrave Macmillan.
Wilson, F. G. (1934). The mixed constitution and the separation of powers. *Southwestern Social Science Quarterly, 15*(1), 14–28.

Christopher H. Achen is the Roger Williams Straus Professor of Social Sciences Emeritus at Princeton University. His primary research interests are public opinion, elections, and the realities of democratic politics, along with the statistical challenges that arise from those fields. He is the author or co-author of six books, including *Democracy for Realists* (with Larry Bartels) in 2016. He has also published many articles. He is a member of the American Academy of Arts and Sciences and has received fellowships from the Center for Advanced Study in the Behavioral Sciences, the National Science Foundation, and Princeton's Center for the Study of Democratic Politics. He was the founding president of the Political Methodology Society, and he received the first career achievement award from the Political Methodology Section of the American Political Science Association in 2007. He has served on the top social science board at the National Science Foundation, and he was the chair of the national council for the Inter-university Consortium for Political and Social Research (ICPSR) from 2013 to 2015. He is also the recipient of an award from the University of Michigan for lifetime achievement in training graduate students and a student-initiated award from Princeton University for graduate student mentoring.

Democracy Erodes from the Top: Public Opinion and Democratic "Backsliding" in Europe

Larry M. Bartels

Abstract Observers have described a "crisis of democracy" in contemporary Europe, with "exploding" popular support for right-wing populist parties fueled by anti-immigrant sentiment, political distrust, and dissatisfaction with democracy itself. However, opinion surveys provide remarkably little evidence of such a "crisis" in public opinion. Across Europe, attitudes regarding immigration, European integration, political trust, and satisfaction with democracy have remained largely unchanged over the past two decades. In the two European countries where democracy has eroded significantly, Hungary and Poland, "backsliding" has been engineered by politicians and imposed from above, not in response to any mandate from voters. Public acquiescence in these developments seems more plausibly attributable to substantial improvements in subjective well-being under illiberal governments than to any popular hankering for authoritarianism.

Keywords Crisis of democracy · Democratic "backsliding" · European integration · Hungary · Immigration · Poland · Political trust · Public opinion · Satisfaction with democracy

An eminent scholar of comparative politics, Adam Przeworski (2019, p. 1), began a recent book on *Crises of Democracy* by declaring that:

> Something is happening. 'Anti-establishment,' 'anti-system,' 'anti-elite,' 'populist' sentiments are exploding in many mature democracies. ... Confidence in politicians, parties, parliaments, and governments is falling. Even the support for democracy as a system of government has weakened.

The 2016 Brexit vote in the United Kingdom, the election of Donald Trump as US president, and the rise of right-wing populist parties in Europe and elsewhere produced an explosion of commentary about the "populist explosion" agitating

---

L. M. Bartels (✉)
Department of Political Science, Vanderbilt University, Nashville, TN, USA
e-mail: larry.bartels@vanderbilt.edu

affluent democracies, a "global wave of populism" (Bremmer, 2017; Judis, 2016; Norris, 2017; Taylor, 2016).

In Europe, at least, the forces propelling this populist "wave" are widely agreed upon. "Two core issues lie at the root of today's rising populism," Michael Bröning (2016) wrote in *Foreign Affairs*, "the challenge of migration and the lingering euro crisis." Jan-Werner Müller (2016, p. 96) cited "a retrenchment of the welfare state, immigration, and, above all in recent years, the Eurocrisis." Benjamin Moffitt (2016, pp. 1, 159–160) likewise argued that "A prolonged global financial downturn, rising unemployment in a number of areas and a loss of faith in perceived elite projects like the European Union are helping fuel the flames" of populism, threatening "a crisis of faith in democracy" in which citizens are "more and more disillusioned with mainstream politics."

All of this does sound portentous. But, at least insofar as the attitudes and preferences of ordinary Europeans are concerned, *virtually none of it is true*. On the whole, Europeans feel significantly warmer toward immigrants than they did 15 years ago. They are, if anything, slightly more enthusiastic about the project of European integration. Trust in national parliaments and politicians has remained virtually constant, as has public satisfaction with the working of democracy. In these and other respects, the conventional wisdom about a "crisis of democracy" in contemporary Europe is strikingly at odds with data from public opinion surveys.

That is not to say that there is no crisis of democracy in contemporary Europe. However, political observers' understanding of the nature of that crisis reflects a significant misunderstanding of the role of public opinion in democratic politics. The "folk theory" of democracy exalts "government of the people, by the people, for the people," as Abraham Lincoln famously put it. Even when citizens' preferences do not directly determine policy, they are supposed to be the primary force animating democratic politics.[1] But if the people rule, however indirectly, then aberrations in the workings of democracy must somehow reflect the people's failings—bad attitudes, rash choices, or insufficient diligence in fulfilling the obligations of citizenship.

The alternative view propounded here might be termed an *elitist* account of democratic crisis. Of course, "elitist" has become a scornful term in modern discourse and especially in the context of discussions of democracy. My aim in employing it here is not to wade into normative debates regarding the appropriate roles of leaders and citizens in democratic political systems. It is simply to underscore the remarkable disconnection of ordinary public opinion from the developments that are commonly taken as indicative of a "crisis of democracy" in contemporary Europe. Nancy Bermeo (2003, p. 221), summarizing her examination of over a dozen full-blown breakdowns of democracy in twentieth-century Europe and Latin America, wrote that "the culpability for democracy's demise lay overwhelmingly with political elites." My argument here is that the culpability for

---

[1] On the "folk theory" of democracy, see Achen and Bartels (2016).

Europe's current crisis of democracy likewise lies overwhelmingly with political elites.

My analysis proceeds in two steps. First, I summarize broad trends in European public opinion from 2002 through 2019, focusing particularly on attitudes commonly taken as symptomatic of a "wave" of populist sentiment or a "crisis of democracy," including antipathy to immigration and European integration, ideological polarization, distrust of political elites, and dissatisfaction with the workings of democracy. In Europe as a whole and in most countries considered separately, those attitudes turn out to be largely unchanged since the turn of the century.

If populist sentiment is essentially stable, how has support for populist parties "exploded"? Mostly, it hasn't. While several countries have seen flare-ups in voting for populist parties in recent years, the overall increase has been very modest—by one account, no more than a few percentage points.[2] Moreover, there is virtually no correlation between support for populist parties at the polls in specific countries, or changes in that support over time, and the extent of populist sentiment in those countries.[3] Electoral support for populist parties seems to depend much more on the "supply" of populist mobilization, and on institutional rules that facilitate or inhibit that mobilization, than on citizens' demand for populism.

Second, I consider the two most prominent examples of democratic "backsliding" in contemporary Europe, tracing the bases of popular support for Fidesz in Hungary before and after its rise to power in 2010 and for the Law and Justice party in Poland before and after its rise to power in 2015. In both cases, I find surprisingly little evidence of public hankering for even "mildly authoritarian" rule.[4] Rather, these were conventional conservative parties swept into office by discontent with unsuccessful incumbents and then maintained in office *despite* their autocratic actions because they presided over significant increases in prosperity and subjective well-being, bolstering trust in political elites and—ironically—satisfaction with the workings of democracy. While ordinary citizens in these cases may be guilty of prioritizing the quality of their day-to-day lives over democratic procedures, democracy has clearly eroded from the top down, not from the bottom up.

---

[2] See Norris and Inglehart (2019, p. 9). By this tabulation, the average vote share for "populist" parties in 32 Western democracies increased from 10.9% in the 1980s and 9.9% in the 1990s to 11.4% in the 2000s and 12.4% in the 2010s.

[3] Of the eight countries with the highest levels of right-wing populist sentiment in 2014–2017, only two (Hungary and France) had right-wing populist parties attracting as much as 10% of the vote. On the other hand, right-wing populist parties flourished in Switzerland, Denmark, and Norway, all of which were among the half-dozen European countries with the *lowest* levels of right-wing populist sentiment in 2014–2017. As Rovira Kaltwasser (2012, p. 188) observed, "populist radical right parties have shown a great success precisely in those regions of Europe where the structural prerequisites for their rise were hardly existent."

[4] The description of Hungary and Poland as "mildly authoritarian regimes" is borrowed from Levitsky and Ziblatt (2018, p. 188).

1 The Extraordinary Normalcy of European Public Opinion

If Europe is experiencing a crisis of democracy, most Europeans seem not to have gotten the message. Over the past two decades, the key attitudes and values that Przeworski saw "exploding in many mature democracies" have, in fact, hardly budged. I focus here on a handful of attitudes that are commonly implicated in discussions of a democratic crisis in contemporary Europe and that are indeed associated with support for right-wing populist parties in many countries.[5] These include attitudes toward immigration and European integration, ideological polarization, trust in parliament and politicians, and satisfaction with democracy.

My analysis of trends in these attitudes is based on the single best collection of longitudinal data on contemporary European public opinion, the European Social Survey. The nine rounds of ESS, conducted biannually from 2002–2003 through 2018–2019, include more than 350,000 respondents in 23 countries, providing an unparalleled record of European public opinion in the twenty-first century.[6] Table 1 shows the ESS sample size in each country and round.[7]

1.1 Support for Immigration

Immigration has emerged as a momentous policy issue and a salient political flashpoint in many of the world's affluent democracies. A 2016 article in *Foreign Policy* warned that "The Immigration Crisis Is Tearing Europe Apart" (Stokes, 2016). Another in *The Washington Post* declared that, in light of demographic projections of "more and more immigrants for decades to come," Europeans' reactions to immigration "raise troubling questions about the ability of political institutions in the developed world to cope with their arrival" (Ehrenfreund, 2016). Friction between natives and immigrants often receives lavish attention from the

---

[5] On the relationship between these attitudes and support for right-wing populist parties, see Bartels (2017).

[6] The 354,829 respondents represent 183 country rounds; the country round samples range in size from 985 to 3,142 and average 1,939. Surveys were not conducted in the remaining 24 country rounds (11.6%). My characterizations of European opinion are based on weighting each country round in proportion to its adult population. My substantive conclusions remain essentially unchanged when each country round is weighted equally.

[7] Data and documentation are available from the ESS website (*http://www.europeansocialsurvey.org/*). My analysis generally includes EU countries as of 2006 and those in the Schengen area. It excludes countries admitted to the EU after 2006 (Bulgaria, Croatia, and Romania), some small countries with little or no ESS data (Cyprus, Iceland, Latvia, Luxembourg, and Malta), and several other countries represented sporadically in the ESS dataset (Albania, Israel, Kosovo, Montenegro, Russia, Serbia, Turkey, and Ukraine).

Table 1 Countries represented in European Social Surveys, 2002–2019

	1	2	3	4	5	6	7	8	9	Total
Austria (AT)	2257	2256	2459	0	0	0	1825	2010	2503	13,310
Belgium (BE)	1899	1778	1798	1760	1704	1869	1769	1766	1769	16,112
Czechia (CZ)	1360	3142	0	2394	2518	2076	2148	2269	2398	18,305
Denmark (DK)	1506	1487	1505	1610	1576	1650	1502	0	0	10,836
Estonia (EE)	0	1989	1517	1954	1935	2452	2111	2019	1905	15,882
Finland (FI)	2000	2039	1921	2340	1878	2197	2087	1925	1755	18,142
France (FR)	1503	1806	1986	2073	1820	2021	1977	2070	2010	17,266
Germany (DE)	2919	2870	2916	2751	3031	2958	3045	2852	2360	25,702
Great Britain (GB)	2052	1897	2394	2352	2422	2286	2264	1959	2211	19,837
Greece (GR)	2566	2406	0	2249	2811	0	0	0	0	10,032
Hungary (HU)	1685	1498	1518	1544	1561	2014	1733	1624	1661	14,838
Ireland (IE)	2069	2304	1814	1764	2576	2628	2433	2757	2216	20,561
Italy (IT)	1207	0	0	0	0	985	0	2653	2746	7591
Lithuania (LT)	0	0	0	0	1677	2109	2250	2122	1836	9994
Netherlands (NL)	2364	1881	1889	1778	1829	1845	1969	1681	1673	16,909
Norway (NO)	2036	1760	1750	1760	1653	1666	1451	1545	1406	15,027
Poland (PL)	2110	1716	1750	1759	1852	1999	1728	1705	1500	16,119
Portugal (PT)	1511	2052	2222	2642	2296	2229	1265	1270	1055	16,542
Slovakia (SK)	0	1512	1766	1810	1856	1847	0	0	1083	9874
Slovenia (SI)	1519	1442	1476	1477	1403	1257	1224	1307	1318	12,423
Spain (ES)	1729	1664	1876	2828	2021	1967	1975	1958	1668	17,686
Sweden (SE)	1999	1948	1927	1830	1497	1898	1829	1551	1541	16,020
Switzerland (CH)	2084	2141	1804	2005	1583	1555	1582	1525	1542	15,821
Total	38,375	41,588	36,288	40,680	41,499	41,508	38,167	38,568	38,156	354,829

Sample size by country and ESS round

media, even in places where public opinion is generally quite favorable toward immigration (Goodman, 2019).

While some of Europe's party systems and political institutions have indeed been rattled by anti-immigrant mobilizations, ordinary Europeans on the whole became significantly *more sanguine* about immigration over the first two decades of the twenty-first century.[8] The European Social Surveys consistently included six questions tapping attitudes toward immigration.[9] The average response to these six questions, scaled to range from zero to ten, gradually increased from 5.3 in 2002–2003 to 5.7 in 2018–2019.[10] Of the 15 countries represented in all nine ESS rounds, 13 became warmer toward immigrants, with the average responses in nine of these countries increasing by a half-point or more on the zero-to-ten scale. Only two countries, Hungary and Poland, experienced declines in average ratings.

Even Europe's refugee crisis, which brought hundreds of thousands of asylum-seekers from war-torn Syria, Afghanistan, and Iraq to Europe in 2015 and early 2016, made no perceptible dent in public support for immigration—except in Hungary, which saw the largest and most sudden influx of asylum-seekers, as well as a vigorous anti-immigrant campaign by Prime Minister Viktor Orbán. In Germany, where Chancellor Angela Merkel's "fierce determination to maintain open borders for the refugees" was hailed internationally as a remarkable act of political courage, public support for immigration held absolutely steady at 6.2 on the ten-point scale through four ESS rounds fielded between late 2012 and early 2019. And Sweden, which has had a high rate of net immigration for more than a decade

---

[8] Because the set of countries represented in each ESS round varies, I track European averages using a statistical analysis including country fixed effects for the whole period. The countries accounting for most of the missing observations—Italy, Greece, and Lithuania—are in some respects unrepresentative, though only Italy is populous enough to have much impact on the European averages. More elaborate statistical procedures designed to account for sample selection produce little evidence of bias due to correlations between countries' opinion climates and their participation in specific ESS waves.

[9] Three questions asked how willing the respondents' country should be to allow immigrants (1) "of the same race or ethnic group as most [country]'s people," (2) "of a different race or ethnic group," and (3) "from the poorer countries outside Europe." Responses to these three questions were recoded to range from zero (for "allow none") to ten (for "allow many"). The other three questions asked (4) whether immigration is good or bad for the country's economy, (5) whether the country's cultural life "is generally undermined or enriched" by immigration, and (6) whether immigration makes the country "a worse or a better place to live." The correlations between responses to the six questions range from .46 to .80, and their loadings on a common factor range from .72 to .85. I included respondents who answered at least five of the six questions, imputing neutral values for the sixth when necessary.

[10] The estimated increase is .42 (with a standard error of .17). The corresponding estimated increases for the six separate items range from .05 (for enriching cultural life) to .63 (for allowing more immigrants of the same race or ethnic group). All of my longitudinal cross-national analyses allow for disturbances in individual survey responses to be correlated within country-waves.

and the second-largest influx of asylum-seekers in 2015, has consistently had the most favorable attitudes toward immigration in Europe by far.[11]

The social tensions associated with immigration, especially immigration from outside the relatively homogenous societies of Europe, are quite real. Political entrepreneurs exploiting those tensions have produced a good deal of ugly rhetoric and even spurred the adoption of some ugly policies. But European public opinion has been remarkably immune to the immigration crisis that is "tearing Europe apart."

1.2 Support for European Integration

The European Union is an unlovable institution under the best of circumstances, a supranational conglomerate operating "by élite consensus and an irritating sort of mild bureaucratic snuffling," as one observer put it (Wood, 2019, p. 63). "Up to the early 2000s," historian Adam Tooze (2018, p. 112) has written, "the EU operated against a backdrop of what political scientists called a 'permissive consensus.' Europe's population accepted the gradual push for ever closer union without enthusiasm but also without protest." But that changed, the story goes, as the EU was paralyzed by rigidity and infighting in the wake of the Great Recession and the European sovereign debt crisis. According to political scientist Sheri Berman (2019, p. 402):

> The EU's technocratic rather than democratic nature generated a backlash against the EU as it became associated with economic problems rather than prosperity.

Yanis Varoufakis (2016, pp. 48–49), an economist-turned-politician on the receiving end of EU rigidity, put it more colorfully:

> when a technocracy harboring a deep, Platonic contempt for democracy attains inordinate power, we end up with an antisocial, dispirited, mindless autocracy. Europeans recognize this in today's Brussels-based bureaucracy.

If we turn to the ESS data to gauge the depth of this public backlash against the EU, we find another anomaly. Seven of the nine ESS waves included a question tapping attitudes toward European integration. Respondents were asked whether "European unification should go further" or whether "it has already gone too far." Response options ranged from zero (for "already gone too far") to ten ("unification should go further"). The responses suggest that support for further unification is neither particularly low nor declining.[12]

---

[11] Dionne (2017), Nolan (2015), Scheppele (2015), Drozdiak (2017), pp. 3–4; Eddy (2017). Data on immigration and asylum-seeking are recorded in the OECD's International Migration Database (*http://stats.oecd.org/*).

[12] A separate item tapped trust in the European Parliament on a zero-to-ten scale. The average level of trust in 2018–2019, 4.4, was only slightly lower than the average level in 2002–2007 (4.5), and only slightly lower than the average level of trust in the respondents' national parliaments (4.6).

For Europe as a whole, the trend in public attitudes toward European integration is mostly flat, with support for further unification having declined slightly in 2006–2007 (a period of EU expansion) and again in 2014–2015, then increased in the two most recent rounds of surveys. The average level of support in 2018–2019 (5.5) was slightly higher than when the question was first asked in 2004–2005 (5.3).[13] Support for further European integration increased substantially over this period in Portugal (1.4 points), Germany (1.0 points), Finland, Belgium, and Sweden. Declines in support were both smaller and rarer. The largest overall decline (0.6 points) was in Switzerland, which has long maintained a determined independence from the EU in any case. Support also declined by about half a point in Poland and Ireland—two countries on the periphery of the EU that have seen much higher rates of economic growth than other parts of Europe.[14]

Nor is there any support in these data for the notion that "Growing disaffection with Europe has become particularly acute among young people, who in the past embraced a borderless Europe" (Drozdiak, 2017, p. xvii). Young Europeans have generally been more supportive of further European integration than their elders—and that is true to about the same extent in recent years as it was before the economic crisis. The average level of support among people born since 1980 has not varied by as much as half a point over the whole period, and in 2018–2019 it was probably higher than at any previous time.[15] The *only* country in which the overall balance of opinion among young people in 2018–2019 was tilted against further European integration was the steadfast outsider Switzerland. Even in Great Britain, where antipathy to the EU among older voters propelled the "leave" side to a stunning victory in the Brexit referendum, the balance of opinion among young people has remained slightly positive. There is simply no evidence here of a generational turn—or, for that matter, any turn at all—away from the project of European integration.

1.3 Political Trust and Satisfaction with Democracy

One of the most worrisome aspects of contemporary European politics, by many accounts, is a profound dissatisfaction among ordinary citizens with their political leaders and institutions and even with democracy itself. In an attention-getting diagnosis by Roberto Foa and Mounk (Foa & Mounk, 2016, pp. 15–16), for example:

---

[13] The estimated increase is .18 (with a standard error of .15).

[14] From 2002 to 2019, the average annual growth rate of real GDP per capita was 4.0% in Poland and, despite a sustained downturn in the wake of the Great Recession, 3.1% in Ireland. The corresponding growth rate for the 19-country Euro area as a whole was 0.8%.

[15] The estimated increase in support for further integration in this cohort from 2004–2005 to 2018–2019 is .14 (with a standard error of .13).

Approval ratings for the continent's leading politicians stand at record lows, and citizens have grown deeply mistrustful of their political institutions.... Even as democracy has come to be the only form of government widely viewed as legitimate, it has lost the trust of many citizens who no longer believe that democracy can deliver on their most pressing needs and preferences.

The ESS questionnaires have consistently included items tapping trust in politicians and in the respondent's country's parliament using zero-to-ten scales ranging from "no trust at all" to "complete trust."[16] For the continent as a whole and for most individual countries, the average responses are closer to "no trust at all" than to "complete trust." However, there is no evidence that "citizens have grown deeply mistrustful of their political institutions" in recent years or even that "Confidence in politicians, parties, parliaments, and governments is falling." The overall level of trust declined by about half a point on the ten-point scale between 2002–2003 and 2012–2013, at the height of the sovereign debt crisis, but has subsequently rebounded almost entirely.[17]

As Tolstoy might have said, trusting countries are all alike, while every distrustful country is distrustful in its own way. Five of the fifteen countries represented in every wave of the ESS—Switzerland, Norway, Sweden, Finland, and the Netherlands—exhibited consistently high and gradually increasing levels of trust in their parliaments and politicians.[18] The countries with roughly average levels of political trust—Germany, France, Great Britain, Belgium, and Ireland—were also fairly consistent, with the average level of trust in each country fluctuating within a band of one point or less on the ten-point scale.

Poland, Portugal, Slovenia, and Hungary were less trusting and also more volatile. However, their several tribulations do not amount to anything like a unified crisis of political distrust. Trust in parliament and politicians reached its nadir in 2004 in Poland, in 2009 in Hungary, in 2012–2013 in Portugal, and in 2014 in Slovenia. In each of these cases, there was a subsequent rebound in trust. Some of the countries less consistently represented in the ESS also had low average levels of political trust—Lithuania, Italy, Greece, Czechia, and Slovakia.[19] But here, too, there is a good deal of heterogeneity in trajectories.

---

[16] Another item tapping trust in political parties did not appear in the first ESS round, but has produced generally similar responses in subsequent rounds. Additional questions regarding trust in the legal system and the police have produced higher ratings and are less strongly correlated with the more specifically political trust ratings.

[17] The cumulative decline amounts to just .05 points (with a standard error of .16 points) on the ten-point scale.

[18] Denmark exhibited an even higher but generally declining level of trust.

[19] Although some of these countries are missing from as many as four or five ESS rounds, the statistical analysis generating the estimated average levels of political trust for Europe as a whole takes them into account by including country fixed effects for the entire period. Tests for selection bias based on relating survey participation to population, economic conditions, protest activity, and immigration rates reveal little evidence of correlation between non-participation and opinion climates within countries over time.

As for democracy itself, the ESS questionnaires have also consistently included an item gauging satisfaction "with the way democracy works" in each respondent's own country. The responses to this item are even more stable than those for trust in parliament and politicians. At its lowest point, in 2010–2011, the average level of satisfaction with democracy in Europe as a whole was 5.0 on the zero-to-ten scale, two-tenths of a point below its level in 2002–2003. By the following wave, it had reached a new high, and in 2018–2019, it stood at 5.4, another twenty-first-century record. While there are certainly "many citizens" dissatisfied with the workings of democracy, there is no evidence here that Europeans' "support for democracy as a system of government has weakened" over the first two decades of the twenty-first century.

Only two countries, Spain and France, saw declines of as much as half a point in satisfaction with democracy between 2002–2003 and 2018–2019. Norway, Switzerland, Ireland, Portugal, Germany, and the Netherlands all saw increases at least that large. But the largest improvement of all—1.3 points on the ten-point scale—came in one of the least likely places imaginable, Poland. When the first ESS wave was conducted in autumn 2002, Poles expressed the lowest average level of satisfaction with "the way democracy works" of the 20 countries in the survey, 4.1. (Next lowest was Slovenia at 4.4, and the European average was 5.2.) By 2018–2019, the average level of satisfaction with democracy in Poland was 5.4, exactly matching the European average.

What makes this increase so perplexing, of course, is that outside observers have been distinctly *dis*satisfied with "the way democracy works in Poland" in recent years. Since the election of the Law and Justice party in 2015, Poland has engaged in democratic backsliding reminiscent of—and, indeed, modeled on—the earlier entrenchment of "illiberal" democracy in Hungary, complete with efforts to pack the courts with party loyalists, stifle the press, and resist the authority of the EU. As one recent report for American readers put it, "If You Think the U.S. is Having a Constitutional Crisis, You Should See What is Happening in Poland" (Perch & Kelemen, 2020).

The juxtaposition of democratic backsliding and public satisfaction with democracy in Poland raises a broader set of questions about the relationship between public opinion and democratic politics. When democratic institutions and procedures do erode, what role do ordinary citizens play in the process, and how do they respond?

2 Public Opinion and the Erosion of Democracy in Hungary and Poland

Concerns about a "crisis of democracy" in contemporary Europe rest in significant part on the illusion of an "explosion" of populist sentiment—growing antipathy to immigrants and the EU, declining trust in politicians, and declining popular attachment to democracy as a political system. But even if these shifts in public opinion were real, the notion that they posed a threat to democracy would hinge on a web of implicit assumptions linking public disaffection to toxic party politics and the breakdown of democratic institutions.

Foa and Mounk's influential account of "deconsolidation" illustrates this quasi-logic. The authors "suspect" that public opinion is "one of the most important factors in determining the likelihood of democratic breakdown." But the path they trace from bad attitudes to autocracy (2016, pp. 15–16) consists of a series of quick jump-cuts:

> Approval ratings for the continent's leading politicians stand at record lows, and citizens have grown deeply mistrustful of their political institutions. Far-right populist parties, such as France's National Front or the Sweden Democrats, have risen from obscurity to transform the party system of virtually every Western European country. Meanwhile, parts of Central and Eastern Europe bear witness to the institutional and ideological transformations that might be afoot: In Poland and Hungary, populist strongmen have begun to put pressure on critical media, to violate minority rights, and to undermine key institutions such as independent courts.

A subsequent book-length analysis by Mounk (2018, pp. 2–3) runs the same movie in reverse, from electoral dictatorships back to populist backsliding stemming from electoral support for "extremists":

> In Russia and Turkey, elected strongmen have succeeded in turning fledgling democracies into electoral dictatorships. In Poland and Hungary, populist leaders are using that same playbook to destroy the free media, to undermine independent institutions, and to muzzle the opposition. More countries may soon follow. In Austria, a far-right candidate nearly won the country's presidency. In France, a rapidly changing political landscape is providing new openings for both the far left and the far right. In Spain and Greece, established party systems are disintegrating with breathtaking speed. Even in the supposedly stable and tolerant democracies of Sweden, Germany, and the Netherlands, extremists are celebrating unprecedented successes.

Regardless of whether the path is traced forward or backward, the frightening route from "supposedly stable and tolerant democracies" to "electoral dictatorships" runs squarely through Hungary and Poland, where "populist leaders" have indeed worked "to destroy the free media, to undermine independent institutions, and to muzzle the opposition." Thus, any assessment of the nature and magnitude of Europe's crisis of democracy must carefully consider how and why these apparently democratic systems have suffered significant erosion.

One problem here is that the term "populist" has varied connotations in different settings. Are "populist leaders" in Hungary and Poland interchangeable with "the far right" in Austria or France or the "extremists" gaining electoral footholds in Sweden and Germany? Is populism itself a threat to democracy? In the course of a broader study of populism in contemporary Europe, political scientists Roger Eatwell and Matthew Goodwin cited Hungarian leader Viktor's attacks on democratic institutions as grounds for worry that populism "may presage the collapse of liberal-democratic freedoms and rights." But they also noted that, contrary to some expectations, supporters of populist parties "are generally not anti-democrats who want to tear down our political institutions. . . . In several of these democracies national populist voters are actually more supportive of representative democracy than the general population" (Eatwell & Goodwin, 2018, pp. 72, 117–120).

Further complicating matters, the rhetoric and behavior of leaders and parties can change over time. The Global Populism Database, which provides content analysis of speeches by political leaders in many countries, characterized Orbán's rhetoric as "somewhat populist" in 2010–2014 and 2014–2018, but "not populist" in his previous stint as prime minister in 1998–2002. Polish strongman Jaroslaw Kaczynski's rhetoric was likewise classified as "not populist" when he served as prime minister in 2006–2007.[20] These assessments raise the question of whether ordinary Hungarians and Poles were really voting for populism, much less for autocracy, when they handed power to their "populist leaders."

Notwithstanding these complexities, Hungary and Poland provide the best leverage we have for understanding the connection between right-wing populist sentiment, populist leadership, and the erosion of contemporary liberal democracy. By sketching the evolution of public opinion, electoral politics, and government in these countries in the first decades of the twenty-first century, I hope to shed light on the nature of threats to liberal democracy elsewhere in Europe.

2.1 *Hungary*

A decade after the fall of communism, Hungary came closer than any other formerly communist country to having a stable two-party system. In 2002 the Hungarian Socialist Party (MSZP) won a narrow plurality over the conservative Hungarian Civic Alliance (Fidesz), 41.4% to 39.8%. In 2006 the Socialists managed to win a narrow plurality of seats and to continue their governing coalition with the smaller Alliance of Free Democrats, despite trailing narrowly in the popular vote (41.4% to 41.6%).

This seeming normalcy was thrown out of kilter 5 months after the 2006 election with the leak of an audio recording of Prime Minister Ferenc Gyurcsány addressing a private meeting of MSZP officials. "We screwed up," Gyurcsány told his comrades:

> Not a little, a lot. No European country has done something as boneheaded as we have. Evidently, we lied throughout the last year-and-a-half, two years.... We lied in the morning, we lied in the evening.[21]

Gyurcsány's obscenity-laced admission of deceit and manifest contempt for the electorate triggered a wave of anti-government protests lasting more than a month. Clashes between protesters and police resulted in hundreds of injuries. Opposition leaders called for Gyurcsány's resignation, but he survived a parliamentary vote of confidence by a 207-165 margin (McLaughlin, 2006; Smith, 2006).

---

[20] Kirk A. Hawkins et al., The Global Populism Database (*https://populism.byu.edu/Pages/Data*)

[21] "We Lied to Win, Says Hungary PM," BBC News, 18 September 2006

The next parliamentary election, in 2010, was dominated by popular disaffection stemming from the Gyurcsány scandal. The governing MSZP lost more than half its popular support (winning just 20.3% of the vote) and more than two-thirds of its seats in the National Assembly. The big winners were the right-wing parties that had spearheaded the protests of 2006 and subsequent opposition efforts. The radical nationalist party Jobbik (the Movement for a Better Hungary) won 16.5% of the vote, making it a not-so-distant third in strength behind the faltering MSZP. Meanwhile, the largest opposition party, Fidesz, won 53.1% of the vote (up from 41.6% in 2006) and, importantly, 263 seats—a bare two-thirds majority—in the National Assembly.

In May 2007, a member of the European parliament affiliated with Fidesz had ascribed the political crisis stemming from Prime Minister Gyurcsány's leaked audio recording to the fact that "a Hungarian prime minister with a parliamentary majority is utterly secure in power; there is no way of removing him or her as long as that majority remains in place. This effectively relieves the prime minister of all responsibility towards society; it is for all practical purposes a semi-democratic system."[22]

When Hungarian voters replaced the discredited MSZP with Fidesz in 2010, the shoe was on the other foot—it was Fidesz's prime minister, Viktor Orbán, who was "utterly secure in power" and effectively relieved "of all responsibility towards society." Orbán's room to maneuver was significantly increased by the fact that Fidesz's slim two-thirds majority in the National Assembly allowed him to amend the constitution. According to Hungarian political scientist Béla Greskovits (2015, p. 34),

> FIDESZ's landslide victory at the 2010 parliamentary elections was a foregone conclusion, whereas the fact that the party acquired two-thirds of the mandate was accidental and is best explained by the Hungarian electoral system. However, it is partly due to this accident that the FIDESZ government could move ahead so fast in rolling back Hungarian democracy by using its overwhelming legislative power to infuse all the democratic institutions with authoritarian and illiberal "checks and balances."

The new government engineered the adoption of a declaration retroactively designating the election outcome as a "voting booth revolution" and the beginning of a new political community:

> The National Assembly declares that a new social contract was laid down in the April general elections through which the Hungarians decided to create a new system: the National Cooperation System.

As Hungarian legal scholar András Pap (2018, pp. 50–51, 68) noted:

> the idea of creating a new political community (or even the adoption of a new constitution) was not part of the political campaign in the elections . . . . The ideological declarations in the new Constitution create the impression that these values were actually expressed in the 'voting-booth revolution.' This retroactive argument logically cannot hold water, due to the very fact that the campaign did not include it.

---

[22] See Schöpflin (2007). Of course, by this standard almost every parliamentary democracy is "a semi-democratic system."

Table 2 Bases of identification with Fidesz before and after Hungary's 2010 election

	2009	2012–2015	2017–2019
Conservative ideology	0.455	0.264	0.180
	(0.029)	(0.025)	(0.018)
Conservative worldview	−0.030	0.168	0.086
	(0.051)	(0.033)	(0.034)
Anti-immigrant sentiment	0.015	−0.004	0.043
	(0.027)	(0.018)	(0.020)
Anti-EU sentiment	−0.014	0.059	0.065
	(0.019)	(0.017)	(0.014)
Dissatisfaction with the economy	−0.020	0.016	−0.145
	(0.029)	(0.019)	(0.024)
Dissatisfaction with democracy	0.035	−0.187	−0.170
	(0.026)	(0.020)	(0.020)
Distrust of parliament and politicians	−0.053	−0.131	−0.137
	(0.028)	(0.018)	(0.018)
2015 wave	–	0.12	–
		(0.06)	
2019 wave	–	–	0.10
			(0.06)
% "close"	23.2%	16.0%	23.1%
Pseudo R-squared	0.25	0.27	0.32
N	1484	3537	3121

Ordered probit regression coefficients (with standard errors in parentheses). Estimated response thresholds not shown

The next major step in the erosion of Hungarian democracy likewise came after, not before, an election. The first election conducted under the new constitution and electoral law stemming from the mythical "new social contract" of 2010 was held in April 2014. An international election-monitoring group reported that it was "efficiently administered and offered voters a diverse choice following an inclusive candidate registration process," but that Fidesz "enjoyed an undue advantage because of restrictive campaign regulations, biased media coverage and campaign activities that blurred the separation between political party and the State."[23] Despite this "undue advantage," Fidesz's vote share declined from 53.1% in 2010 to 44.5% in 2014—just a few points higher than before the Gyurcsány scandal and hardly a rousing popular endorsement of Hungary's "new social contract." Nonetheless, a few months after the election, Orbán took further steps to consolidate what he now famously referred to as an "illiberal" democracy in Hungary.

The statistical analyses reported in Table 2 shed light on the changing bases of support for Fidesz before and after its authoritarian turn. The analysis reported in the first column of the table is based on data from the 2009 ESS, more than 2 years into

---

[23] Office for Democratic Institutions and Human Rights, Limited Election Observation Mission Final Report, 11 July 2014 (*https://www.upr-info.org/sites/default/files/document/hungary/session_25_-_may_2016/osce-odihr_upr25_hun_e_annexe1.pdf*)

the anti-Gyurcsány mobilization but a year before the crucial 2010 election. At that point, there is no indication at all that support for Fidesz was grounded in anti-democratic sentiment or even in "populist" attitudes more generally. The most important predictor by far of identification with Fidesz was conservative ideology. Dissatisfaction with democracy had little or no effect, while trust in parliament and politicians was, if anything, positively related to identification with the party. The other factors generally associated with support for Europe's right-wing populist parties—opposition to immigration and to the EU and conservative worldviews—were equally irrelevant.[24]

By late 2012, more than 2 years after the beginning of Hungary's democratic "backsliding," conservative worldviews had emerged as a significant predictor of identification with Fidesz, but opposition to immigration and to European integration were still irrelevant. Moreover, satisfaction with democracy and trust in parliament and politicians were now strongly positively associated with support for Fidesz—an indication that the party was increasingly seen, at least by its supporters, as Hungary's political establishment. Only in 2015—5 years after Orbán came to power and as Europe's refugee crisis began to overwhelm Hungary—did opposition to immigration and to the EU begin to register as significant factors in support for Fidesz. Perhaps Orbán's fiery rhetoric scapegoating immigrants and the EU attracted new supporters. More likely, it encouraged people who already backed Fidesz to express more negative views about immigrants and European integration than they had previously.

2.2 Poland

The erosion of democracy in Poland reveals some striking similarities to events in Hungary. As in Hungary, Poland had a relatively stable two-plus party system, with the combined vote share of the center-right Civic Platform (PO) and the Law and Justice party (PiS) increasing from 51% in 2005 to 74% in 2007 and 69% in 2011. Civic Platform garnered 41.5% of the vote in 2007 and 39.2% in 2011, in each case forming a governing coalition with the smaller Polish People's Party. It was the first time in the history of modern Polish democracy that a prime minister served two successive terms.

---

[24] My measure of conservative worldviews is based on responses to ten ESS items tapping the importance of security, tradition, creativity, diversity, and the like. It is only modestly correlated with left-right ideology (R=.15). The scale runs from zero (for people who ascribed maximal importance to liberal values and minimal importance to conservative values) to ten (for those who ascribed maximal importance to conservative values and minimal importance to liberal values). I included respondents who answered at least nine of the ten questions, imputing neutral values for the tenth when necessary. On the political relevance of these attitudes, see Stenner (2005) and Hetherington and Weiler (2018).

In the run-up to the next election in 2015, it looked like Civic Platform might win a third consecutive term. But support for the party dropped precipitously that summer "when several government officials were caught making profane and impolitic comments on illegal wiretaps"—a striking echo of the events leading to the demise of MSZP in Hungary. On Election Day in late October, Civic Platform's vote share fell precipitously to 24.1%, while the Law and Justice party's share surged to 37.6%. The latter figure was enough to secure 235 of 460 seats in the Sejm, making Law and Justice the first party in Poland's post-communist era to win an absolute majority of seats (Bartyzel & Skolimowski, 2015; Lyman, 2015).

In light of subsequent developments, it is essential to note that the 2015 election outcome was by no means a popular ratification of even a mildly authoritarian program. According to a BBC News analysis:

> Law and Justice won big because they offered simple, concrete policies for the many in Poland that feel untouched by the country's impressive economic growth. It offered higher child care benefits and tax breaks for the less well-off. After eight years in office many Poles had grown weary of the governing centrist Civic Platform's unfulfilled promises, scandals and what was perceived by some to be an aloof attitude. Law and Justice also stuck with its winning formula of presenting a more moderate face than its rather combative leader Jaroslaw Kaczynski. That moderate face belongs to Beata Szydlo, a 52-year-old miner's daughter and avid reader, who will become the country's next prime minister. (Easton, 2015)

A subsequent scholarly assessment echoed this account, noting that the Law and Justice party "softened its image. It placed signs of authoritarian leanings as well as controversial personalities (including Jaroslaw Kaczynski himself) out of public view. Running on the slogan 'Good Change,' PiS leaders called for compassionate conservatism, and sought to offer undecided voters an alternative to the 'boring' PO" (Fomina & Kucharczyk, 2016, pp. 60–61).

The Poles who supported the Law and Justice party in 2015 were hardly unusual in preferring "good change" to "boring" incumbency; there is a strong tendency in democratic politics for incumbent parties to lose support over time. Perhaps Poles should have been wary of the party's authoritarian proclivities in light of some of the initiatives it had pursued the last time it held power, in 2006–2007, including attempts to ban marches by pro-gay activists and to bolster its control over journalists and prosecutors. But that had been 8 years earlier, with a mostly different cast of characters, and in the context of a coalition government with two socially conservative parties whose "democratic credentials" were "very much in doubt."[25]

The seventh round of ESS interviews in Poland, conducted in the spring of 2015, provides a snapshot of popular support for the Law and Justice party on the eve of its return to power 5 months later. The statistical analysis of these data presented in the first column of Table 3 provides little evidence of popular enthusiasm for an

---

[25] According to Albertazzi and Mueller (2013, pp. 358–361), the League of Polish Families' youth wing "was staffed by large numbers of skinheads, quite open about their Nazi sympathies and responsible for attacks against gay and feminist groups, members of ethnic minorities and others," while Self-Defence had been organized in the early 1990s "as a militia aimed at defending farmers from debt collectors and it had not been a stranger to violence in the past."

Table 3 Bases of identification with Law and Justice before and after Poland's 2015 election

	2015	2016–2017	2018–2019
Conservative ideology	0.307	0.236	0.351
	(0.023)	(0.029)	(0.031)
Conservative worldview	0.190	0.194	0.225
	(0.042)	(0.046)	(0.046)
Anti-immigrant sentiment	0.013	0.045	0.086
	(0.028)	(0.026)	(0.028)
Anti-EU sentiment	−0.019	0.048	0.021
	(0.018)	(0.017)	(0.020)
Dissatisfaction with the economy	0.055	−0.013	−0.061
	(0.028)	(0.027)	(0.037)
Dissatisfaction with democracy	0.052	−0.138	−0.092
	(0.026)	(0.028)	(0.032)
Distrust of parliament and politicians	−0.031	−0.148	−0.151
	(0.026)	(0.023)	(0.029)
% "close"	11.5	14.5	17.1
Pseudo R-squared	0.18	0.27	0.33
N	1693	1670	1442

Ordered probit regression coefficients (with standard errors in parentheses). Estimated response thresholds not shown

authoritarian turn. Perhaps most obviously, only 11% of Poles (43% of those who chose a party) reported feeling close to the Law and Justice party in spring 2015.[26] Moreover, Law and Justice identifiers were distinguished overwhelmingly by conservative ideology and worldviews—the same factors that had predicted identification with the party for almost a decade, although both relationships were stronger in 2015 than previously. Dissatisfaction with democracy was modestly related to identification with Law and Justice. However, the main drivers of support for populist parties elsewhere in Europe seem to have had remarkably little traction. Neither anti-EU sentiment nor anti-immigrant sentiment seemed to matter, while distrust of political elites was, if anything, probably *negatively* related to identification with the Law and Justice party.

Notwithstanding the limited breadth of popular support for the Law and Justice party, Poland's new leaders did not hesitate to translate their parliamentary majority into an assault on checks and balances comparable to Orbán's in Hungary. Indeed, party chair Jaroslaw Kaczynski said of Orbán, "You have given an example, and we are learning from your example." Within 2 months of the election, the Sejm passed a law reorganizing the Constitutional Court, and early the next year it passed a law initiating the process of giving the government full control of state radio and television. Later, the formerly independent National Council of the Judiciary was

---

[26] Weighting all countries and ESS rounds by population, 4.5% of the respondents said they were "very close" to some party, 27.3% "quite close," 14.8% "not close" or unspecified, and 1.3% "not at all close"; the remaining 52.1% said they did not feel closer to any particular party.

packed with party loyalists, and Polish judges were prohibited from implementing rulings by the European Court of Justice (Kingsley, 2018; Perch & Kelemen, 2020).

As in Hungary, popular reaction to the Law and Justice party's power grab has been mixed. In 2019 parliamentary elections, Law and Justice's vote share increased by six percentage points, but the party lost seats and control of the Senate. In the 2020 presidential election, incumbent Andrzej Duda won 51% of the runoff vote—virtually identical to the 51.5% he had won 5 years earlier.

In the ESS data, the proportion of Poles who said they felt close to the Law and Justice party gradually increased from 11% in 2015 to 14% in 2016–2017 and 16% in 2018–2019. Perhaps more importantly, the bases of that support (summarized in the second and third columns of Table 3) shifted in ways that parallel the shift in support for Fidesz in Hungary. Although conservative ideology and worldviews remained the most important bases of identification with the Law and Justice party, support for the party began to be associated with opposition to immigration and, to a lesser extent, with opposition to European integration. In addition, Poles who felt close to the Law and Justice party reported significantly greater levels of satisfaction with democracy and trust in parliament and politicians. Whether these attitudes were a cause or an effect of identification with the Law and Justice party is, of course, unclear.

2.3 Public Opinion and Democratic "Backsliding"

Hungary and Poland fit few of the stereotypes often associated with the "crisis of democracy" in contemporary Europe. In stark contrast to the familiar notion of economic crisis or social stagnation pushing disgruntled masses into the arms of authoritarian leaders, these were among the more stable and prosperous places in Central and Eastern Europe. Despite some egregious mismanagement, the economy of Hungary (as measured by real GDP per capita) grew by 25% in the decade leading up to the election of Viktor Orbán in 2010, while Poland's economy grew by a spectacular 45% in the decade leading up to the Law and Justice party's election in 2015. While both countries were rocked by significant political scandals, the "mildly authoritarian regimes" that emerged from those disruptions were not in any obvious sense products of economic or social distress.[27]

Some scholars of Western European politics have focused on the "hollowing-out" of civil society as a worrisome indicator of democratic decline. However, that line of analysis seems to be similarly unhelpful in accounting for developments in Hungary and Poland. Indeed, applying a variety of indicators of "hollowing-out" to ten East Central European democracies in the first decade of the twenty-first century,

---

[27] Analyzing the success of populist parties in 27 countries in Europe and the Americas, Castanho Silva (2019, p. 280) concluded that "elite collusion and corrupt governments are the most important factors behind the rise of populists."

Greskovits (2015, pp. 32–35) ranked Hungary as the *least* "hollowed" among them, with "a vibrant and mobilized civil society." He concluded that "what really matters for the solidity or backsliding of democracy is not the vibrancy vs hollowness of the system, or the strength vs weakness of civil society per se," but:

> the *liberal/democratic rather than illiberal/authoritarian ideology and purpose of the actors* who mobilize civil society organizations and their members for political participation.[28]

It is true that citizens' trust in political leaders and institutions in these countries was quite low and with good reason. In Hungary, the rise of Fidesz to majority status was certainly facilitated by Prime Minister Gyurcsány's remarkable 2006 admission of persistent deceit and bad faith. In Poland, governments of the center, left, and right successively got bogged down in major corruption scandals. Yet there is remarkably little evidence in the ESS data that political distrust *produced* support for Fidesz or for the Law and Justice party. Indeed, the statistical analyses reported in Tables 2 and 3 suggest that identification with both parties was, if anything, *positively* related to trust in parliament and politicians on the eve of their electoral breakthroughs and (less surprisingly) even more strongly positively related thereafter.

Nor is there much support for the notion that these democracies succumbed to political polarization. In a comparative analysis of democratic decline in Hungary, Turkey, and Venezuela, political scientists Robert Kaufman and Stephan Haggard (Kaufman & Haggard, 2019, pp. 419–420) argued that all three countries:

> experienced reinforcing cycles of democratic dysfunction, social polarization, and declining support for moderate, democratic political forces and institutions. These stresses on democratic rule were compounded by polarizing political appeals that cast competitors as enemies and even existential threats to the nation and the people. . . . Once in office, Orbán's effort to further polarize the electorate continued, with attacks on the EU, on outsiders such as George Soros, and a full-throated exploitation of the European migrant crisis to stoke racial and ethnic anxiety.

Contemporaneous evidence from public opinion surveys in Hungary provides little support for this account. In 2009, on the eve of the election that propelled Orbán to power, ideological polarization was higher than in most other European countries, but comparable to levels in France and Sweden, and significantly lower than in Czechia and Slovenia. The level of ideological polarization in Hungary has subsequently increased by about 11%, but that increase mostly reflects shifts to the political left, not the right, in response to Orbán's rule.[29] Similarly in Poland, ideological polarization was only moderately high on the eve of the Law and Justice

---

[28] Here, too, there is a strong parallel with Bermeo's (2003, p. 232) conclusion that democratic breakdowns in twentieth-century Europe and Latin America often occurred "where civil society was relatively *dense.*" On "hollowing out," see Mair (2013).

[29] The standard deviation of left-right placements in Hungary increased from 2.29 in 2009 to 2.55 by 2019. The proportion of respondents placing themselves at 0, 1, or 2 on the zero-to-ten left-right scale increased from 8.7% to 13.4% (an estimated 4.7% increase with a standard error of 1.3), while the proportion placing themselves at 8, 9, or 10 *decreased* from 21.5% to 20.5% (an estimated 1.0% decrease with a standard error of 1.8).

party's election in 2015, though it subsequently increased (by about 7%, reflecting slight shifts to both the left and the right on the ideological spectrum).[30]

In her historical survey of breakdowns of democracy, Nancy Bermeo argued that political elites rather than ordinary people were generally "the key actors" in precipitating these breakdowns. "There were a few cases where anti-democratic movements became electorally successful political parties," Bermeo (2003, p. 234) wrote, "but in the vast majority of our cases, voters did not choose dictatorship at the ballot box." With due allowance for the significant distinction between "dictatorship" and the "mildly authoritarian regimes" considered here, the same might be said of contemporary Hungary and Poland. Voters in these countries did not choose authoritarians at the ballot box. Rather, they chose the only readily available alternatives to unsatisfactory incumbent governments, only to have their votes rather transparently trumped up by the winners into a "voting booth revolution" justifying "a new social contract" expanding the power of the ruling party at the expense of the courts, the media, and other political actors.

These developments call to mind Susan Stokes's (2001) account of "neoliberalism by surprise" in late twentieth-century Latin America. However, in that context supposedly left-wing governments faced significant economic and political pressures to pursue neoliberal policies once in office. The "illiberalism by surprise" pursued by Orbán in Hungary beginning in 2010 and by Kaczynski in Poland beginning in 2015 seems to have been much more a matter of choice than of duress. They engineered the dismantling of democratic checks and balances not in response to any overwhelming external or internal pressures, but simply because they could.

Popular responses to this democratic backsliding provide a final parallel to Bermeo's account of breakdowns of democracy. "Ordinary people generally were guilty of remaining passive when dictators actually attempted to seize power," she wrote (Bermeo, 2003, pp. 222, 235). While they "generally did not polarize and mobilize in support of dictatorship, they did not immediately mobilize in defense of democracy either." There has certainly been some mobilization of opposition to the ruling parties in Hungary and Poland. However, neither has faced massive resistance; indeed both have enjoyed substantial public support. The ESS survey data shed some light on the bases of that support.

Table 4 summarizes public opinion in Hungary in four distinct periods: (1) from 2002 through 2007, under the MSZP (Socialist) government; (2) in 2009, on the eve of Fidesz's electoral breakthrough; (3) in the first 5 years of democratic backsliding under Orbán; and (4) in the two most recent ESS rounds, in 2017 and 2019. The entries are average responses for the entire population, not just Fidesz supporters. The final column shows changes in public sentiment from 2009, the year before Orbán's election, to the most recent reading in 2019.

---

[30]The standard deviation of left-right placements in Poland increased from 2.32 in 2015 to 2.42 in 2016–2017 and 2.47 in 2018–2019. The proportion of respondents placing themselves at 0, 1, or 2 on the zero-to-ten scale increased from 7.9% to 9.3% (an estimated 1.4% increase with a standard error of 1.1), while the proportion placing themselves at 8, 9, or 10 increased from 24.3% to 25.5% (an estimated 1.2% increase with a standard error of 1.7).

Table 4 Subjective well-being in Hungary before and after the 2010 election of Fidesz

	2002–2007	2009	2010–2015	2017–2019	Δ 2009 to 2019
Satisfaction with national economy	3.37 (0.04)	1.70 (0.05)	3.45 (0.03)	4.78 (0.04)	+3.04 (0.08)
Satisfaction with incumbent government	3.53 (0.05)	1.81 (0.07)	3.84 (0.04)	4.54 (0.05)	+2.70 (0.10)
Trust in parliament and politicians	3.47 (0.04)	2.19 (0.06)	3.56 (0.03)	4.19 (0.05)	+2.10 (0.09)
Satisfaction with democracy	4.15 (0.04)	2.89 (0.08)	4.35 (0.04)	4.68 (0.05)	+1.64 (0.11)
State of health services	3.43 (0.04)	3.78 (0.08)	3.76 (0.03)	3.85 (0.05)	−0.03 (0.10)
State of education	4.70 (0.04)	4.50 (0.07)	4.76 (0.03)	4.87 (0.05)	+0.34 (0.10)
Satisfaction with life as a whole	5.56 (0.05)	5.23 (0.08)	5.76 (0.03)	6.29 (0.04)	+.95 (0.10)

Average values on zero-to-ten scales (with standard errors in parentheses)

These data document a remarkable transformation of the social and political climate of Hungary. Average satisfaction with the economy increased by three points on the zero-to-ten scale between 2009 and 2019, a massive improvement. Satisfaction with the national government improved almost as much. Trust in parliament and politicians nearly doubled, and even satisfaction with "the way democracy works in Hungary" increased dramatically. Perhaps most impressively, the average level of satisfaction with "life as a whole nowadays" increased by almost a full point on the ten-point scale. Moreover, by every one of these indicators, life in Hungary has continued to improve over the course of Orbán's tenure.

Hungarians' subjective well-being was at a low ebb in 2009, more than 2 years into the crisis set off by the Gyurcsány scandal and just months after the government accepted a humiliating €15 billion bailout from the EU, IMF, and World Bank.[31] However, even if they took the earlier, less dire years of MSZP rule (represented by the first column of Table 4) as a baseline, Hungarians would have considered themselves significantly better off—economically, socially, and politically—under Fidesz, especially in recent years.

Poland in the spring of 2015, 5 months before the election that brought the Law and Justice party to power, was not in a crisis comparable to Hungary's in 2009. The various indicators of subjective well-being in the 2015 ESS data, reported in the

---

[31] Kate Connolly and Ian Traynor, "Hungary Receives Rescue Package, With Strings Attached," *The Guardian*, 29 October 2008 (*https://www.theguardian.com/business/2008/oct/29/hungary-economy-imf-eu-world-bank*). "Hungary Offered A Tripartite Bailout—With Strings," *Forbes*, 29 October 2008 (*https://www.forbes.com/2008/10/29/hungary-imf-aid-markets-economy-cx_vr_1029markets7.html#4ae90d1c3404*)

Table 5 Subjective well-being in Poland before and after the 2015 election of the Law and Justice Party

	2002–2013	2015	2016–2017	2018–2019	Δ 2015 to 2019
Satisfaction with national economy	3.86 (0.02)	4.05 (0.05)	4.84 (0.05)	5.76 (0.06)	+1.72 (0.08)
Satisfaction with incumbent government	3.21 (0.02)	3.07 (0.05)	4.04 (0.07)	4.64 (0.07)	+1.57 (0.09)
Trust in parliament and politicians	2.63 (0.02)	2.40 (0.05)	2.93 (0.05)	3.43 (0.06)	+1.03 (0.08)
Satisfaction with democracy	4.47 (0.02)	4.37 (0.06)	4.66 (0.06)	5.41 (0.07)	+1.04 (0.09)
State of health services	3.64 (0.02)	3.44 (0.06)	3.91 (0.06)	4.25 (0.06)	+.81 (0.08)
State of education	5.35 (0.02)	5.41 (0.06)	5.69 (0.06)	6.03 (0.06)	+0.62 (0.09)
Satisfaction with life as a whole	6.61 (0.02)	6.94 (0.06)	7.14 (0.05)	7.06 (0.05)	+0.12 (0.08)

Average values on zero-to-ten scales (with standard errors in parentheses)

second column of Table 5, are roughly comparable to the average levels from the previous decade in the first column of the table. Nonetheless, the two surveys conducted since Jaroslaw Kaczynski began to follow Viktor Orbán's example of "illiberal" entrenchment show improvements in well-being similar in flavor, if smaller in magnitude than those under Orbán in Hungary. Here, too, the most striking improvement—1.7 points on the zero-to-ten scale from 2015 to 2019—was in satisfaction with the economy. Here, too, satisfaction with the government increased almost as much, while trust in parliament and politicians and satisfaction with democracy also increased by a full point. Unlike in Hungary, ratings of the state of health services and education also improved markedly, though satisfaction with life as a whole remained essentially unchanged.

By these measures, at least, ordinary Hungarians and Poles have flourished even as outside observers have recorded substantial declines in the quality of their democracies.[32] Under the circumstances, it is hardly surprising that many seem to have accommodated themselves—after the fact—to Orbán's and Kaczynski's "illiberal" entrenchments. And even if they have been less troubled by the erosion of checks and balances than democratic theorists might wish, it is very hard to see them as active proponents of authoritarianism, much less as its primary agents. They have

---

[32] In the V-Dem project's annual assessments of "Liberal Democracy," Hungary's rating fell from .782 in 2009 to .370 in 2019. Poland's rating fell from .811 in 2014 to .533 in 2019. By way of comparison, France and Germany's ratings in 2019 were .798 and .838; Bulgaria and Romania's were .513 and .467.

gone about their political lives in much the way that democratic citizens generally do.

3 Public Opinion as It Is

Why have so many well-informed observers been so wrong about the basic contours of public opinion in contemporary Europe? In *The Phantom Public*, Walter Lippmann (1925, p. 200) wrote of:

> immense confusions in the current theory of democracy which frustrate and pervert its action. I have attacked certain of the confusions with no conviction except that a false philosophy tends to stereotype thought against the lessons of experience. I do not know what the lessons will be when we have learned to think of public opinion as it is, and not as the fictitious power we have assumed it to be.

Almost a century later, we are still struggling to learn to "think of public opinion as it is." Much writing about democratic politics remains, as E. E. Schattschneider (1960, p. 130) put it 60 years ago, "essentially simplistic, based on a tremendously exaggerated notion of the immediacy and urgency of the connection of public opinion and events." If right-wing populist parties are gaining footholds in European parliaments, it must be because "'populist' sentiments are exploding." If immigration is "tearing Europe apart," it must be because anti-immigrant attitudes are on the rise. If political elites are embroiled in squabbles about European integration, there must be "a backlash against the EU." And if democratic systems succumb to backsliding, it must be because "support for democracy as a system of government has weakened."

The evidence presented here casts considerable doubt on "the immediacy and urgency of the connection of public opinion and events" in contemporary Europe. Significant developments are afoot, ranging from increased electoral support for populist parties in some countries to social frictions stemming from immigration to isolated instances of real, disturbing erosion of democratic checks and balances. But none of these developments seems to be immediately or urgently connected to shifts in public opinion, either in Europe as a whole or in specific countries.

In the most influential essay ever written about public opinion, Philip Converse claimed that "The broad contours of elite decisions over time can depend in a vital way upon currents in what is loosely called 'the history of ideas.' These decisions in turn have effects upon the mass of more common citizens. But, of any direct participation in this history of ideas and the behavior it shapes, the mass is remarkably innocent" (Converse, 1964, p. 255).

This characterization has sometimes been criticized as belittling the democratic capacity of ordinary citizens. But when the currents of ideas in play involve anti-immigrant agitation and other manifestations of "populist" extremism, the word "innocent" has a rather different connotation.

Developments in Hungary and Poland underline another respect in which democratic theory has tended "to stereotype thought against the lessons of experience." As John Zaller has argued, public opinion "is capable of recognizing and focusing on its own conception of what matters."[33] But "what matters" to ordinary citizens may not be what matters to democratic theorists. For more than half a century, empirical research has found citizens expressing allegiance to high-minded democratic values in the abstract while often flouting those values in specific cases.[34] In Hungary and Poland, citizens experiencing substantial improvements in subjective well-being under "mildly authoritarian" regimes have registered significant increases not only in political trust and approval but also in satisfaction with "how democracy works," demonstrating a good deal of willingness to overlook some "cracking down on judges and the news media, refusing to take in migrants and lashing out at the European Union" in exchange for prosperity, order, and validation of their national identities (Karasz, 2017; Szakacs, 2019). That willingness may be egregious from the standpoint of democratic theory; but when theory and political behavior collide, "it is at least as likely that the ideal is wrong as it is that the reality is bad" (Schattschneider, 1960, p. 128).

Even if the public's "own conception of what matters" in these instances is considered "bad," it can hardly be considered surprising. One of the primary lessons of experience in democratic systems is that citizens care much more about outcomes than about procedures. When the corruption or incompetence of political leaders seems to impinge on their well-being, they will register their disapproval through whatever channels are most readily available to them. When they experience peace and prosperity, they will mostly be happy to let the people in charge carry on. If the results in either case amount to a "crisis of democracy," that is first and foremost a crisis of political leadership, not a crisis of public opinion.[35]

---

[33] Zaller (1998, p. 186) interpreted President Bill Clinton's popularity in the wake of a major scandal as demonstrating "just how relentlessly the majority of voters can stay focused on the bottom line," meaning not just prosperity but, more broadly, "political substance." He noted that the public might not be "either wise or virtuous. For one thing, its sense of substance seems, in the aggregate, rather amoral—usually more like 'what have you done for me lately' than 'social justice'."

[34] Important early works include Prothro and Grigg (1960) and McClosky (1964). Two recent examples are Bartels (2020) and Graham and Svolik (2020).

[35] I am grateful to Vanderbilt's May Werthan Shayne Chair for financial support, to Nancy Bermeo for advice and encouragement, to Kaitlen Cassell for splendid research assistance, and to Cassell, Benjamin Page, John Sides, and participants in the Vanderbilt Political Science faculty workshop for helpful criticism of a preliminary draft of this report.

References

Achen, C. H., & Bartels, L. M. (2016). *Democracy for realists: Why elections do not produce responsive government.* Princeton University Press.

Albertazzi, D., & Mueller, S. (2013). Populism and liberal democracy: Populists in government in Austria, Italy, Poland and Switzerland. *Government and Opposition, 48,* 343–371.

Bartels, L. M. (2017). The 'wave' of right-wing populist sentiment is a myth. *Washington Post Monkey Cage,* 21 June 2017. Available at: https://www.washingtonpost.com/news/monkey-cage/wp/2017/06/21/the-wave-of-right-wing-populist-sentiment-is-a-myth/

Bartels, L. M. (2020). Ethnic antagonism erodes republicans' commitment to Democracy. *Proceedings of the National Academy of Sciences,* 117. Available at: https://www.pnas.org/content/pnas/117/37/22752.full.pdf

Bartyzel, D., & Skolimowski, P. (2015). Poland hands unprecedented ballot win to Conservative Party. *Bloomberg,* 25 October 2015. Available at: https://www.bloomberg.com/news/articles/2015-10-25/poland-ousts-government-as-law-justice-gains-historic-majority

Berman, S. (2019). *Democracy and dictatorship in Europe: From the Ancien Régime to the present day.* Oxford University Press.

Bermeo, N. (2003). *Ordinary people in extraordinary times: The citizenry and the breakdown of democracy.* Princeton University Press.

Bremmer, I. (2017). The wave to come. *Time,* 11 May 2017. Available at: https://time.com/4775441/the-wave-to-come/

Bröning, M. (2016). The rise of populism in Europe: Can the center hold?" *Foreign Affairs Snapshot,* 3 June 2016. Available at: https://www.foreignaffairs.com/articles/europe/2016-06-03/rise-populism-europe

Castanho Silva, B. (2019). Populist success: A qualitative comparative analysis. In K. A. Hawkins, R. E. Carlin, L. Littvay, & C. R. Kaltwasser (Eds.), *The Ideational Approach to Populism: Concept, Theory, and Analysis* (pp. 305–319). Routledge.

Converse, P. E. (1964). The nature of belief systems in mass publics. In D. E. Apter (Ed.), *Ideology and Discontent* (pp. 206–261). Free Press.

Dionne, Jr., E. J. (2017). Germany's political crisis. *Washington Post,* 2 December 2015.

Drozdiak, W. (2017). *Fractured continent: Europe's crises and the fate of the West.* W. W. Norton & Company.

Easton, A. (2015). Poland elections: Conservatives secure decisive win. *BBC News,* 26 October 2015. Available at: https://www.bbc.com/news/world-europe-34631826

Eatwell, R., & Goodwin, M. (2018). *National populism: The revolt against liberal democracy.* Pelican Books.

Eddy, M. (2017). A year after the Berlin market attack, Germany admits mistakes. *New York Times,* 19 December 2017. Available at: https://www.nytimes.com/2017/12/19/world/europe/berlin-attack-memorial.html

Ehrenfreund, M. (2016). Europe's immigration crisis is just beginning. *Washington Post Wonkblog,* 1 July 2016. Available at: https://www.washingtonpost.com/news/wonk/wp/2016/07/01/europes-immigration-crisis-is-just-beginning/

Foa, R. S., & Mounk, Y. (2016). The democratic disconnect. *Journal of Democracy, 27,* 15–16.

Fomina, J., & Kucharczyk, J. (2016). Populism and protest in Poland. *Journal of Democracy, 27,* 60–61.

Goodman, P. S. (2019). The Nordic model may be the best cushion against capitalism. Can it survive immigration?" *New York Times,* 11 July 2019. https://www.nytimes.com/2019/07/11/business/sweden-economy-immigration.html

Graham, M. H., & Svolik, M. W. (2020). Democracy in America? Partisanship, polarization, and the robustness of support for democracy in the United States. *American Political Science Review, 114*(2), 392–409.

Greskovits, B. (2015). The hollowing and backsliding of democracy in East Central Europe. *Global Policy, 6*(2015), 34.

Hetherington, M., & Weiler, J. (2018). *Prius or pickup? How the answers to four simple questions explain America's great divide*. Mariner Books.

Judis, J. B. (2016). *The populist explosion: How the Great Recession transformed American and European politics*. Columbia Global Reports.

Karasz, P. (2017). Leaders of Hungary and Poland chafe at E.U., but how do their people feel?" *New York Times*, 6 September 2017. Available at: https://www.nytimes.com/2017/09/06/world/europe/hungary-poland-eu.html

Kaufman, R. R., & Haggard, S. (2019). Democratic decline in the United States: What can we learn from middle-income backsliding? *Perspectives on Politics, 17*, 419–420.

Kingsley, P. (2018). As West fears the rise of autocrats, Hungary shows what's possible. *New York Times*, 10 February 2018. Available at: https://www.nytimes.com/2018/02/10/world/europe/hungary-orban-democracy-far-right.html

Levitsky, S., & Ziblatt, D. (2018). *How democracies die*. Crown.

Lippmann, W. (1925). *The phantom public*. Harcourt, Brace and Company.

Lyman, R. (2015). Right-wing party roars back in Polish elections. *New York Times*, 25 October 2015. Available at: https://www.nytimes.com/2015/10/26/world/europe/poland-parliamentary-elections.html

Mair, P. (2013). *Ruling the void: The hollowing-out of western democracy*. Verso.

McClosky, H. (1964). Consensus and ideology in American Politics. *American Political Science Review, 58*(8), 361–382.

McLaughlin, D. (2006). 150 injured as Hungarians riot over PM's lies. *The Guardian*, 19 September 2006. Available at: https://www.theguardian.com/world/2006/sep/19/1

Moffitt, B. (2016). *The global rise of populism: Performance, political style, and representation*. Stanford University Press.

Mounk, Y. (2018). *The people vs. democracy: Why our freedom is in danger and how to save it*. Harvard University Press.

Müller, J. W. (2016). *What is populism?* University of Pennsylvania Press.

Nolan, D. (2015). Hungary government condemned over anti-immigration drive. *The Guardian*, 2 July 2015. Available at: https://www.theguardian.com/world/2015/jul/02/hungary-government-condemned-over-anti-immigration-drive

Norris, P. (2017). So is the wave of populist nationalism finished? Hardly. *Washington Post Monkey Cage*, 17 May 2017. Available at: https://www.washingtonpost.com/news/monkey-cage/wp/2017/05/17/so-is-the-wave-of-populist-nationalism-finished-hardly/

Norris, P., & Inglehart, R. (2019). *Cultural backlash: Trump, Brexit, and authoritarian populism*. Cambridge University Press.

Pap, A. L. (2018). *Democratic decline in Hungary: Law and society in an illiberal democracy* (p. 2018). Routledge.

Perch, L., & Kelemen, R. D. (2020). If you think the U.S. is having a constitutional crisis, you should see what is happening in Poland. *Washington Post Monkey Cage*, 25.

Prothro, J. W., & Grigg, C. M. (1960). Fundamental principles of democracy: Bases of agreement and disagreement. *Journal of Politics, 22*(2), 276–294.

Przeworski, A. (2019). *Crises of democracy*. Cambridge University Press.

Rovira Kaltwasser, C. (2012). The ambivalence of populism: Threat and corrective for democracy. *Democratization, 19*(2), 184–208.

Schattschneider, E. E. (1960). *The semisovereign people: A Realist's view of democracy in America*. Dryden Press.

Scheppele, K. L. (2015). Orban's police state: Hungary's crackdown on refugees is shredding the values of democracy. *Politico*, 14 September 2015. Available at: https://www.politico.eu/article/orbans-police-state-hungary-serbia-border-migration-refugees/

Schöpflin, G. (2007). Democracy, populism, and the political crisis in Hungary. *Eurozine*, 7 May 2007. Available at: https://www.eurozine.com/democracy-populism-and-the-political-crisis-in-hungary/?pdf=

Smith, C. S. (2006). Clashes disrupt Hungary's celebration of anti-Soviet revolt. *New York Times*, 24 October 2006. Available at: https://www.nytimes.com/2006/10/24/world/europe/24hungary.html

Stenner, K. (2005). *The authoritarian dynamic*. Cambridge University Press.

Stokes, B. (2016). The immigration crisis is tearing Europe apart. *Foreign Policy*, 22 July 2016. Available at: http://foreignpolicy.com/2016/07/22/the-immigration-crisis-is-tearing-europe-apart/

Stokes, S. C. (2001). *Mandates and democracy: Neoliberalism by surprise in Latin America*. Cambridge University Press.

Szakacs, G. (2019). Hungary could resume anti-EU campaigns, says PM Orban. *Reuters*, 24 March 2019. Available at: https://www.reuters.com/article/us-hungary-eu-orban-idUSKCN1R50GV

Taylor, A. (2016). The global wave of populism that turned 2016 upside down. *Washington Post World Views*, 19 December 2016. Available at: https://www.washingtonpost.com/news/worldviews/wp/2016/12/19/the-global-wave-of-populism-that-turned-2016-upside-down/

Tooze, A. (2018). *Crashed: How a decade of financial crises changed the world*. Viking.

Varoufakis, Y. (2016). *And the weak suffer what they must? Europe's crisis and America's economic future*. Nation Books.

Wood, J. (2019). Can you forgive her? How Margaret Thatcher ruled. *The New Yorker*, 2 December 2019.

Zaller, J. (1998). Monica Lewinsky's contribution to Political Science PS. *Political Science and Politics, 31*(2), 182–189.

Larry M. Bartels holds the May Werthan Shayne Chair in Public Policy and Social Science at Vanderbilt University. He joined Vanderbilt in 2011, following stints at Princeton University (1991–2011) and the University of Rochester (1983–1991). He received BA and MA degrees from Yale University and a PhD in political science from the University of California, Berkeley. His teaching and research focus on public opinion, electoral politics, public policy, and representation. His books include *Unequal Democracy: The Political Economy of the New Gilded Age* (2nd edition), *Democracy for Realists: Why Elections Do Not Produce Responsive Government* (with Christopher H. Achen), and *Presidential Primaries and the Dynamics of Public Choice*. He is also the author of numerous scholarly articles and of occasional pieces in *The New York Times*, *The Washington Post*, *Los Angeles Times*, and other media outlets. His professional honors include the Warren E. Miller Prize from the American Political Science Association's Elections, Public Opinion, and Voting Behavior section, the Society for Political Methodology's Career Achievement Award, and Vanderbilt University's Earl Sutherland Prize for Career Achievement in Research. He is a past vice president of the American Political Science Association and a member of the American Academy of Arts and Sciences, the American Academy of Political and Social Science, the National Academy of Sciences, and the American Philosophical Society.

Part II
Defining the Limits of Democratic Governance

On the Limits of Democracy

Geoffrey M. Hodgson

Abstract This essay discusses the practical limits to democratic participation in decision-making. While defending representative democracy, it looks at some experiments with deliberative, participatory, or direct democracy which reveal a number of problems. Among these are establishment of incentives for voters to become adequately informed on issues, including the many questions that require specialist knowledge and skilled judgement. Contemporary advocates of 'maximum' or extensive democracy have overlooked the evidence we have about the difficulties involved. There is danger that reckless extensions of democratic participation will fail and help to undermine democracy itself.

Keywords Representative democracy · Direct democracy · Deliberative democracy · Participatory democracy · Duty · Incentives

Today, democracy faces major challenges. It has outright opponents and empowered manipulators. In several countries, representative democracy is under attack. This essay is about the limitations of democracy. It argues that while representative democracy is vital, direct and participatory democracy are not the panaceas that some people uphold. There are dangers in hyper-democracy as well as in anti-democracy.[1]

Thoughtful democrats have long accepted that democracy should not be used to undermine crucial rights. James Madison (Madison, 1787) warned that a 'factious' majority might 'sacrifice to its ruling passion or interest both the public good and the rights of other citizens'. His remedy involved elected representatives constrained by rules and laws, rather than direct democracy or self-rule by citizens themselves. In

---

[1] These wider issues are considered in Hodgson (2021, ch. 9), from which some material for this present essay is taken. The author thanks Christopher Achen, Larry Bartels, David Gindis and Gerhard Schnyder for discussions.

G. M. Hodgson (✉)
Institute for International Management, Loughborough University London, London, UK
e-mail: G.Hodgson2@lboro.ac.uk

© The Author(s), under exclusive license to Springer Nature Switzerland AG 2022
E. M. L. Economou et al. (eds.), *Democracy in Times of Crises*,
https://doi.org/10.1007/978-3-030-97295-0_4

1840, Alexis de Tocqueville ([1840] 2003) worried that political powers in a representative democracy may become over-centralized and abused, leading to a 'democratic despotism'. He stressed the importance of the countervailing powers of 'associations of ordinary citizens' and of freedom of the press. In 1859, John Stuart Mill (1859) also cautioned against the possibility of a majority depriving a population of their rights. Quintin Hogg, Lord Hailsham (1976), warned of the dangers of increasing executive power in the UK, and diminishing parliamentary scrutiny, using the phrase 'elective dictatorship'. A government could be elected by popular mandate and still concentrate too much power in its hands.

Another challenge for democracy is less obvious. Oddly, it comes from those who wish to spread democracy much further throughout society. There is something appealing in this sentiment. In suitable circumstances (discussed below), it can be of practical value. But calls for participatory democracy have vastly exceeded any detailed discussion of their feasibility and usefulness, especially in the context of a highlight complex economy depending on specialist knowledge. Pushing democracy too far without attention to practical details and possible adverse outcomes is a danger to democracy itself. Any failure in the attainment or operation of extended participatory democracy could cause an anti-democratic reaction. And for reasons outlined in this essay, failures are more likely than many envisage.

Today we have to avoid the real danger of growing illiberal democracy from one quarter while resisting calls for an unfeasible hyper-democracy from another. First consider some assertions that democracy should be radically extended.

1 Extending Democracy

Proposals for an extension of democratic participation can be found in the writings of Jean-Jacques Rousseau, Pierre-Joseph Proudhon, John Stuart Mill, G. D. H. Cole and many others (Pateman, 1970). Marxists have often heralded a democratic socialist future. Vladimir Ilyich Lenin (1967, vol. 2, pp. 334–335) promised in 1917 that the Bolshevik revolution would bring 'an immense expansion of democracy' for working people. But of course it quickly turned out to be very different. Nevertheless, during the twentieth century, the extension of democracy became a prominent maxim.

John Dewey was an influential exponent of extended participatory democracy. Dewey (1916, pp. 100–101, 304) widened the meaning of democracy and claimed that it is 'more than a form of government; it is primarily a mode of associated living, of conjoint communicated experience'. Dewey envisioned that 'democratic social organization' would provide 'direct participation in control'. Dewey (1940, p. 224) added:

> Democracy is a way of personal life controlled not merely by faith in human nature in general but by faith in the capacity of human beings for intelligent judgment and action if proper conditions are furnished.

His declared 'faith' in extensive democratic participation was held with a religious tenacity, without substantiation of its feasibility and against growing evidence of its problems.

In his book on Dewey's thought, Robert Westbrook (1991, pp. 293–318) conceded that Walter Lippmann (1922) had won his dispute with Dewey (1927) over the nature and formation of public opinion and the limits of democracy. Dewey failed to explain the institutions and mechanisms of his proposed participatory system. While he was right to stress the social nature of knowledge, he was extraordinarily optimistic about how it could be accessed, harnessed and communicated. He neglected the tacitness and context dependence of knowledge. He was also unclear on how individuals could be incentivized to become better informed. His vision of an extensive participatory democracy has never been detailed or put into practice. Dewey died in 1952. But his vision of a participatory democracy endured. It was formative for the New Left in the 1960s. In particular, as Westbrook (1991, p. 549) noted:

> Perhaps nowhere did Dewey's ideals echo more resoundingly than in the "Port Huron Statement" of the Students for a Democratic Society (SDS, 1964).

The Port Huron Statement was originally drafted by Tom Hayden, who was heavily influenced by Dewey and the two Mills. The SDS made the widespread extension of participatory democracy its central motif. It declared that the 'means of production should be, open to democratic participation and subject to democratic social regulation'. Details and practicalities were ignored. But the maxim of participatory democracy became hugely influential.

More recently, the US socialist politician Bernie Sanders promoted 'democratic control over the factories and shops to as great a degree as you can' (Ben-Meir, 2015). Similarly, Jeremy Corbyn, socialist leader of the UK Labour Party from 2015 to 2020, argued for 'public, democratic ownership and control of our services and utilities' (Trade Unions for Energy Democracy 2018). Little consideration was given to how this would work in practice. Would everyone vote on everything, or would we vote for representatives who would act on our behalf? Little thought was given to the democratic structures, to checks and balances, to the competence of the voters to decide on complex or technical issues, to the problems of information overload in a modern complex economy, and so on. Panaceas without practicalities can be dangerous.

Yanis Varoufakis, the Marxist former Finance Minister of Greece, founded the Democracy in Europe Movement 2025 (DiEM25). It has Julian Assange, Noam Chomsky, James K. Galbraith, Naomi Klein, Ken Loach, Caroline Lucas and several others on its Advisory Panel. DiEM25 aims in its Manifesto to 'maximise democracy in workplaces, towns, cities, regions and states' (Democracy in Europe Movement 2025, 2020). What would *maximizing* democracy mean? Why should democracy be maximized and not justice, welfare, rights, equality, or living standards? Maximizing democracy would probably mean diminishing some of these other virtues. Maximizing time spent in democratic workplace meetings would reduce economic output and prosperity. Democracy could be used to restore the death penalty, expel immigrants or legalize torture. Pushing for more democracy, to the point where it surpasses practical or ethical limits, is a severe threat to the survival of the liberal foundations of democracy itself.

For some, the mantra of 'democratic control' has become an excuse to avoid complex ethical debates about justice and rights. For them, making something 'democratic' trumps any other moral consideration. Instead of grappling with complex ethical and organizational problems, some hyper-democratic politicians abdicate leadership and suggest we 'put it to the people' in a vote. The result is then regarded as moral or just, simply because it is democratic. Hyper-democratic rhetoric enables a dereliction of justice, duty or virtue.

Hyper-democracy faces practical questions of feasibility and credibility. There are severe functional constraints, as well as the moral danger of the tyranny of a local or national majority against the rights of minorities. These limits are considered too rarely. There is substantial but often neglected evidence of the difficulties involved, some of which is discussed below. Another danger here is that by extolling democracy as a goal, and as a solution to every problem, expectations are over-inflated. Calls for maximal democracy can create a combination of frustration and discord that fractures the stabilizing institutions upon which any democracy depends. The inevitable failure of hyper-democracy could lead to an anti-democratic reaction.

Robert Michels (1915) showed in his book on *Political Parties* that hyper-democracy was unfeasible in any large-scale organization. All complex social systems require routinized bureaucracy. No-one is able to have a complete understanding of what is happening or of what is possible. But leaders and top administrators are more involved: they amass more knowledge and power than others. They have greater awareness of, and access to, key information. In political parties and trade unions, ordinary members have other major demands on their time and are hence less able to become immersed in the details. Democratic votes on everything of significance would be impossible. For reasons of both practicality and efficacy, votes have to be restricted to guiding constitutional rules, elections of representatives or a limited number of issues where voters are better informed.

Possible increases in democratic involvement have to be appraised in the light of real-world experience. Voter incentives for democratic participation and knowledgeable involvement have to be considered. There are practical limits, such as the number of meetings and time required to make a large number of informed collective decisions. Short cuts, such as Internet voting, may not provide sufficient incentives for voters to become better informed. Without adequate expert knowledge, the outcomes could be disastrous. Where would it be feasible and beneficial to extend democracy? What kinds of democracy do we need to promote and defend?

This essay considers different kinds of democracy, including (a) deliberative democracy (such as citizens' assemblies), (b) participatory democracy (including in the workplace) and (c) representative democracy. Using empirical evidence and theoretical argument, greater practical virtue is found in (b) and (c). Direct democracy, as practised in Ancient Athens and promoted today by the Italian Five Star Movement, is evaluated elsewhere (Hodgson, 2021, ch. 9), where it is concluded that this too has major limitations.

2 Democracy Is Not a Voting Machine

Is the purpose of democracy simply to reflect popular opinion? Or does it have other important functions? The Benthamite view, that policies should somehow be derived from an aggregation of individual utilities, takes existing preferences as sovereign. Similarly, the Pareto criterion – that no-one's utility should be reduced—also makes current individual preferences supreme.

But actual or workable democracy is not a process by which individual preferences are fed into a voting machine, with an obedient government that then implements those policy choices. The theory of social choice, as developed by (the economist and socialist) Kenneth Arrow and others, and by some political thinkers, has sustained this mistaken view of democracy as a machine to aggregate preferences. Arrow showed that no rank-order voting system can comply with three reasonable criteria of fairness. This result prompted multiple responses, ranging from attempts to ameliorate this problem to dismissals of democracy *tout court*. But the basic problem is the assumption that democracy is a voting machine to reflect individual preferences. As Jonathan Aldred (2019, p. 82) argued it in his critique of Arrow (1951):

> Democracy is more than voting systems which add up citizens' sacrosanct fixed preferences. In a democracy, preferences are *not* sacrosanct ... we try to persuade citizens to change their minds. More generally, democracy involves public deliberation, debate and persuasion, hopefully bringing about some reconciliation of different points of view.

The famous theory of voting developed by Anthony Downs (1957) assumes that political parties attempt to identify and respond to the preferences of voters. Christopher Achen and Larry Bartels (2016) saw such assumptions as part of as 'folk theory of democracy' and provided extensive evidence that it does not stand up to critical examination. As Joseph Schumpeter (Schumpeter, 1942, pp. 284–285) insisted:

> democracy does not mean and cannot mean that people actually rule in any obvious sense of the terms "people" and "rule." Democracy means only that the people have the opportunity of accepting or refusing the men who are to rule them.

Representative democracy cannot and should not be a machine for aggregating individual preferences. As Burke (1774) argued long ago, parliamentary representatives are not delegates. Another once-member of the UK Parliament, John Stuart Mill (2008 [1861], p. 143), made a similar point: a representative should be 'of such calibre as to be intrusted with full power of obeying the dictates of his own judgment'. Their job is to interpret and protect the interests of their electorates, not to act as mandated functionaries who simply relay the opinions of their voters. Being elected is only the beginning of a complex and uncertain process of representation and legislation. Their decision-making involves the interpretation of expert opinion, multiple processes of engagement with the civil service and the legal system and negotiations with other politicians concerning acceptable compromises.

Public administration is an immensely complex process. Those involved directly in government have to engage with multiple loci of expertise and interests. It is not even possible for a parliamentary or popular assembly to scrutinize all the detail involved. As Mill ([1861], 2008 pp. 62, 69) put it:

> a popular assembly is still less fitted to administer, or to dictate in detail to those who have the charge of the administration. ... Every branch of public administration is a skilled business, which has its own peculiar rules ... none of them likely to be duly appreciated by persons not practically acquainted with the department.

Mill thus argued that a role of an ordinary parliamentary representative 'is to watch and control the government; to throw the light of publicity on its acts'. Well-functioning parliamentary government entails a system of checks and balances. Representative democracy involves exploration and testing of the feasible and desirable. It is not a delegatory machine for automatically enacting the popular will.

In his *Against Democracy*, Jason Brennan cited substantial evidence that voters are poorly informed. Hence the translation of their opinions into policies would be dysfunctional. He assumed that democracy is a machine to translate voter preferences into government actions. But this is not the purpose of representative democracy. The developmental processes of representation, legislation and engagement with state bureaucracy are missing from Brennan's analysis. In his brilliant review of Brennan's book, Shany Mor (2019) wrote:

> The book never adequately differentiates the competence to make important public decisions from the competence to participate in an election, but these surely are not the same skill set. ... Voting is not the same as democracy. Ruling is not the same as electing. Competence is not the same as suffrage. Governing is not the same as lawmaking. And appointing, even by election, is not the same as representing. Yet, throughout his book, Brennan continually conflates or elides these differences.[2]

Democracy often produces bad government. Does that mean that democracy is bad? Democracy has other consequences. Amartya Sen argued that democracy helps to sustain political and liberal rights. Brennan (2017, p. ix) himself admitted that democracies 'do a better job of protecting economic and civil liberties than non-democracies'.

Brennan (2017, pp. vii–ix) mentioned some of the defects of the Brexit referendum, and he noted the 2016 election of Trump with less popular votes than his opponent. These particular problems have relatively simple fixes. Many countries restrict referendums or require super-majorities—such as 60 per cent or more in favour – for votes that change or remove people's rights. A major defect in the US presidential election system is the use of the Electoral College, which makes it possible for a candidate with less popular votes to win. This can be fixed by abolishing the outdated Electoral College and aggregating individual votes over the whole country.

---

[2] In his review of Brennan (2017), Mounck (2018) and Runciman (2018), Mor (2019) pointed out that none of these authors paid much attention to processes of representation, including formative engagement by representatives with the legislative system.

Democracy must be seen as a developmental process, where current preferences are not sacrosanct. Supporters of deliberative democracy see it as a possible solution to problems with voter ignorance and misinformation. We now turn to the real-world experience of deliberative democracy.

3 Deliberative Democracy

If voters were better informed, then democracy would be enriched. Hence Mill, Dewey and many others argued that democracy should operate within a wider context of popular discussion and deliberation over key issues. Similarly, John Rawls (1971, p. 359) opined:

> the effects of common deliberation seem bound to improve matters ... Discussion is a way of combining information and enlarging the range of arguments.' It was argued that widespread political discussion would enliven and improve democracy.

Deliberative democracy refers to arrangements and procedures that aim to bring representative samples of citizens together, from different genders, ethnicities, regions and income groups to argue and listen, weigh up pros and cons and develop their own views through conversations with others. It involves a small representative sample of the population as a whole. Through an egalitarian, open-minded and inclusive conversation, deliberation is hoped to create greater empathy with others and a deeper understanding of everyone's interests. Often participants are asked to give reasons for their opinions and to explain how their proposals would serve the common good.

By the 1990s, deliberative democracy had become a great hope for progressives and democrats. It was expected that it would help fulfil the promises of Mill, Dewey and Rawls that democracy could become an educative and enlightening process. Substantial influence over political decisions could be extended to the wider population (Bohman & Rehg, 1998; Elster, 1998; Fishkin, 2018; Gutmann & Thompson, 1996; Habermas, 1989, 1996, 2001; Mansbridge, 1983).

There is a large amount of empirical research on deliberative democracy. It has revealed some benefits, but a multitude of problems. A lengthy survey by Tali Mendelberg (2002, pp. 154, 156, 158) found 'thin or nonexistent empirical evidence for the benefits that deliberative theorists expect'. She noted studies that showed that while deliberation can facilitate cooperation between individuals, it can undermine it between groups. Cass Sunstein (2000, 2002) provided evidence that, under some conditions, deliberation can drive different groups toward more extreme views. Other experiments showed that deliberation sometimes added little to mutual awareness: groups first expressed their preferences without discussion, and there was little further benefit from adding deliberation.

Faced with difficult and controversial problems, some participants in a deliberative democracy duck the issues, to avoid disputes. Jane Mansbridge (1983) argued that pressure for deliberation can backfire by antagonizing participants, and non-deliberative procedures can sometimes be superior. Similarly, Diana Mutz (2006, pp. 3, 133) showed that deliberation can often lead to conflict, which in turn discourages participation:

> Although diverse political networks foster a better understanding of multiple perspectives on issues and encourage political tolerance, they *discourage* political participation, particularly among those who are averse to conflict. ... My results suggest that, within any given individual, enthusiastic participation rarely coexists with ongoing exposure to diverse political viewpoints and careful consideration of the political alternatives.

Complexity creates further disincentives for involvement and increases the amount of time and effort required. In his extensive review of the evidence, David Ryfe (2005, p. 51) noted:

> Especially in the face of difficult, complex issues, people seek to 'pass the buck' in an effort to avoid responsibility for decision making .... Their sheer extensiveness and complexity make them difficult issues amenable to no easy answers. Their extensiveness means that any rational individual will seek to forego the burden of participation because she is not likely to directly affect the result....

Participation in deliberation is often highly unequal (Mansbridge, 1983; Mendelberg, 2002, pp. 163–173, 176). Studies of trial juries show that higher-status participants 'tend to speak more, to offer more suggestions, and to be perceived as more accurate in their judgments'. Those most skilled in rhetoric can sway the decision in their favour. Often the more educated people dominate. But this does not necessarily mean that the decision outcomes are superior. Experiments show that even educated people often select evidence that supports a pre-conceived view and ignore evidence that counters it. Mendelberg's (2002, p. 80) survey concluded that 'deliberation should not be attempted under all circumstances as a cost-free solution to costly problems, nor should it be rejected wholesale'.

Ryfe (2005, pp. 49–50) noted that 'to some extent the empirical literature is driven by the passion and vision of deliberative theorists'. He continued:

> Nonetheless, one cannot ignore the fact that the empirical findings have been mixed. Under certain conditions, it appears that deliberation can produce more sophisticated, tolerant, and participative citizens ... but these outcomes are not automatic and in fact may be rare ... Combined with the fact that institutionalizing deliberation can be quite costly ... this finding suggests a need for more reflection.

Ryfe (*ibid*., pp. 62–63) concluded that 'deliberation is not easy':

> It seems to require a mixture of knowledge/skills, motivation, and civic identity. It is difficult to create conditions to bring these elements together. It is perhaps even more difficult to sustain them once they are created.

In another overview of the evidence on deliberative democracy, Dennis Thompson (2008, pp. 499–500) also gave a cautionary verdict:

> The general conclusion of surveys of the empirical research ... is that taken together the findings are mixed or inconclusive ... The main reason for the mixed results is that the success or failure of deliberation depends so much on its context.... The conditions under which deliberative democracy thrives may be quite rare and difficult to achieve.

Most people do not seem to enjoy deliberative democracy. They prefer to avoid the rigours of deliberative reasoning. Ryfe (2005, p. 56) explained that in normal circumstances people rely on habitual thought patterns rather than logical arguments to make decisions:

> Deliberation represents a disturbance of everyday reasoning habits. People prefer to rely on routine scripts to navigate through their social world. Being jolted out of these scripts is, generally speaking, a disconcerting experience.

Despite this evidence, deliberative democracy still has many enthusiastic advocates. They point to the success of the Irish Citizens' Assembly prior to the 2015 and 2017 referendums that led to the legalization of gay marriage and abortion. A randomly selected group of people deliberated extensively on several issues. Their views helped the Irish government to frame and promote the changes in the referendums. But they also deliberated on other important questions, which the government ignored. Among the strongest effects of the Irish Citizens' Assembly was that it convinced elected politicians that formerly taboo reforms, concerning abortion and gay marriage, in a largely Catholic country, had a chance of passing in referendums (O'Leary, 2019).

Experiments with citizens' assemblies in other countries have had mixed results. An assembly in Canada in 2004 made recommendations on electoral reform that were not approved by the public. Electoral reform recommendations made by a citizens' assembly in the Netherlands in 2006 were rejected by the government (Pal, 2012). In the UK, a 2017 citizens' assembly charged with finding an acceptable Brexit policy was described by its organizers as a 'great success'. It explored the complex issues pretty thoroughly. But it gave first preference to an improbable, have-cake-and-eat-it proposal, where the UK retained full freedom to conduct its own international trade policy while maintaining a frictionless border with the EU (Renwick et al., 2017).

There have been some successful citizens' assemblies on climate change. Generally, these are advisory. Participants learn more about the issues and can make innovative and useful recommendations about individual behaviour and community action. But they cannot always cope with the complex trade-offs and cost-benefit evaluations that guide government policy. Instead, their effective roles are advisory and educational.

Citizens' assemblies can be useful, but only if they are carefully managed. They are not a political panacea. They are expensive to run. They are often perceived as unrepresentative. Their members lack the accountability of elected representatives, who are subject to re-election. They can serve important advisory and educational purposes. But, given the evidence, the idea that citizens' assemblies should be given powers to veto or even make legislation is romantic and reckless (Fishkin, 2018; Warren, 1996, 2009). The following section gives further reasons for this verdict.

4 Alongside Duty, Other Incentives Matter

Any act of voting itself takes time and incurs costs. These inconveniences are small but significant. In terms of benefits, the marginal effect of any single vote in a large electorate is likely to be negligible, unless the voting is close to a tie. A tied outcome is rarely expected. Hence generally the costs of voting greatly exceed the expected payoffs.

It is difficult to explain individual voting in functional cost-benefit terms. This is known as the *paradox of voting*. Utility analysis would predict a zero turnout, unless it is assumed, in an ad hoc manner, that people somehow gain utility simply by casting their vote. If our understanding of motivation also involves duty or virtue, then more plausible explanations are forthcoming. Many people vote because they feel duty bound to do so. They may wish to construct a civic minded identity for themselves and be regarded as virtuous citizens. But this does not mean that costs and benefits are unimportant. They should be considered when addressing problems of low or falling turnout in many democracies. Duty and other incentives all matter.

The sense of duty can be nurtured and encouraged by good leaders and governments. But duty alone cannot make democracy work well. Incentives, particularly to become better informed, matter hugely too. It is one problem to get people to vote. It is another to ensure that they are adequately informed.

Both deliberative and direct democracy assume that citizens can become adequately informed about crucial details. This requires motivation, time and effort. We may debate how much knowledge is adequate. But even modest estimates would suggest a substantial amount of time is needed. The impact of one vote is small, while the time and effort involved to become adequately informed is large.

This problem is severe within nationwide models of direct democracy, as proposed by the Italian Five Star Movement. An individual vote becomes influential only if the results are close to a tie. But with tens of millions of voters, the probability of a tie is negligible. The possible benefits of casting one vote are miniscule. So why spend hours researching the topic of the vote?

Mill, Dewey, Rawls and others argued that democracy would encourage political education and social responsibility. But acquiring and evaluating political information take considerable time. They incur costs that are much greater than the act of voting itself. Becoming well informed on a political topic such as socialism, liberalism, conservatism, climate change, evolution, constitutional theory, macroeconomics, international trade or public finance would take months or more. The personal costs of political education are substantial.

Again, the marginal benefits for the individual are negligible. So why bother to become educated about these issues? Sure enough, the dutiful or virtuous citizen will feel obliged to seek some information, but few if any of us have the time to go into more than a small fraction of the sample issues above. Political education has large costs but infinitesimal marginal benefits for voters at the ballot box. Appeals to duty or virtue cannot resolve this, even if everyone were dutiful and virtuous. There are not enough hours in the day.

Table 1 Costs and benefits (functional and moral) for an individual voter

	Costs		Benefits	
Functional costs and benefits	Cost of casting a vote, in terms of time, money and inconvenience	A (small)	Benefit of casting of vote, in terms of the individual's influence on the outcome	B (very small)
Moral costs and benefits	Cost of becoming adequately informed about the complex issues involved	C (large)	Benefit of casting of vote, in terms of fulfilling a sense of duty, or being recognized as a virtuous citizen	D (varies from individual to individual)

Table 1 summarizes the costs and benefits for an individual voter. *Functional* costs are the minimum costs of casting a vote, in terms of time, money and inconvenience. *Functional* benefits concern no more than the perceived degree of influence of the individual on the outcome. By definition, these costs and benefits exclude further matters of duty or virtue. The 'paradox of voting' emerges because B is generally less than A. Functional costs (A) exceed functional benefits (B), so why do many people vote?

To answer this question, we bring in issues of duty or virtue. By definition here, *moral* costs and benefits are additional to functional costs and benefits. They arise because of matters of duty, virtue or the common good. (Functionality may involve morality, and vice versa, but these nuances need detain us no further.) Many people vote because their moral benefits in D overcome their functional costs A. They vote out of a sense of duty, or because voting upholds their identity as a virtuous citizen. But D varies greatly from individual to individual, depending on their moral development.

At least from the point of view of society as a whole, and of the health of its democratic institutions, burden C must also be considered. Democracy works better when the voters are adequately informed. Becoming cognizant could be regarded as a citizen's duty. It serves the common good. But the costs for the individual here, for any reasonable criterion of adequacy, are large. The time and other costs involved in C are much greater than in A, and the tiny value of B acts as little incentive to become better informed on political issues. While public authorities should encourage senses of duty, virtue and moral obligation, they will generally be insufficient to overcome the cost to the individual of becoming adequately informed.

Of people 'living in democracies', de Tocqueville ([1840] 2003 pp. 780–781) noted that it is:

> Only with some effort that these men wrench themselves from their private business to turn their attention to communal affairs; their natural inclination is to leave responsibility for them to the ... permanent representative which is the state.

He continued:

> The growing love of prosperity and the ... love of public peace ... naturally inclines citizens to grant or surrender endless new rights to central government.

In short, people trust in representative government rather than giving their scarce attention to complex political matters and messy public affairs and disputes.

This helps to explain the widespread preference for involvement in private issues over public politics. People typically have much more influence over their immediate or private lives than they do over political systems. The costs of effective involvement are also different. In our homes, communities and workplaces, we are always hearing about things that affect us immediately in our daily lives. It would require much greater time and effort to become well-informed in complex political matters.

Citizens' assemblies involve large information costs for participants, which are greater when issues become highly complex. This makes deliberation burdensome. Many free-ride on the deliberative and investigatory efforts of others. The cost of becoming well-informed in a citizens' assembly must be weighed against the low chances of a vote having a decisive effect.

Of course, citizens' assemblies involve far fewer people than the entire electorate. Consequently, a single vote is likely to matter more. But how much more? Most citizens' assemblies consist of between 50 and 200 participants. The chances of a tied vote are higher with these much lower numbers, but they are still insufficient to provide strong incentives (Margolis, 1977).

Similar considerations should be applied to a national parliament. But there is at least one big difference between elected parliaments and appointed citizens' assemblies. Members of a parliament are accountable to their voters, and they can be removed if their electorates are dissatisfied. They would lose their salaries. So they worry about their popularity. Typically, members of a citizens' assembly have no such accountability, salary or concerns about popular support. Hence members of parliament have a greater incentive to become informed. We know from experience that far too many are below par. Parliamentary democracy is far from perfect. But citizens' assemblies could be even worse. Generally, the ordinary citizen has limited incentives to becoming well informed on political and economic issues.

Political activists are the exception, not the rule. It partly results from the incentives structures in any sizeable community. As Achen and Bartels (2016, pp. 1, 9) reported: 'evidence demonstrates that the great majority of citizens pay little attention to politics'. This is explicable:

> Human beings are busy with their lives. Most have ... a job consuming many hours of the day. They also have meals to prepare, homes to clean, and bills to pay. ... Sorting out which presidential candidate has the right foreign policy toward Asia is not a high priority for them. Without shirking more immediate and important obligations, people cannot engage in much well-informed, thoughtful political deliberation, nor should they.

Most people are interested only occasionally in issues of government. Individuals have much greater incentives to invest thought and care in important personal decisions over which they can have greater influence. Consider a choice to get married or divorced, to buy a home, to purchase a new car or to change jobs. Incentives for thoughtful investigation and prudence are here much greater because the direct outcomes for the individual can be substantial.

Consequently, people will think or talk endlessly about actual or potential partners or friends, or infidelities, or mortgage finances, or fitted kitchens, or the fuel consumption of the latest car, or of frictions with their current boss. Those things are of immediate importance. Most people will think or talk much less about national politics. While duty and moral virtue are paramount, other incentives matter too.

Advocates of direct or deliberative democracy are fond of Ancient Athens. In 1819 the liberal Benjamin Constant ([1819] Constant, 2017, p. 4) noted two crucial differences between Athenian and modern democracies. First, the Athenian citizenry were numbered in thousands, not millions. Second, slavery liberated a minority from toil: 'The abolition of slavery has deprived the free population of all the leisure they used to have when slaves did most of the work. Without the slave population of Athens, 20,000 Athenians couldn't have gathered in the public square for discussions, every day'. Athenian direct democracy was made possible by slavery. The enslavement of the majority, plus the support of unenslaved women who managed households, increased the possibilities for extensive debate and discussion for the fortunate male minority. Slavery and gender subjugation reduced the opportunity costs (C in Table 1) for male citizens of becoming adequately informed.

But that cost reduction was not enough. Plato and Aristotle claimed that many Athenian citizens were insufficiently educated to rule. Getting citizens to attend the assembly (the *ekklesia*) was also a problem (because of costs A). At one point it was agreed to pay them to appear (thus increasing benefits B). The classical scholar Loren Samons (2004, p. 6) noted that 'the people who gave rise to and practiced ancient democracy left us almost nothing but criticism of this form of regime'. Samons showed that the history of democratic Athens was 'marked by numerous failures, mistakes, and misdeeds—most infamously, the execution of Socrates'. The Athenian assembly pursued a belligerent colonial foreign policy. Athenian direct democracy was highly flawed.

Perhaps someday we shall have robots that will liberate us from the Biblical curse of toil and give us all time to engage in more discussion and reflection. Maybe. Even then, as all evidence so far suggests, major problems with direct and deliberative democracy will endure.

Politics, in its narrow sense of pertaining to government power, is a separate sphere from everyday life. Politics is the deliberate mobilization of 'pressures for collectively binding resolutions', as Mark Warren (1996, pp. 247, 258) put it. Most social relations involve power, but they are not all political, in this sense of the word. With its insistence on principles and rules, political engagement is in many ways a departure from the muddling-through humdrum of everyday life. For any individual, 'there must exist a balance between those relationships that are politicized and those that are not'. Much is not overtly political in the narrower sense, nor should it be.

5 Worker Participation and Cooperatives

What about participation in decision-making at work? Employees have strong incentives to become informed about issues that directly affect their work, their work environment and their livelihood. Because of the lower numbers involved, the impact of one worker's vote in the workplace is likely to be greater than in a political constituency. Consequently, some worker participation in decision-making can ostensibly be valuable and productive.

There are different kinds of worker participation. Derek Jones (2018) has refined a typology that operates in two dimensions, namely, control rights by workers and the rights of workers to a share in the profits. Return rights can range from a zero share of the profits to a majority share, as in the case of some employee share-ownership schemes. Control rights range from zero, through routine consultation on important issues by management, to some form of dominant control, either directly or through elected representatives.

Worker-owned cooperatives exhibit high return and control rights. Examples include the Mondragon cooperatives in Spain. By contrast, quality circles—where a group of employees meet regularly to solve problems at work—typical involve some participation in control, but often without return rights. Employee representation on the board of directors involves greater control rights but not necessarily any more return rights.

Although return rights and control rights interact and are not mutually independent, our primary concern here is with control rights. What are the effects of greater democratic control by workers in the workplace? Some major surveys have indicated that greater control rights often have a positive effect on firm performance. Some particular studies have compared worker cooperatives with more conventional capitalist firms, finding that cooperatives either match or outperform their capitalist counterparts. Other studies have looked at German-style codetermination, finding a positive relationship between the existence of works councils and productivity. The view of some mainstream economists that worker participation in management would reduce efficiency has been refuted (Burdin, 2014; Dow, 2003; Fakhfakh et al., 2012; Hübler & Jirjahn, 2003; Mueller & Stegmaier, 2017; Pencavel, 2013).

There is a trade-off between the time spent in meetings and the time devoted to productive work. This restricts involvement in decision-making. Even with weekly meetings, individual workers will be allocated tasks or projects in the meantime—often these cannot await a weekly vote. Individuals or small teams need to make their own decisions frequently, especially with complex and highly skilled work. These numerous everyday decisions cannot for practical reasons be put to a poll. Voting on everything would bring production to a standstill. Democracy can come into play in a small minority of decisions only.

Yet the evidence suggests that this small amount of democratic involvement in the workplace can have positive economic and welfare effects. It is also a question of scale: in smaller workplaces, workers have greater incentives to be informed and to be involved. To a degree, workers in any firm sink or swim together. Market competition pressures workers to cooperate, for the survival and prosperity of the enterprise (Hodgson, 2019, ch. 2).

Does democratic participation increase political awareness and involvement? With worker participation or cooperatives, there are relatively strong incentives to become better-informed and to participate in decisions at work. Worker participation can enhance the democratic spirit. But there is little evidence to suggest that it brings wider political knowledge or involvement.

What about community participation? Evidence suggests that people in communities tend to interact with subsets of like-minded people. Consequently, in local neighbourhoods, often people congregate together with those others who are more similar in terms of their culture, profession or beliefs. Schemes for democratic participation in community decision-making have to deal with this problem. Empirical studies suggest that unless there are strong incentives to work together, lines of political or other conflict can emerge, leading to the breakdown of cooperation in the community. On the other hand, incentives for cooperation can be heightened by a common threat, such as a disruptive construction project or the need to deal with a hazard such as fire or flooding. But otherwise, schemes of community participation face the difficulty of bonding people together for long periods of time. And again, the larger the number of people, the lower the incentives to become informed or be involved (Mutz, 2006).

In contrast, with worker cooperatives or participatory firms, greater bonding pressure emanates from the need to work together to ensure the survival of the firm in a competitive market environment. For these and other reasons, as Diana Mutz (2006, p. 29) argued:

> If one wants to harness the power of social networks for the kinds of purposes envisioned by advocates of deliberative democracy, voluntary associations and neighborhoods are probably *not* the best places to start. ... Of the various social contexts identified, the workplace appears the most promising....

6 Conclusion: Defending Democracy from Its Enemies and Friends

Representative democracy is flawed. But it is vital to defend it. The Biblical four horsemen of the apocalypse are conflict, war, famine and death. Their threat can be diminished through societies with representative democratic institutions and respect for human rights (Sen, 1981, 1999). Research also shows that open democracies with political competition and pressure groups are more effective than autocracies in dealing with environmental pollution. Representative democracy is vital to deal with the climate crisis as well (Binder & Neumayer, 2005; Fredriksson et al., 2005; Li & Reuveny, 2006).

Representative democracy is not a machine for translating individual preferences, or the assumed general will, into government policies. This is a utopian fantasy based on empirically refuted claims about human psychology and how and why people vote. Democratic government cannot be the political will of a nation, whatever that may be. As Warren (1996, p. 248) argued:

> Democracy is not ... an expression of a social totality. It is not the expression of a community, a "we," the will of the people. Metaphors of popular sovereignty are misleading at best.

Achen and Bartels (2016, p. 4) provided evidence that:

> Even the most informed voters typically make choices not on the basis of policy preferences or ideology, but on the basis of who they are – their social identities.

In reality, voting is less an expression of preferences and more about personal identity.

Representative democracy is vital for different reasons:[3]

1. **Legitimation of government**. Representative democracy is a means of legitimating government. For Max Weber (Weber, 1947), legitimation is a process where the public confer prestige upon a government and accept its powers and authority. Stanley Milgram (1974) showed that humans have string dispositions to obey what is perceived as legitimate authority. Instead of appealing to a Divine right to rule, or to other stories that are supposed to legitimate power, modern democracies attain legitimacy through mechanisms of political election.

2. **Acceptance of outcomes.** Partly because of their perceived legitimacy, elections deliver (often imperfect) outcomes that most people agree to accept, even if they are uncomfortable with them. This is called 'losers' consent' (Anderson et al., 2005). Consider some cases when an electoral system produced a challengeable result. In the UK in 1951 the Labour Party was replaced in government by the Conservatives, who obtained slightly less votes overall. In the UK in February 1974, the Conservative Party got slightly more votes, but Labour won more parliamentary seats and came to power as a minority government. The result of the 2000 presidential election in the USA hangs on a few hundred disputed votes in swing state Florida. The US Electoral College system has delivered presidents with less votes than their closest rival in 1876, 1888 and 2016. In all these UK and US cases, the results were accepted by the defeated party. Whether they liked it or not, most people tolerated the outcome. By contrast, President Trump did not accept defeat in 2020. His ungrounded claims of huge election fraud undermined public respect for democracy. This is a rare exception that proves the rule. Acceptance of outcomes is important for social cohesion and stability.

3. **Government turnover.** Representative democracy provides the legal and peaceful possibility of removing a government from power. This does not necessarily mean that is removed for good reasons or that the incoming government is any better. But a change of government is possible. As Achen and Bartels (2016, p. 317) observed: 'This turnover is a key indicator of democratic health and

---

[3]The reasons given here in favour of representative democracy modify and supplement the arguments of Achen and Bartels (2016, pp. 316–319).

stability. It implies that no one group or coalition can become entrenched in power, unlike in dictatorships or one-party states where power is often exercised persistently by a single privileged segment of society'.

4. **Incentives to be responsive.** Because they can be removed by the voters, politicians in a democracy will have some incentive (however slight) to please their electorates. This would help explain why there have been few famines in democracies, and why democracies that tolerate organized public pressure groups seem to be better in dealing with pollution and other overt problems. Compared with dictatorships, politicians in a democracy have a greater incentive to satisfy the people. The downside of this is that the majority of the electorate may harbour nationalist, punitive, intolerant or authoritarian prejudices. Politicians may pander to these too. The benefits of responsiveness depend on the virtues of the sentiments to which they are responding.

5. **Some constraint on bad behaviour.** The possibility of removal from power can also place constraints on the behaviour of politicians and reduce manifest breaches of widely accepted ethical norms. These constraints are not always effective, and they depend on public sentiment. But they are there.

6. **Protecting human rights.** There is evidence that, under specific conditions, democracies with effective and socially representative inter-party competition can help reduce violations of human rights. Politicians in power tend to be more careful about such abuses if they are threatened by an effective opposition that can be fuelled by public anger (Davenport & Armstrong, 2004; De Mesquita et al., 2005).

7. **Toleration of opposition.** Electoral competition in democracies teaches politicians and electorates to tolerate opposition. In the UK, the main opposition party is institutionalized with the title 'Her Majesty's Most Loyal Opposition'. Achen and Bartels (2016, pp. 317–318) again: 'The notion that citizens can oppose incumbent rulers and organize to replace them, yet remain loyal to the nation, is fundamental both to real democracy and social harmony'. When this tolerance is eroded, then democracy and social order are endangered. Some tolerance is vital to sustain appropriate moderation on all sides.

8. **Development of a civic culture.** Finally, while Mill and Dewey may have exaggerated the educative benefits of representative democracy, there is still evidence that democratic political engagement helps to develop citizenship and a civic culture. Normally, the right to vote is itself a token of citizenship and equal worth (Finkel, 1985, 1987; Pateman, 1970).

Some of these points provide indicators for constitutional reforms and other actions to improve the effectiveness of democracy. Addressing points (3), (4), (5) and (6), some preference must be given to electoral systems that make representatives vulnerable to replacement in elections. So-called 'first past the post' systems based on geographical constituencies, as found in the UK and USA, perform badly on that score. In those systems, many parliamentary representatives have large majorities, and they are less likely to be removed. Limits on their additional earnings and employments would also encourage representatives to be more focused on and responsive to their electorates. The maximum time between elections should also not be too high.

Points (6) and (7) underline the importance of effective and representative inter-party competition, both within electoral constituencies and through the system as a whole. Party competition should not simply represent the interests of rich elites. There needs to be limits on party expenditures in elections. Some state funding of political parties could also help counterbalance the disproportionate influence of rich donors. All of the above eight points indicate a need for public political information and sustained ethical debate. There also needs to be ongoing and effective civic education of adults as well as of children.

Socialists often hide their passion for widespread public ownership behind the rhetoric of a vastly extended democracy. They press for a 'democratic socialism' involving extended participation and deliberation. Yet copious past experience with direct or deliberative democracy should engender much more caution. Hyper-democratic slogans are no substitute for ethical principles or political programmes. They cannot provide a collective identity for a stressed and fragmented population. They offer no substantive vision that can deal with the threat of illiberal nationalism, which builds on the nostalgic identities of the excluded and resentful.

We should defend representative democracy and vastly improve its workings, learning from the best practice in other countries. Democracy should not be confined to national or local government. It is vital to cultivate the democratic habit. There is scope for further careful experimentation with participatory democracy in the workplace and elsewhere. But any extension of democracy along these or other lines has to consider the individual incentives to be involved and better informed. We should learn from past experience and avoid vague formulations of 'democratic control' and dangerous slogans like 'maximizing democracy'.

Major constitutional reform is required in many countries (including the UK and USA) to ensure that democracy works better and does not become an elective dictatorship. The emergence of illiberal democracy in several countries underlines the need for checks, balances and protected rights. The independence of the judiciary has to be safeguarded. The rule of law has to be upheld. Corruption must be minimized. Democracy is not enough.

The is a lot to be done to improve modern democracy, but we should not ignore the abundant evidence of what does work and what does not. The enhancement of democracy must be evidence-based. Numerous real-world surveys and experiments testify to the difficulties involved in such endeavours. Democracy is a plant that must be carefully nurtured in the right location and soil. It is not a magic potion to solve all political problems and moral dilemmas.

References

Achen, C. H., & Bartels, L. M. (2016). *Democracy for realists: Why elections do not produce responsive government*. Princeton University Press.

Aldred, J. (2019). *Licence to be bad: How economics corrupted us*. Allen Lane.
Anderson, C. J., Blais, A., Bowler, S., Donovan, T., & Listhaug, O. (2005). *Losers' consent: Elections and democratic legitimacy*. Oxford University Press.
Arrow, K. J. (1951). *Social choice and individual values*. Wiley and Chapman Hall.
Ben-Meir, I. (2015). Bernie Sanders despised democrats in 1980s, said a JFK speech once made him sick. *BuzzFeed News*, 16 July. Available at: https://www.buzzfeed.com/ilanbenmeir/bernie-sanders-despised-democrats-in-1980s-said-a-jfk-speech?utm_term=.wmVM4dxppX#.trN5owqLL1
Binder, S., & Neumayer, E. (2005). Environmental pressure group strength and air pollution: An empirical analysis. *Ecological Economics, 55*(4), 537–538.
Bohman, J., & Rehg, W. (Eds.). (1998). *Deliberative democracy: Essays on reason and politics*. MIT Press.
Brennan, J. (2017). *Against democracy*. Princeton University Press.
Burdin, G. (2014). Are worker managed firms more likely to fail than conventional companies? Evidence from Uruguay. *Industrial and Labor Relations Review, 67*(1), 202–238.
Burke, E. (1774). *Speech to the electors at Bristol*. Retrieved April 30, 2020, from http://press-pubs.uchicago.edu/founders/documents/v1ch13s7.html
Constant, B. (2017). *The liberty of the ancients compared with that of the moderns*, translated by Jonathan Bennett from the text of 1819. Retrieved November 26, 2020, from https://www.earlymoderntexts.com/assets/pdfs/constant1819.pdf
Davenport, C., & Armstrong, D. A. (2004). Democracy and the violation of human rights: A statistical analysis from 1976 to 1996. *American Journal of Political Science, 48*(3), 538–554.
De Mesquita, B. B., Downs, G. W., Smith, A., & Cherif, F. M. (2005). Thinking inside the box: A closer look at democracy and human rights. *International Studies Quarterly, 49*(3), 439–457.
De Tocqueville, A. (2003). *Democracy in America*, (E. Gerald, Trans. Bevan from the volumes of 1835 and 1840, with an Introduction by Isaac Kramnick). Penguin.
Democracy in Europe Movement 2025 (DiEM25). (2020). *Manifesto*. Retrieved May 18, 2020, from https://diem25.org/manifesto-long/
Dewey, J. (1916). *Democracy and education: An introduction to the philosophy of education*. Macmillan.
Dewey, J. (1927). *The public and its problems: An essay in political inquiry*. Holt.
Dewey, J. (1940). Creative democracy – The task before us. In Conference on Methods in Philosophy (Ed.), *The philosopher of the common man: Essays in Honor of John Dewey to Celebrate his Eightieth Birthday* (pp. 220–228). Putnam's Sons.
Dow, G. K. (2003). *Governing the firm: Workers' control in theory and practice*. Cambridge University Press.
Downs, A. (1957). *An economic theory of democracy*. Harper and Row.
Elster, J. (Ed.). (1998). *Deliberative democracy*. Cambridge University Press.
Fakhfakh, F., Pérotin, V., & Gago, M. (2012). Productivity, capital, and labor in labor-managed and conventional firms: An investigation on French data. *Industrial and Labor Relations Review, 65*(4), 847–879.
Finkel, S. E. (1985). Reciprocal effects of participation and political efficacy: A panel analysis. *American Journal of Political Science, 29*(4), 891–913.
Finkel, S. E. (1987). The effects of participation on political efficacy and political support: Evidence from a West German panel. *Journal of Politics, 49*(2), 441–464.
Fishkin, J. S. (2018). *Democracy when the People are thinking: Revitalising our politics through public deliberation*. Oxford University Press.
Fredriksson, P. G., Neumayer, E., Damania, R., & Gates, S. (2005). Environmentalism, democracy, and pollution control. *Journal of Environmental Economics and Management, 49*(2), 343–365.
Gutmann, A., & Thompson, D. (1996). *Democracy and disagreement*. Harvard University Press.
Habermas, J. (1989). *The structural transformation of the public sphere: An inquiry into a category of bourgeois society*, translated from the German by T. Burger. MIT Press.

Habermas, J. (1996). *Between facts and norms: Contributions to a discourse theory of law and democracy*, translated from the German edition of 1992. MIT Press.
Habermas, J. (2001). *Moral consciousness and communicative action*. MIT Press.
Hailsham, L. (1976). *Elective dictatorship*. BBC.
Hodgson, G. M. (2019). *Is Socialism feasible? Towards an alternative future*. Edward Elgar.
Hodgson, G. M. (2021). *Liberal solidarity: The political economy of social democratic liberalism*. Edward Elgar.
Hübler, O., & Jirjahn, U. (2003). Works councils and collective bargaining in Germany: The impact on productivity and wages. *Scottish Journal of Political Economy, 50*(4), 471–491.
Jones, D. C. (2018). The economics of participation and employee ownership (PEO): An assessment. *Journal of Participation and Employee Ownership, 1*(1), 4–37.
Lenin, V. I. (1967). *Selected works in three volumes*. Lawrence and Wishart.
Li, Q., & Reuveny, R. (2006). Democracy and environmental degradation. *International Studies Quarterly, 51*(4), 935–956.
Lippmann, W. (1922). *Public opinion*. Macmillan.
Madison, J. (1787). *Federalist No. 10. The same subject continued: The Union as a safeguard against domestic faction and insurrection*. Retrieved December 20, 2020, from https://guides.loc.gov/federalist-papers/text-1-10#s-lg-box-wrapper-25493273
Mansbridge, J. J. (1983). *Beyond adversary democracy*. University of Chicago Press.
Margolis, H. (1977). Probability of a tie election. *Public Choice, 31*, 135–138.
Mendelberg, T. (2002). The deliberative citizen: Theory and evidence. In M. X. Delli Carpini, L. Huddy, & R. Y. Shapiro (Eds.), *Research in micropolitics: Volume 6: Political decision making, deliberation, and participation* (pp. 151–193). Elsevier.
Michels, R. (1915). *Political parties: A sociological study of oligarchical tendencies of modern democracy*, translated from the German edition of 1911. Hearst.
Milgram, S. (1974). *Obedience to authority: An experimental view*. Harper and Row, and Tavistock.
Mill, J. S. (1859). *On liberty*. John Parker & Son.
Mill, J. S. ([1861] 2008). *Considerations on representative government*. Serenity.
Mor, S. (2019). Nobody understands democracy anymore. *The Tablet,* 13 August. Retrieved May 8, 2020, from https://www.tabletmag.com/jewish-news-and-politics/289489/nobody-understands-democracy-anymore
Mounck, Y. (2018). *The people vs democracy: Why our Freedom is in danger and how to save it*. Harvard University Press.
Mueller, S., & Stegmaier, J. (2017). The dynamic effects of works councils on labour productivity: First evidence from panel data. *British Journal of Industrial Relations, 55*(2), 372–395.
Mutz, D. C. (2006). *Hearing the oher side: Deliberative versus participatory democracy*. Cambridge University Press.
O'Leary, N. (2019). The myth of the citizens' assembly'. *Politico,* 18 June. Retrieved May 11, 2020, from https://www.politico.eu/article/the-myth-of-the-citizens-assembly-democracy/
Pal, M. (2012). The promise and limits of citizens' assemblies: Deliberation, institutions and the Law of Democracy. *Queen's Law Journal, 38*, 259–294.
Pateman, C. (1970). *Participation and democratic theory*. University of Cambridge Press.
Pencavel, J. H. (2013). *The economics of worker coops*. Edward Elgar.
Rawls, J. (1971). *A theory of justice*. Harvard University Press.
Renwick, A., Allan, S., Jennings, W., McKee, R., Russell, M., & Smith, G. (2017). *The Report of the Citizens' Assembly on Brexit*. Constitution Unit, University College London. Retrieved October 16, 2020, from https://citizensassembly.co.uk/wp-content/uploads/2017/12/Citizens-Assembly-on-Brexit-Report.pdf
Runciman, D. (2018). *How democracy ends*. Profile.
Ryfe, D. M. (2005). Does deliberative democracy work? *American Review of Political Science, 8*, 49–71.

Samons, L. J. (2004). *What's wrong with democracy? From Athenian practice to American worship*. University of California Press.
Schumpeter, J. A. (1942). *Capitalism, socialism and democracy*. George Allen and Unwin.
Sen, A. K. (1981). *Poverty and famines: An essay on entitlement and deprivation*. Clarendon Press.
Sen, A. K. (1999). *Development as freedom*. Knopf and Oxford University Press.
Students for a Democratic Society. (1964). *The Port Huron Statement*, reprint of the 1962 version. Students for a Democratic Society.
Sunstein, C. R. (2000). Deliberative trouble? Why groups go to extremes. *Yale Law Journal, 110*, 71–119.
Sunstein, C. R. (2002). The law of group polarization. *Journal of Political Philosophy, 10*(2), 175–195.
Thompson, D. F. (2008). Deliberative democratic theory and empirical political science. *Annual Review of Political Science, 11*, 497–520.
Trade Unions for Energy Democracy. (2018). Jeremy Corbyn speech to Alternative Models of Ownership Conference. *Trade Unions for Energy Democracy*, 11 February. Retrieved May 17, 2020, from http://unionsforenergydemocracy.org/corbyn-calls-for-public-democratic-con trol-and-ownership-of-energy-in-order-to-transition-to-renewables/
Warren, M. E. (1996). What should we expect from more democracy? Radically democratic responses to politics. *Political Theory, 24*(2), 241–270.
Warren, M. E. (2009). Citizen representative. In M. E. Warren & H. Pearse (Eds.), *Designing deliberative democracy, the British Columbia citizens' assembly* (pp. 50–69). Cambridge University Press.
Weber, M. (1947). *The theory of social and economic organization*, edited with an introduction by Talcott Parsons. Free Press.
Westbrook, R. B. (1991). *John Dewey and American democracy*. Cornell University Press.

Geoffrey M. Hodgson is Emeritus Professor in Management at Loughborough University London. He was formerly at the University of Hertfordshire and the University of Cambridge. He is author of many academic books including *Liberal Solidarity* (2021), *Is there a Future for Heterodox Economics?* (2019), *Is Socialism Feasible?* (2019), *Conceptualizing Capitalism* (2015), *From Pleasure Machines to Moral Communities* (2013) and *Darwin's Conjecture* (2010, with Thorbjoern Knudsen). He has published over 150 articles in academic journals. He is Editor in Chief of the *Journal of Institutional Economics* and a founder of the World Interdisciplinary Network for Institutional Research (WINIR). He has over 40,000 citations on Google Scholar and is ranked as one of the 100 most influential living economists in the world today.

The Battle of Salamis and the Future of Democracy

George C. Bitros

Abstract The *Ecclesia of Demos* heeded to the pleas of Themistocles in 483/2 BCE and committed enough resources from the Laurion silver mines to build 200 triremes. Three years later, the triumph in the Battle of Salamis proved that the Athenian democracy could act prudently, when the common good was at high stake. By contrast, while the United States ought to remain strong in view of China's uprising, it nurtures two deficits, one in the public finances and another in the quality of democracy, which by growing almost out of control place democracy in the United States, and hence in the world, in harm's way. Thus, thinking ahead, the best act of prudence would be to introduce a bold reform by replacing the *representative party democracy*, which suffers from several irreversible drawbacks, with *digital direct democracy*. This model of self-government is superior because, first, it is free from unpalatable deficiencies and, second, it is endowed with several distinct advantages. In particular, it matches policy choices to citizen preferences. It offers institutional flexibility and efficiency. Citizens as shareholders of the state engage and take responsibility for the institutions of democracy, and the problems of asymmetric information and management coordination are confronted through discussion in the *electronic Ecclesia of Demos*.

Keywords Prudence in statecraft · Democracy in deficit · Democratic deficit · Representative party democracy · Athenian democracy · Digital direct democracy

JEL Codes D7 · F5 · H1 · H5 · H6

G. C. Bitros (✉)
Athens University of Economics and Business, Athens, Greece
e-mail: bitros@aueb.gr; https://www.aueb.gr/sites/default/files/aueb/Bitros-CV.20-21.pdf

© The Author(s), under exclusive license to Springer Nature Switzerland AG 2022
E. M. L. Economou et al. (eds.), *Democracy in Times of Crises*,
https://doi.org/10.1007/978-3-030-97295-0_5

1 Introduction

In the 186 years, from its formal establishment by Cleisthenes in 508 to 322 BCE, when it succumbed to the Macedon forces in the Lamian War, the Athenian democracy faced an existential threat only once. This was by the Persians, who attempted to conquer Greece twice. The first time in 490 BCE they were beaten in the plain of Marathon. But they came back 10 years later more determined with superior land and naval forces. The defeat that the Spartans suffered in Thermopylae and the retreat of the Athenians in Artemisium in 480 BCE placed Greeks in a desperate situation. Retreating Athenians did not have a land army of significant strength to defend their city. But still together with the Corinthians, Aegeniteans, and other Greek city-states they had a respectable fleet of triremes with well-trained men. Thus, they abandoned Athens and made a last stand in the narrow straits between the shores of Attica and the island of Salamis. The naval battle that took place in 480 BCE under the leadership of the Athenians and plans laid out by Themistocles ended in triumph of the Greek forces. Finally, in the following year, an emboldened allied land army led by Spartans dealt on the Persians such a devastating defeat in the Battle of Plataea that they were forced to rush out of Greece.

Due to the light that it can shed on a wide range of issues, which vary across time and space but remain always timely, the Battle of Salamis continues to attract significant scholarly attention. For a purposely selected example, consider the problem of *prudence* in statecraft by drawing on Sternberg (2005). When Persians were defeated in Marathon, ordinary Athenians returned to their daily lives and most likely forgot the damage they had inflicted to the prestige of Persia, which was the greatest empire known in the world up to that time. Yet according to Themistocles, the odds were high that they would return and he advised Athens to embark on a bold program of public works to bolster its defenses. By upgrading and expanding the navy, he sensed, Athens would not strengthen only militarily. Employment opportunities for the low-income citizens who would become mariners and rowers in the new triremes would increase spectacularly, thus enhancing democracy and social cohesion. The economy would get a strong transformative shock, which would stir a sizable flow of workers out of agriculture and into the building of skills and new trades mostly related to manufacturing, maritime, and "international" commerce (Bitros et al., 2020). Personal incomes and wealth would increase and spill over to the budget of the state. Last, but not least, although eventually the posture of the enlarged fleet might not deter Persians from returning, if all went well and Athens survived, it could develop into an incontestable sea-power in the Eastern Mediterranean and beyond.

However, all these strategic advantages might be secured, if only the necessary resources became somehow available. Now we know what happened 3 years before the Battle of Salamis. In 483 BCE, Athens discovered a new rich vein of silver in the nearby mines of Laurion, and the issue among citizens came down to the distribution of the riches that would result for the state. In the ambivalent debates that followed in the *Ecclesia of Demos*,[1] Themistocles was successful in passing a motion toward committing 100 talents for two consecutive years to build and operate 200 triremes. What we do not know is how Athenians managed to construct so many new ships, upgrade those they had already in place, and deploy all of them ready for combat in that pivotal morning of September 20, 480 BCE. Undoubtedly, instrumental among the factors that contributed were the prudential arguments of Themistocles, which mobilized citizens to offer their best for the common good, and this proves above all else that what triumphed in the Battle of Salamis was the Athenian democracy in the mode of self-government, which had grown robust in the previous three decades.

With this proposition in hand, it is convenient now to raise the question: If a Salamis-like challenge confronted the most powerful democracy in the world today, that is, the United States (US), can we say with confidence that it would come out victorious? Searching for an answer, it is natural to ponder about possible adversaries among the present and prospective superpowers. In the light of the outcomes in the Second World War and the First Cold War that followed, which resulted in the dissolution of the Soviet Empire in 1992, one would be encouraged to answer that the future of the US democracy, and hence that of the free world, is safe. But the answer is much less certain if one contemplates the possibility of a sharp engagement with China, and particularly so if the latter's growing power is viewed in the context of the assessments submitted long ago by Russell (1922).[2] For, since in this case the US democracy would confront a huge communist state erected on the foundations of a society having 5000 years of civilization and brewed with the social values of Confucianism, the odds become *precarious*, and the future depends on the willingness to self-insure via the mechanism of *prudence*. By implication, the answer to the above question depends on the answers to the questions: Does the United States apply adequate *prudence* in view of China's uprising?[3] If not, first, what are the reasons? And second, what should be done to improve the odds for the triumph of

---

[1] *Ecclesia of Demos* or *Assembly* was the top decision-making body with all legislative and select ultimate-degree judicial and auditing powers. Members of the *Assembly* were all male Athenian citizens over 30 years of age; the quorum for the meetings was 6000 in a male population that ranged from 30,000 to 60,000, depending on the period; and the number of meetings was at least once a month.

[2] His assessments of the implications from the ascendance of China in the world are scattered everywhere in the book. However, in my view, the one of interest here is the following:

> The danger of patriotism is that, as soon as it has proved strong enough for successful defense, it is apt to turn to foreign aggression. China, by her resources and her population, is capable of being the greatest Power in the world after the United States. It is much to be feared that, in the process of becoming strong enough to preserve their independence, the Chinese may become strong enough to embark upon a career of imperialism (Chapter XV, The Outlook for China).

[3] As we see the world today, only a coalition of democracies led by the USA, the most powerful of them all, will have any chance to win a new cold war with China. For this reason, looking forward what counts most is whether or not the USA prepares for such a contingency. This explains why the focus in this paper is on the USA.

democracy, whenever the occasion arises, hopefully in the longer than in the shorter future?

The objective in this paper is to shed some light on these questions. For this purpose, in the next section, the focus is on two indices, which are known to proxy well for the prospects of any nation, namely, the state in the US public finances and the quality of democracy. Drawing on the course of these indices over the post-war period, it is found that the United States is experiencing growing deficits on both counts. Then, given that these protracted deficits hold grave risks for democracy, even in the absence of challenges from abroad, Sect. 3 looks at the root causes for the apparent lack of volition on the part of the United States to act prudently by bringing these ominous deficits under control. To no surprise, the analysis corroborates that what is now at full play are the structural deficiencies that remain latent in the *representative party democracy* mode of self-government.[4] In this light, Sect. 4 lays out a proposal for a bold reform along the lines prescribed by the Athenian model of self-government, whereas Sect. 5 comments on the advantages of the proposed reform and the technological advances that render it tenable. Finally, the paper closes in Sect. 6 with a brief summary of the main findings and the conclusions in the context of the timeless lessons for today from the Battle of Salamis.

2 Twin Deficits and Lack of Prudence

By all accounts of experts from international organizations, academic research centers, and independent think tanks, the crisis that erupted in the United States in 2008 and spread quickly throughout the world had all the makings to become catastrophic. Several immediate drivers instigated it. One was the US dollar, another the process of globalization, and still another the revolutionary technological advances in the electronic transmission of speech, text, and icons over long geographical distances, which weakened even further the capability of democratic governments to respond with timely enactment and enforcement of pertinent remedial policies. However, none of these drivers would have been able either individually or collectively to stir a crisis of such cliff-hanging proportions, if democracy in the United States had not grown dysfunctional in preceding decades.

On the front of economic policies, the calls that something was going wrong became increasingly lauder and clearer from early in the postwar period. The battleground of ideas centered less on Keynes (1936, 1942) and more on the convenient interpretations and adaptations of his propositions by the so-called Keynesians. When Hayek (1960, pp. 304–305) penned down his warning, he

---

[4]The debacles of the USA in Vietnam, in the late 1960s and early 1970s, and in Afghanistan recently, highlight the existence of a most precarious vicious circle. In particular, they suggest that over time the lack of *prudence* exacerbates these structural deficiencies, leading in turn to decision-making under a state of *urgency* and *impatience*.

remained hopeful that democracy did have the capability to learn from its follies and reverse course away from systematic deficit spending and debt accumulation. However, he proved too optimistic because ever since democracy in the United States has continued on the same dead-end track.

In particular, when payments imbalances under the Bretton Woods agreements came to a heading in 1971, instead of committing to reestablishing budget discipline, the United States abandoned the agreements altogether and unilaterally abrogated the convertibility of the US dollar into gold. What this decision signaled was that from then on they would adopt fiscal and monetary policies and by implication foreign exchange policies, which would serve their national interests rather than those of the alliance of free nations that they led since the victorious big war. As a result, by the time of Buchanan and Wagner (1977), *democracy in deficit* had been established already as the new normal. Entitlements kept increasing at unsustainable real rates of growth. Servicing of the unproductive public debts absorbed ever-increasing chunks of gross domestic product (GDP), along with aggravating income and wealth inequality. The public sector expanded by crowding out the more productive private sector and limiting almost by a third its share in the country's GDP. As Gordon (2016), Bitros (2020), and many others have confirmed, long-term economic growth nosedived into the region of secular stagnation, precisely as Hayek had predicted in the above citation. Regulatory arrangements designed to keep the markets open to actual and potential competition became part of the problem rather than the solution by failing repeatedly to perform effectively according to their mandates. Last, but not least, the United States from creditor turned into a debtor country, thereby eroding the value of the US dollar as the preeminent currency of the world.

The crisis in 2008 presented another opportunity for the United States to return to time-honored economic policies. Instead, by adopting unorthodox initiatives, they pushed budget deficits, public debt, and monetary accommodation to levels never seen before. The federal government used taxpayer money to save financial and industrial concerns from bankruptcy. Independent regulatory authorities gave in to the too-big-to-fail doctrine, which was invoked by politicians to save unscrupulous financial enterprises. The US Federal Open Market Committee went into three consecutive rounds of "quantitative easing" by printing money like there was no tomorrow. And, when by 2019 the economy had been propped up to achieve economic growth rates even above its productive potential, unemployment declined to historical lows; asset valuations rose way above their pre-2008 levels, etc.; policy makers rejoiced for a job well done. Therefore, when a few months into 2020, the news about the COVID-19 pandemic broke open, and the economy went into a sharp tailspin, extending spectacularly on the practices of *democracy in deficit* to forestall a catastrophe was hardly surprising.[5]

---

[5] Some well-intentioned observers ask: What else could the US government do to avert a catastrophe? The answer is that US governments ought to have exercised *prudence* in the postwar period to be prepared for the contingency of a pandemic like the present one. If governments under

The economic policies of *democracy in deficit* gained traction and took hold among US voters because of their appeal to the socially desirable economic outcomes that Keynesians evangelized in abundance. In reality though, these policies were propagated by politicians, lobbyists, advertisers, and, in general, a wide range of agents who are known to pursue their interests through the government and the public sector. As a result, gradually organized minorities captured the institutions of democracy, the latter stopped catering to the interests of the many, and this development has given rise to various sources that feed into the so-called *democratic deficit*. To highlight its trend, consider Barber's (2003, pp. xxxiii, ix–x) related assessments in 1984 and again in 2003. From them, it follows that back in the 1970s, due to non-transient misalignments in the functioning of the political parties, US voters started to loose trust in democracy. An increasing percentage of them became alienated and stopped taking part in the electoral process, and by the 1990s, this trend developed into a participation crisis of such proportions that it was difficult to tell whether the United States remained in the family of true practicing democracies.[6]

Moreover, even if there were no issues of legitimacy, the drivers of the *democratic deficit* are many and very significant to ignore. For a brief account, consider Levinson (2007). He cites two types of deformities. On the one hand, there are those that the political parties introduce in their competition to win and retain the power to govern and, of course, enjoy the privileges that come with it. Arrangements like the use of private money in the electoral campaigns, gerrymandering of legislative districts, loopholes in the administration of elections, etc. fall in this category. On the other hand, there are certain provisions in the US Constitution that limit seriously the sovereignty of citizens to determine the mode of self-government that serves best their interests.

To conclude, in the absence of determination for bold prudential reforms, the twin deficits described above will continue to widen, to erode social cohesion, and to weaken democracy in the United States from inside. The analysis below of the inherent deficiencies of *representative party democracy* corroborates further this onerous outlook.

---

representative party democracy cannot act prudently, this variant of democracy comes into strong question, because governments stop serving a very critical aspect of the common good.

[6]In the 2020 elections, voter participation reached an all-time record of 149 million. However, whether this is a temporary shift in the behavior of voters due to the particular circumstances of the elections or a more permanent change in the long trend of relatively low participation rates remains to be seen.

3 Innate Deficiencies in Representative Party Democracy

In principle under democracy, all powers originate from the citizens. But, in difference to classical Athens, where democracy was *direct* in the sense that governance was in the hands of citizens themselves, contemporary democracies have been set up on the presumption that the vast majority of citizens lack the specialized knowledge and skills that are required to analyze complicated issues, or implement the necessary decisions. For this reason, state governance is *indirect* in that it is assigned through formal elections to certain citizens who are expected to have the appropriate knowledge, skills, and integrity. Thus, the elected officials-politicians become, in essence, *representatives* or *agents* of the citizens as *principals*. At this level, representation per se is problematic. The task in this section is to explain why this is the case.

3.1 Impossibility of Representation in Groups

The key question is this: Can citizens delegate through elections their choices over policies in a consistent way and hold politicians accountable for their implementation? The answer that emerges from the following analysis is in the negative.[7]

Suppose a candidate for the US Congress from a district in New York wishes through his campaign to get a precise idea about the ordering of the priorities of his prospective voters. In his speeches he presents a large assortment of policies supported by his party and shortly before the elections he asks from those present in a town hall meeting to order for him from the most to the least urgent a select number of policies suitable for the district. Can he expect to come out from their responses enlightened? In other words, will he be able to obtain an ordering that, if elected, he can take to Washington and state to his colleagues in the party that this is the order of priorities that represents the preferences of his constituents, irrespective of whether they voted for him or not? Assuming that the constituents we are talking about satisfy certain reasonable criteria concerning their autonomy and rational structure of preferences over the policies in question, there is no way to construct a "collective ordering" such that every one of those who took part in the process would be able to recognize as his own.[8]

---

[7] For a more extensive discussion of the theoretical foundations of the analysis as well as references to key literature, see Bitros et al. (2020, pp. 227–241).

[8] At times, it is suggested that the relative frequencies of items mentioned in opinion surveys may be considered a good proxy of the "collective ordering" of the preferences of the people who participate. However, even if the sample of the respondents is representative of the wider population in statistical terms, the said frequencies are not a proper index of the ordering sought because, after the results of an opinion survey are announced, many of those who take part disagree that the frequencies coincide with their ordering. For the pioneering analyses in this area, see Arrow (1951) and Buchanan, Tullock (1962).

Being unable to obtain a "collective ordering" out of the stated preferences of his constituents, if elected, by necessity the Congressman will vote according to his own perception of this ordering, hoping that he may guess correctly. If he does, most likely he will get re-elected. If not, he stands a good chance to become a one-term Congressman. However, this uncertainty is unlikely to leave his congressional behavior unaffected. For, having started eager to serve his district, and thereby his homeland, he will view his presence in the US Congress as a one-off opportunity for self-promotion. And when that happens, the problems for democracy start, because in his voting calculus his short-term personal and party's interests will take precedent over the longer-term ones of his constituents and his country.

3.2 Asymmetry of Information

Beyond the thorny issue of representation in groups, contemporary democracy is beset by a second fundamental problem known in the literature as the *principal-agent problem* or *dilemma*. Let us see how it arises in the context of the preceding example.

Upon entering into the US Congress, the Congressman will be appointed to committees tasked with various subjects. Naturally in carrying out his duties, he will gain a lot of information available only to a very narrow circle of people and hence potentially of considerable monetary value. Will he be tempted to use it for his own advantage? The paramount odds are that he will succumb to the uncertainty about his re-election, but also because of self-excuses as if others in his position would do the same, electoral campaigns are costly and so on. As a result, given that informational asymmetry confers exploitable advantages to the political system as a whole, one must ask: Can citizens do something about it, and if so, how may they deter politicians from deceiving them? The answers found in the literature follow two general approaches. The first maintains that the mandate citizens give to politicians should be specified in strict terms. In other words, what this approach recommends is that the government should be assigned a specific range of policies or projects, without any discretion to deviate from certain explicitly defined limits (*strict agency*). The second approach suggests that the mandate should be completely open (*free agency*).[9] That is, once elected politicians should be free to decide according to their own perception of correctness, without even taking into account the preferences of their voters. History and experience show that only the latter approach has been adopted, since, for example, when they are called to govern, political parties do not abide even by their own pre-election commitments. Hence, it is not surprising that as a rule in contemporary *representative party democracies*, elected officials deceive citizens and introduce measures to strengthen their authority, quash accountability, and insulate themselves from the control of the public.

---

[9]This distinction was already made in the eighteenth century by Burke (1774).

The problems that emanate from asymmetric information become insurmountable when we turn to the implementation of the enacted policies. For then, the ultimate principals, i.e., the citizens who pay the bills, are passive, the immediate principals are the elected politicians who act autonomously and quite likely for their own interests, and agents are the unelected employees in the narrow and the wider public sector. Since they are the latter who produce and control the data on any one subject and as a rule provide the continuity of service in the public administration, while their political supervisors come and go, the asymmetries of information they enjoy may enable them individually and collectively through their labor unions to act as "a state within a state." To be sure, the installation of digital monitoring systems in recent decades may have stemmed widespread attempts by employees in the public sector to take advantage of hidden knowledge and hidden actions. On the other hand, the continuing enlargement of the state may enhance the opportunities for such aberrant behaviors, and hence on balance the situation has been worsening.[10]

3.3 The Deleterious Role of Political Parties

As their views had been shaped by the study of the Athenian democracy and their experiences under the British rule, most of the founders of the US democracy were distrustful of political parties. Madison in particular appears in his essay *On factions* to believe that they would not emerge. Yet he and the other founding fathers were proven wrong because already in the 1790s, two parties were established and started to compete fiercely. As a result, even though the *Constitution* does not make any mention to them, from very early political parties became a de facto institutional complement of representative democracy in the United States.[11]

The general assessment by experts is that in the nineteenth century, the political parties contributed significantly to the establishment and operating maturity of the principles and institutions that the founders provided for in the US constitutional order. They managed to create governing majorities by focusing electoral campaigns on the issues rather than on the personal traits of the politicians that were involved. However, in the twentieth century and particularly after the Second World War, the political parties lost their orientation. Already in the first quarter of the last century, when Weber (1921/1946, p. 94) was writing by drawing on his visits to the United States, it did not escape from his sharp observational lenses that "The management

---

[10] Political scientists have long been trying to devise mechanisms in order to mitigate the undesirable consequences from a social point of view of the *principal-agent problem* both in policy design and policy implementation. The results so far are not encouraging because controlling of the practice of opportunism by politicians and bureaucrats carries exorbitant costs on the part of citizens. For an assessment of this literature, see, for example, Lane (2013).

[11] Madison did not take long to realize that the great dispersion of power that he had embedded in the *Constitution* would render the formation of governing majorities extremely difficult. That is why, according to Postell (2018), he started to doubt about the usefulness of political parties.

of politics through parties simply means management through interest groups."[12] Yet the capture of the political parties by special interests was still in its infancy at the time, and Weber thought that only large, organized parties could oppose bureaucracy as a tendency toward a caste of mandarins, removed from the common people by expert training, examination certificates, and tenure of office. Had he lived into the 1980s, most likely he would have concurred with Barber's (2003, pp. xxxiii, ix-x) assessments.

In short, experience and evidence demonstrate that political parties behave as large enterprises, acting to maximize the interests primarily of their organized members, secondarily of their sponsors, and lastly of their supporters in the electoral body, as foreshadowed by Franklin (2005, p. 87), rarely maximizing the interests of the country. These assessments are based on at least the following considerations. First, and foremost, is the pretext of the need for governmental stability. Gehl and Porter (2017) have established that the political market has been transformed into a tightly controlled oligopoly with no real competition and two large parties alternating in power. In turn, this structure, supported by multifaceted legal and other constraints, renders the entry of new parties exceptionally difficult and allows the political system to become autonomous and hence indifferent to the preferences and interests of citizens. Second, as the political system becomes autonomous, the relationship of representation deteriorates; voters become alienated from politics, stop caring about the common good, and resort to maximizing their own private interests by attaching to the clientelist system of the political parties or rent-seeking. Third, voter alienation erodes solidarity and social cohesion.[13] To counterbalance this process, political parties introduce costly and inefficient programs, mainly in the context of the "welfare state," in which the beneficiaries feel more allegiant toward the initiators of these programs rather than to the citizens who pay the costs through their taxes. Fourth, by attaching to the political parties, the citizens become addicted to the restrictions of their rights and liberties and become tolerant to the enlargement of the state at the expense of the private economy. Fifth, even worse than all the above, is that the problem political parties pose for contemporary democracy becomes insoluble, because as stressed by Lyon (1996):

> Parties and businesses, however, have a strong vested interest in restricting competition. In the case of business, government regulations limit the ability of corporations to choke off competition. But parties control the only body-the government-that can regulate them.

---

[12] One finds even bleaker views about the nature of political parties in Michels (1911).

[13] In certain democracies where the parties often alternate in government, either through implicit or explicit agreements, changes are introduced for perpetuating their hold on power. In the United Kingdom, for example, a government can hold majority in the parliament, despite receiving only one third of the votes of the electorate, enabling it to vote for laws opposed by the vast majority of the population. Governments that are elected by non-proportional electoral systems inspire doubt about their representativeness, thereby undermining the quality of democracy. In turn, the lack of representativeness induces citizens to perceive government decisions as illegitimate and to resort to behaviors that aim to annul the results intended by the laws.

Against the above negative views about the role of political parties, one finds in the literature proponents who argue favorably. For example, Aldrich (1995) maintains that political parties are indispensable because they a) mobilize citizens by arousing their interest in the social, economic, and other policies by ideologically driven arguments, (b) educate citizens by making them aware of the alternative choices on the various issues, and (c) act as facilitating mechanisms in the legislative process. Others assert that citizens lack the information they would need to carry out the functions of governance and that, even if they had it, they lack the incentives to act for the common good; and still some others misinterpret the analysis of bureaucracy by von Mises (1944, pp. 47–49) to deny that responsible to a significant extent for the uncontrollable expansion of the state in the twentieth century was party politics.

3.4 Uncoordinated Administrative Polycentrism

Large multinational companies have manufacturing facilities in many countries, and at the close of each day, despite the time differences among various geographical regions, they are able to know the results of their operations as well as the main problems they face in each country. How do they achieve this remarkable coordination? They achieve it through decentralized management systems, in which their managers in each country may decide freely within certain general limits set by the center and expressed in terms of market shares, profitability, and other indicators of measurable performance for which they are held accountable. But why even in the United States, the mightiest *representative party democracy* of them all, the government is unable to govern effectively? This is a difficult question and answering it would require writing a separate paper. So consider the following brief remarks.

Governments are unable to govern effectively because, among other shortcomings, they lack the prerequisites that have been worked out by contemporary management science. In particular, the objectives they set to achieve are at best broad and uncertain. Their information lags constantly behind the current state of the economy or of the problems they are called to face. The ministers in the various ministries, including their advisors, rarely know the operation of the civil service departments they undertake to work with, thus leaving much leeway to the technocrats and bureaucrats to undermine the enacted policies for their own purposes. Since the objectives pursued are often obscure and immeasurable, growing conflicts among ministers allow them to pull the efforts of the government in various directions, etc.

However, none of the above organizational weaknesses undermines so decisively the effectiveness of governments than the lack of automatic mechanisms to coordinate the information which is necessary to confront a problem of general national interest and which is diffused across many ministries and state agencies and organizations. It follows from experience how all these administrative units safeguard their importance by sitting tightly on the information they collect regarding the tasks to which they have been assigned, so it is safe to surmise that the difficulty of elected governments to control the centers of power within the public sector is an inherent weakness of *representative party democracy*.

3.5 Sum Up

In general, *representative party democracy* suffers from several deficiencies. Some cited frequently in the literature are bureaucracy, rent-seeking, regulatory capture, the corrupting power of private money in politics, etc. However, these are secondary in the sense that emanate from at least four deficiencies that are inherent in this mode of self-government. These are "the impossibility of representation in groups," "the asymmetry of information," "the state capture by the political parties," and the "uncoordinated administrative polycentrism." In the United States, for 150 years, the latter deficiencies did not hinder the functioning of democracy because the public sector was extremely limited and the secondary deficiencies were absent. But beginning from the great depression in 1929, and particularly after the Second World War, the public sector expanded into the private economy and became in essence center for redistribution of income and wealth in the service of organized minorities. As a result, there emerged two deficits, which are growing without any control in sight by those responsible leaders who ought to act prudentially for the common good.

If on this assessment one surmised that the future of *representative party democracy* in the United States, and hence in the free world, is bleak, one would be fully justified. For, if these deficits continue to be left unchecked, eventually the US democracy may fall prey to its internal deficiencies. In that event, military strength would become superfluous and, should China turn imperialist as per the quotation of Russell in the introduction,[14] liberty and individual freedoms will be seriously threatened. For this reason, preventing the grim outlook of such a predicament renders reforming contemporary democracy along the lines of the Athenian model of self-government an act of outmost prudence. What this would entail and why the proposed bold reforms are now technically feasible are issues taken up in the following two sections.

---

[14] Presently, the odds that China may succumb eventually to hegemonic temptations may be small. Besides, in the coming decades China will have to expand within a multipolar world where several superpowers will strive for mutual accommodation. However, since the future is unknown, the best policy for democracies to hedge against even these small odds is to exercise prudence by strengthening their domestic fronts and building strong and cohesive alliances, as Athenians did to face off the great Persian Empire.

4 The Athenian Model of Self-Government

Voluminous research in recent centuries has established that in classical times Athens accomplished a level of achievements that have marked indelibly the history of the world and particularly that of Western civilization, from the architectural marvels of the monuments we so admire today to the millions of citations across all fields of knowledge. Moreover, from politics and ethics to economics and the arts, it is not an overstatement to say that in the fifth and fourth centuries BCE, Athens reached an apex of military, economic, political, cultural, and scientific influence in the world comparable to that of the United States in the post-1929 period.

To be sure, this astonishing feat came about because of many strategic choices by great Athenians leaderships, the norms and values of Athenian citizens themselves, and not to a small extent because of exceptionally good luck, when the odds were heavily against Athens, like in the Battle of Salamis. But, if one were asked to single out only one key factor that made the difference, this would have to be the institutions of the Athenian democracy. The following presentation aims at providing evidence for this proposition.

Democracy in classical Athens was ruled by three entities:[15] the *Ecclesia of Demos* (congregation of citizens) or *Assembly*; the *Council of 500* or *Boule*; and the *Dikastiria* or *Courts*. The *Assembly*, in which participated all adult male Athenian citizens, exercised the decision-making authority, including legislative, supervisory, and select ultimate-degree judicial and auditing powers. It convened four times during each *prytany* (tenth of the conciliar year), which lasted from 36 to 39 days, and at least 40 times per year in total (Thorley, 1996, p. 30). It could be in session only when more than 6000 citizens were present. One of the four meetings of each *prytaneia* was devoted to discussion and decision-making on issues of governance, defense, foreign policy, and provisioning of food and other supplies, including welfare, while the other three dealt with various issues.

The *Council* consisted of 10 groups with 50 members each from the 10 tribes of Athens. The group of 50 members of each tribe served for one tenth of each year, and it was replaced by another group at the end of each *prytany*. In practical terms, each tribe that held this post actually ruled the city-state with full executive rights (Lyttkens, 2013, pp. 59, 76). Among the main duties of the *Council* were (a) to prepare the so-called probouleumata (preliminary decrees) and submit those which were approved for final discussion and voting in the *Assembly* (Demosthenes, *Against Neaera*, 59.4); (b) to prepare the agenda for each meeting of the *Assembly*, (c) to care for the arming and manning of warships as well as the cavalry; (d) to supervise the execution of the budget, the management of the *temples*, which serve also as *treasuries of the gods*, the operations of the *mint*, and a wide range of special purpose funds; and (e) to be in constant contact and monitor the performance of the nine *archons*, the ten *strategoi* (generals), and several hundreds of public officials

---

[15] For a detailed indexing of the sources of evidence on which the presentation in this section is based, please see Bitros and Karayiannis (2012) and Bitros et al. (2020).

(magistrates), most selected by lot and appointed to manage the affairs of the state on a daily basis in conjunction with the services of the *public administration* (Aristotle, *Athenian Constitution*, 46.1, 49.1-2).

As for the judicial powers, these rested with the *Courts*, which heard cases in the civil, maritime, and penal domains. Competent to adjudicate civil disputes were the *Dikasteric Courts* (Popular Courts or People's Courts). These dealt with most cases, albeit scarcely in a law-based fashion. On the contrary, as argued by Cohen (1973) and Lanni (2008), the *Maritime Courts* and the *Areiopagos*, which handled maritime disputes and most homicides, respectively, functioned in a precedent-setting manner from a legal standpoint. The Supreme Court called *Heliaia* comprised 6000 judges and served as a *Court of Appeals*.[16]

In the above institutional setting, state governance was exercised by the *prytaneis*, the nine *archons*, the ten *strategoi* (generals), and the *magistrates* in their dedicated functions, all assisted by the *public administration*. The nine *archons*, all of whom were equal among themselves, although one had the title of *eponymous* (the most important of the nine *archons*), carried out specific projects and responsibilities. For example, the *archon* in charge of defense was responsible for collecting all public revenues earmarked for the financing of the army and paying all related expenses (Tridimas, 2012, p. 4). The ten *strategoi*, each coming from one of the ten Athenian tribes, oversaw the armed forces. Their service was annual, and depending on the evaluation of their performance by the *Council*, they could be reappointed (Lyttkens, 2013, p. 52). The *public administration* consisted of various departments, providing services to enable compliance with building codes, enforcement of regulations regarding food and other supplies, orderly conduct in the markets, and the design, construction, and maintenance of public infrastructure, among others. At the end of each *prytaneia*, a vote was taken as to whether they had performed their duties adequately and those who were found inadequate lost their office.[17] As for the institutions in charge of the state's budget and the currency, they were embedded in the above organizational structure with enough autonomy from the central authorities to pursue effectively their tasks, but also under close supervision and brevity of tenure to discourage corruptive practices on their part.

Figure 1 displays the institutions of state governance in the Athenian model of democracy in classical times. The separation of state powers is shown by the double-

---

[16] *Heliaia* convened very rarely in its full membership. The bulk of cases were brought in front of the *Popular* or *People's Courts*, which constituted particular chambers of *Heliaia*, specialized according to the nature of the law they applied and the importance of the cases they heard. For example, the *Maritime Courts* was a chamber of *Heliaia* dealing with maritime cases. The higher the social importance of the cases a chamber dealt with, the larger its membership was in terms of participating judges. Worth noting is also that before the reforms of Ephialtes and Pericles in the 460s and 450s BCE, respectively, the judicial functions of *Heliaia* were performed by the *Assembly*, which stood as court.

[17] Pritchard (2012, 48–49, 2014, 8) argues that the *strategoi* were often required to finance by themselves the means to perform their *strategia*, i.e., to fulfill their annual responsibilities as generals.

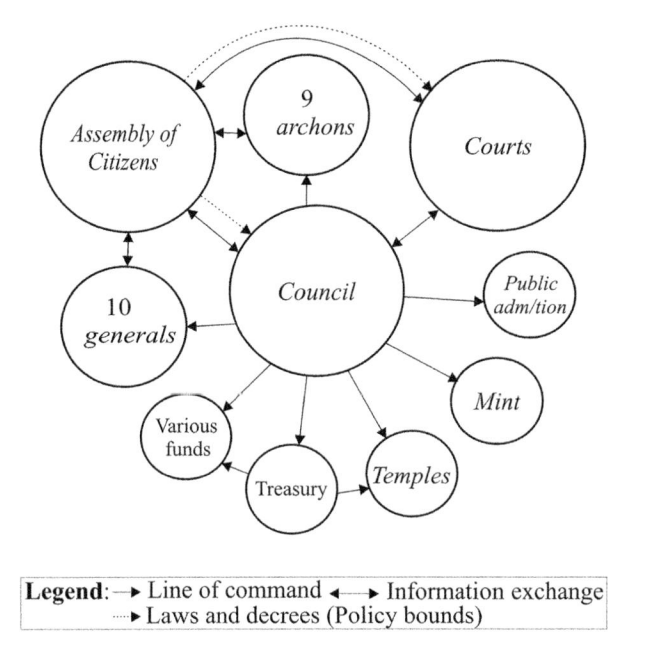

Fig. 1 Institutions of state governance in the Athenian model of democracy in classical times

headed arrows. Among the centers connected by them, there was exchange of information in an environment of cooperation and mutual respect for their institutional independence. On the contrary, single-headed arrows denote the lines of hierarchical command and in reverse the obligation for reporting on the results and possible problems in the course of governance.

This institutional setup emerged neither suddenly nor by design at some particular period. It took a certain form under the reforms by Cleisthenes in 508 BCE. Nevertheless, it evolved mostly over time through judicial trial and error by applying, among others, three fundamental principles. Namely, first, unequivocal ownership of the institutions of democracy by citizens; second, the greatest possible dispersion of state powers among citizens; and third, absolutely no one was to be trusted in the management of state affairs.[18]

It was the first ever and only system of state governance in which, allowing for the arrangements of monitoring and auditing that they had put in place to control corruption to a minimum, the interests of those who governed coincided with the interests of those who were governed. That is why, according to this norm, it was to the benefit of all to manage the state's affairs as per Adam Smith's (1776/1977, pp. 456–457) dictum that:

---

[18] The term "citizen" refers here to male Athenians over 20 years of age who had the right to participate in the *Assembly of Citizens*. Between 20 and 30 years of age, Athenians could not hold public office because they were considered as lacking maturity.

What is prudence in the conduct of every private family can scarce be folly in that of a great kingdom.

5 Advantages of Digital Direct Over Representative Party Democracy

Aside from being free from the deficiencies that were analyzed in Sect. 3, in the absence of political parties, *digital direct democracy* has several advantages that render it far superior to *representative party democracy*. Main among them are that it allows citizens first to arrive at consistent orderings of their preferences over policies, second to implement them promptly and efficiently, third to engage in the governance of the state based on fairness and merit, and fourth to ameliorate the issues of asymmetric information and uncoordinated government polycentrism. The aim in this section is to explain briefly the sources from where these advantages emanate.

5.1 *Unbundling of Policies*

Presumably, by voting for a political party, citizens under *representative party democracy* vote for the package of policies that the particular party proposed during the electoral campaign. Hence, due to its very nature, this type of self-government does not permit citizens the possibility of unbundling, that is, to vote for the policy option, say on education, proposed by party A, on health by party B, on defense by party C, etc. What this difficulty implies is that the ordering of citizen preferences is not revealed, at least not precisely. On the contrary, in the *Assembly of Citizens*, the decisions are taken by voting on a case-by-case basis, and the true order of citizen priorities is arrived at by applying the majority rule among those who vote. Thus, by matching policy choices to citizen preferences, *managerial democracy* delivers what is the true essence of democracy.

5.2 *Superior Flexibility and Efficiency*

To highlight this advantage, consider the case of the British exit from the European Union (EU), i.e., Brexit. British citizens had second thoughts about leaving the EU and the popular sentiment in favor of holding a second referendum gained momentum. However, institutionally this presented considerable problems at both the political and the legislative levels. It was a difficult issue for the prime minister, the ministers, members of the parliament of all parties, etc. Under *managerial democracy*, the solution would be simple and straightforward and could be implemented fast. An initiator would just have to propose a new vote in the *Assembly of Citizens*, and if the outcome were different from the previous one, the new decision would be implemented. A famous example in this regard is the one reported by Thucydides (*History of the Peloponnesian War*, 3.36–49).

In 427 BCE, the *Assembly* decided to punish the rebellious citizens of Mytilene (a member of the Athenian League) by putting to death all adult males upon their surrender after a long siege. An Athenian ship sailed bringing the order of execution to the Athenian general on the island. The next day, the Athenians had second thoughts on the harshness of the punishment and the *Assembly* took a decision to annul the previous one and to execute only the leaders of the revolt. A second ship was sent, countermanding the previous order, with its Athenians commanders promising the rowers extra pay as an incentive, if they arrived in time to save the Mytileneans. The second ship did overcome the first and the Mytileneans were saved. Presumably, if Athens followed Brexit procedures, the decision would have not changed at all or not in time to save the citizens of the island, and the *Assembly* would have committed a terrible mistake.[19]

5.3 Institutional Arrangements for Every Citizen to Engage in State Governance

Tough conditions, more or less similar to those for appointment in the *Council*, applied across the board in classical Athens. Every citizen had the right and the obligation to serve in some capacity based on merit and qualifications, but even then, since none was to be trusted due to the frivolity of human nature, with few exceptions, Athenians kept the term of service to 1 year and, with few exceptions, the selection among the candidates for office was effected by lot or sortition. By implication, the system assured that (a) all qualified and interested citizens had an equal chance of holding public office; (b) factionalism was minimized, since there was no point making promises to win over key supporters; and (c) clientelism in the form of distributing state benefits to particular groups of voters so as to get re-elected was absent. All these merits would render *direct democracy* a vastly better functioning democracy in comparison to *representative party democracy* which, as the quotation from Barber (2003, p. xiv) suggests, vitiates the essence of democracy per se:

> When the public yields its basic governing functions to representatives, it has begun a process of alienation that in the end taints the very idea of public goods and common ground.

---

[19] The evidence is that Athenian democracy in the fourth century became less radical in the sense that after 403 BCE they introduced two new institutions, i.e., "graphe paranomon" and "nomothetai," which acted as further checks and balances mechanisms regarding the decisions of the *Assembly*. Readers interested in the role of these institutions may start with Lyttkens et al. (2018), regarding the former, and Harris (2013), regarding the latter.

This alienation in turn trivializes democracy, transforming what should be ongoing deliberative participation in governance into a cynical preoccupation with media-hyped elections. ... In a word, then, privatization, alienation, and the abuse of civic deliberation are actually easier in a representative democracy than in a strong participatory democracy-which is one more argument in strong democracy's favor.

5.4 Procedural Counterbalancing of Informational Asymmetries

The Athenians who participated in the *Assembly of Citizens* and served in the *Council* and the other state services came from all occupations. They were not presumed to have expert knowledge on any of the multifaceted functions of the state. The only thing they were presumed to have was common sense and motivation to serve the "common good." By culture and values, Athenian citizens were trained to listen and being guided by those more knowledgeable and experienced among them (Economou & Kyriazis, 2019). For an example, consider the case of *Nicophon's law*, which was introduced in 375/374 BCE and concerned matters of the currency. Nicophon was a monetary expert in the service of the *Assembly of Citizens*. To win support for his proposals, he should have strived to explain what the objectives of his draft law were and how they might be achieved. Speaking in the presence of at least 6000 people, the great majority of whom knew little or no monetary economics, he had to communicate his ideas in simple but not simplistic terms. In the process, every citizen present shared the same information, which formed a basis for his vote. Therefore, the asymmetry of information between Nicophon and the prospective voters in his audience was reduced, and the decision was carried out with a better understanding of the pros and cons by those who voted and would share in the consequences, if the law were adopted.

In this context, one may argue that the *Assembly of Citizens* and the *Council* functioned as markets for the exchange and competition of "ideas" and "courses of action." A participant brought forward and tried to "sell" a proposal, for which he had to offer convincing information (arguments) that would make it superior to another proposal on the same issue. In turn, this exchange of arguments among all present counterbalanced informational asymmetries and established a common ground, which facilitated "informed" choices. Helpful in this regard was also that (a) those who participated spoke the same language, shared the same code of ethics, and adopted the same practices in politics, and (b) whoever wished to speak, propose, or even accuse somebody was free to do so, knowing that what he said could be potentially used against him.[20]

---

[20]The process of discussion and decision-making in the *Assembly of Citizens* was much more sophisticated than the above brief description may suggest. For more details to this effect, see Economou and Kyriazis (2019, pp. 64–69).

5.5 Coordination Through Accountability, Personal Responsibility, and Commitment

All public servants remained personally responsible and accountable for the way they conducted themselves in the service of the state until they were relieved by the auditors. In addition, for an Athenian, as honorable as it was to serve in a public post, the same held true when one assumed the mantle of the defender of the public interest. Between them, these rules inspired discipline in the lines of service and precision in the execution according to the prescribed job tasks. Therefore, it would not be farfetched to surmise that coordination in state governance in classical Athens was at least as effective as in contemporary multinational companies.

Athenians, but ancient Greeks in general, believed that election to all state posts particularly by lot is one of the cornerstones of democracy and they would understand neither today's proliferation of non-elected officials heading the ever-expanding plethora of regulatory bodies and independent quasi-state authorities nor the formation of labor unions and their practices in the public sector. This is a crucial difference with today's democracies.

6 Summary of Findings and Conclusions

To the outcome in the Battle of Salamis certainly contributed many uncontrollable factors. Even the direction of the morning breeze that rises to the present day in these straits helped the speed of the Athenian triremes to smash with force onto the Persian ships. But the triumph would not have occurred, and democracy would have eclipsed if the *Ecclesia of Demos* had hot heeded to the pleas by Themistocles to sacrifice the immediate gratification of distributing the riches from Laurion for consumption and instead build the 200 triremes. The Athenian democracy, which at times was driven astray by populist and shortsighted leaders, such as Cleon, proved that it could listen to rational thinking and act in prudence when the common good was at risk. That is why, the lesson for today from that battle is that the future of the US democracy, and hence that of the free world, depends on acting prudently by strengthening its military and economic might, as well as the quality of its democracy.

Unfortunately, at a period when the communist China is expanding its power on all fronts, the United States appears to have lost the ability to act prudently. As the public sector increased, particularly after the war, it was captured by organized minorities, and instead of serving the common good, it allowed democracy to sink, on the one hand, into ever-increasing deficits and debt and, on the other, into citizen indifference and social strife. In view of these developments, anyone concerned cannot help but surmise that the future of democracy is bleak and that, if the twin deficits in question are left unchecked, eventually *representative party democracy* may succumb to its innate deficiencies, to the detriment of liberty and individual freedoms. Thus, thinking ahead, the best act of prudence would be to reform democracy by adapting to the present circumstances the Athenian model of democracy. For, in this context, self-government is superior to *representative party democracy* because, first, it is free from the latter's innate deficiencies and, second, it is endowed with several distinct advantages. In particular, it matches policy choices to citizen preferences. It offers superb institutional flexibility and efficiency. Citizens engage and take ownership of the institutions of democracy, and the problems of asymmetric information and management coordination are confronted through the widest possible discussion among citizens of the issues under consideration.[21]

To be sure, such a revolutionary reform demands preparation on many fronts. Some are technical and fall in the purview of specialists in Information and Communications Technologies (ICTs). For example, two fundamental are how the US Congress might be replaced by an *Electronic Ecclesia of Demos* and the US Government by an *Electronic Council of Federal Directors*.[22] Owing to the advances in ICTs, preparedness in these fronts may be relatively easy to achieve. However, in fronts such as politics, public administration, central and commercial banking, etc., which have served traditionally as bastions of the established mode of self-government, short of some monumental social upheaval, progress is highly unlikely because:

> In today's political climate, with elite corporate interests firmly in control of most Western governments, the prospects for any radical changes being implemented in a way that actually serves popular interests are very slim indeed. The simple truth is that those interests currently in the ascendancy would be blind fools to allow system changes that seriously threatened the control over the political process that they now enjoy (Moore, 1999, p. 56)

Lastly, there are fronts in which citizens can and should mobilize to gain control over future developments. One such front is the ethos built into children in their formative years, because the model of *digital direct democracy* sketched in this paper presumes free-minded and responsible citizens, as the Athenians were. And

---

[21] From my cursory visit to the political science literature in this area, I gather that the dominant view is that the proposed approach to *direct democracy* would be marred by far worse deficiencies than *representative party democracy*. To the Athenians, the substance of democracy did not depend on the complexity of the problems they faced. Democracy was practiced at the local and the state levels. In the latter level, if a very complex problem arose, they would appoint experts to advise the *Assembly of Citizens*, they would discuss the pros and cons of a solution, and at the end they would make up their minds by voting. As I have argued in Bitros (2021), the same approach is practiced by the great multinational companies of our time, and the results for their stakeholders are astonishing by any comparison. If politicians, political scientists, institutionalists, sociologists, and other students of society wish to bypass the core idea of governance by the *demos*, as the substance of *direct democracy*, surely they can invent all sorts of seemingly rational excuses. But the example of Athens 25 centuries ago, and the marvels of governance in present-day multinationals, will be there to remind that true democracy is governance by the *demos* for the *demos*, not by its proxies.

[22] The proposed reforms do not affect the institutional structure built into the constitutions of contemporary *representative party democracies*. Only the technology by which they function is upgraded in the light of the phenomenal advances in the information and communications technologies (ICTs).

children will be the citizens of tomorrow. Hence, change in this direction should start right away by attending to the appropriate upbringing and education of children.

Acknowledgments I should like to thank the editors of this volume and particularly Emmanouil M. L. Economou for helping me debug several obscurities and oversights in this paper. To him I also extend my sincere appreciation for the opportunity I have enjoyed, through our joint research in recent years, to get a good glimpse into what an inexhaustible source ancient Greek literature is for fresh ideas and insights to confront problems of the modern world. However, any remaining errors of fact or interpretation are my own.

References

Aldrich, J. H. (1995). *Why parties? The origin and transformation of political parties in America*. The Chicago University Press.
Aristotle. (1952). *Athenian Constitution*, (Engl. Trnsl. H. Rackham). Harvard University Press/ William Heinemann Ltd./Perseus Digital Library.
Arrow, K. J. (1951/1963). *Social choice and individual values* (2nd ed.). Wiley & Sons.
Barber, B. R. (2003). *Strong democracy: Participatory politics for a new age*. MacMillan Press.
Bitros, G. C. (2020). Demand adjusted capital input and potential output in the context of U.-S. economic growth. *Journal of Economic Asymmetries, 21*, e00140.
Bitros, G. C. (2021, forthcoming). Overhauling democracy by switching to corporate-like governance. *International Journal of Electronic Governance*. Inderscience Publishers.
Bitros, G. C., Economou, E. M. L., & Kyriazis, N. C. (2020). *Democracy and money: Lessons for today from Athens in classical tines*. Routledge.
Bitros, G. C., & Karayiannis, A. (2012). The city-state of ancient Athens as a prototype for an entrepreneurial and managerial society. In G. P. Prastacos, F. Wang, & K. E. Soderquist (Eds.), *Leadership and management in a changing world: Lessons from ancient East and West philosophy* (pp. 289–304). Springer-Verlag.
Buchanan, J. M., & Tullock, G. (1962). *The calculus of consent: Logical foundations of constitutional democracy*. University of Michigan Press.
Buchanan, J. M., & Wagner, R. E. (1977). Democracy in deficit: The political legacy of Lord Keynes. In *The Collected works of James M. Buchanan* (Vol. 8). Liberty Fund.
Burke, E. (1774). *Speech to the electors of Bristol*. Available at: http://peter-moore.co.uk/blog/edmund-burke-speech-to-the-electors-of-bristol-1774
Cohen, E. E. (1973). *Athenian maritime courts*. Princeton University Press.
Demosthenes. (1949). Speeches: LIX, *Against Neaera*, (Engl. Trnsl. N. W. DeWitt, N. J. DeWitt). Harvard University Press/William Heinemann Ltd./Perseus Digital Library
Economou, E. M. L., & Kyriazis, N. C. (2019). *Democracy and economy: An inseparable relationship since ancient times to today*. Cambridge Scholars Publishing.
Franklin, B. (2005). In P. Conn (Ed.), *The autobiography of Benjamin Franklin*. University of Pennsylvania Press.
Gehl, K. M., & Porter, M. E. (2017). Why competition in the politics industry is failing America: A strategy for reinvigorating our democracy. *Harvard Business School*. Available at: https://www.commonwealthclub.org/events/2019-03-29/katherine-gehl-and-michael-porter-why-competition-politics-industry-failing
Gordon, R. J. (2016). *Beyond the rainbow: The rise and fall of growth in the American standard of living*. Princeton University Press.
Harris, E. M. (2013). *The rule of law in action in democratic Athens*. Oxford University Press.
Hayek, F. A. (1960). *The constitution of liberty*. University of Chicago Press.

Keynes, J. M. ([1936] 1949). *The general theory of employment, interest and money*. Macmillan & Co.
Keynes, J. M., (1942). "Budgetary Policy". In: Activities 1940-1946 shaping the post-war employment and commodities. In D. Moggridge, (Ed.), *The Collected Writings of John Maynard Keynes*, (vol. XXVII, pp. 277–278). Macmillan, 1989.
Lane, J. E. (2013). The principal-agent approach to politics: policy implementation and public policy-making. *Open Journal of Political Science, 3*, 85–89.
Lanni, A. (2008). *Law and justice in the courts of Classical Athens*. Cambridge University Press.
Levinson, S. (2007). *The democratic deficit in America*. Available at: https://harvardlpr.com/online-articles/the-democratic-deficit-in-america/
Lyon, V. (1996). *Parties and democracy: A critical view*. Available at: https://democraticreform.net/parties-and-democracy-a-critical-view
Lyttkens, C. H. (2013). *Economic analysis of institutional change in ancient Greece. Politics, taxation and rational behavior*. Routledge.
Lyttkens, C. H., Tridimas, G., & Lindgren, A. (2018). Making direct democracy work: A rational-actor perspective on the graphe paranomon in ancient Athens. *Constitutional Political Economy, 29*, 389–412.
Michels, R. (1911). *Political parties: A sociological study of the oligarchical tendencies of modern democracy.*, Engl. Trnsl. From Germen, E. Paul, C. Paul. The Free Press.
Moore, R. K. (1999). Democracy and cyberspace. In B. N. Hague & B. D. Loader D. (Eds.), *Digital democracy: Discourse and decision making in the information age* (pp. 39–59). Routledge.
Postell, J. (2018). *The rise and fall of political parties in America*. The Heritage Foundation. Available at: https://www.heritage.org/political-process/report/the-rise-and-fall-political-parties-america
Pritchard, D. M. (2012). Costing festivals and war: Spending priorities of the Athenian democracy. *Historia, 61*(1), 18–65.
Russell, B. (1922). *The problem of China*. The Century Co.
Smith, A. (1776/1977). *An inquiry into the nature and causes of the wealth of nations*. Chicago University Press.
Sternberg, E. (2005). Classical precariousness vs. modern risk: Lessons in prudence from the Battle of Salamis. *Humanitas, XVIII*, 141–163.
Thorley, J. (1996). *Athenian democracy*. Routledge.
Thucydides. (1881). *History of the Peloponnesian War.*, Engl. Trnsl. B. Jowett. Clarendon Press. Perseus Digital Library.
Tridimas, G. (2012). Constitutional choice in ancient Athens: The rationality of selection to office by lot. *Constitutional Political Economy, 23*, 1–21.
von Mises, L. (1944). *Bureaucracy*. Yale University Press.
Weber, M. (1921/1946). "Politics as a vocation", in the Engl. Trnsl., by Gerth, H. H. & C. W. Mills. *From Max Weber: Essays in Sociology*, (pp. 77–128). Oxford University Press.

George C. Bitros is Emeritus Professor of Economics at the Athens University of Economics and Business. He holds a PhD and an MA in Economics from New York University and a BA from the Athens School of Economics and Business. In 1976, he returned from the United States to Greece in the position of Senior Research Associate in the Bank of Greece, and 3 years later he moved to the Athens University of Economics and Business where he served as Professor of Economics until his retirement in 2007. He has taught at New York University and Fordham University of New York; he has served as research associate in the National Bureau of Economic Research (USA); and he has published extensively in major scholarly journals as well as books with several prestigious international and domestic publishers. While over the years his teaching and research focused on general equilibrium analysis, industrial organization, managerial economics, cost-benefit analysis, and the fields of capital theory and investment, more recently his research interests have centered on the linkages of institutions to social stability and economic growth.

Part III
Policies Towards Improving the Quality of Democratic Governance

Policy Making by Randomly Selected Citizens: The Perspective of Elected Politicians

George Tridimas

Abstract An institutional reform proposal which recently seems to have gained currency is to introduce at least in some areas policy making by citizens' assemblies, that is, population samples whose members are selected from the public by lot. Analysts and commentators offer an array of sound arguments in support of this reform. However, short of enacting this institutional change by revolution, its adoption relies on elected politicians-legislators accepting it. But policy making by randomly selected assemblies of ordinary citizens decreases the domain of policy areas decided by politicians, and consequently it reduces their authority and prestige. Under what circumstances, if any, would politicians consent to such a change in policy making? This is the issue investigated here. The paper explores a model of institutional choice under uncertainty and examines the payoffs of politicians-legislators under different policy rules. Using the spatial decision framework, it identifies circumstances where an elected politician may be willing to grant policy making powers to a randomly drawn assembly of citizens. The choice is found to depend on the interplay of the following factors: the probability that he wins the election and so he implements his ideal policy compared to the probability that the assembly implements his ideal policy; the cost of fighting an election versus the (lower) cost of policy making by a randomly selected assembly; the policy difference with his rival politician; the deviation between assembly decision and his preferred policy; the size of office rents from winning an election; and the marginal utility of the policy compared to the marginal utility from holding office.

Keywords Citizen's assembly · Appointment to office by lot · Election · Constitutional choice · Institutional reform

G. Tridimas (✉)
Ulster Business School, Department of Accounting, Finance and Economics, Newtownabbey, Co, Antrim, UK
e-mail: G.Tridimas@ulster.ac.uk

© The Author(s), under exclusive license to Springer Nature Switzerland AG 2022
E. M. L. Economou et al. (eds.), *Democracy in Times of Crises*,
https://doi.org/10.1007/978-3-030-97295-0_6

1 Introduction

The prevailing system of representative government faces serious challenges from among other issues voter dissatisfaction with a remote political class, failure to engage popular participation, unfair economic outcomes, and the rise of extremist parties. Recent attempts to address dissatisfaction with majoritarian politics have included experiments in decision making by assemblies of randomly selected citizens, known as "Citizens' Assemblies" or "Juries" or "Mini-publics" or "Allotted Chambers". Such experiments are based on the idea that the deliberation of an assembly which is a portrait in miniature of the population increases the fidelity of the representation and the quality of decision making. In a citizens' assembly, a sample of citizens is selected by lot to deliberate on a specific issue of public policy and is informed by concerned parties, politicians, interest groups, and experts in an open and reflective manner where participants listen as well as speak. The group is then expected to reach sound conclusions which may benefit public policy making.[1] Calls for decision making by such randomly selected assemblies of citizens aim to improve democratic outcomes in comparison to decision making by elected representatives, who as professional politicians are an elite distant from voters and may no longer represent the citizenry. Appointment to public office by lot is known as sortition, and its application goes back to ancient Athens where many public posts were filled by citizens randomly selected by lot.

Proposals to replace majority voting with random selection raise pressing questions about the nature of democracy, representation of voters, and selection of government officials. A large literature has developed scrutinising the plethora of theoretical and practical questions of sortition. Its focus is the advantages of policy making by a randomly selected deliberative group of citizens against policy making by politicians elected through majority voting. Even if one accepts that there are welfare benefits from policies decided by a random sample of the population, there is one glaring omission in this literature, namely, whether elected politicians, who under the existing institutional framework decide policy, may accept policy making by randomly selected assemblies of citizens. Since in a democracy any institutional change in policy making will have to be approved by elected politicians as constitutional writers or post-constitutional legislators, it is their choices which determine the introduction of randomly drawn assemblies (rather than arguments about efficiency, equity, etc.). Deciding public policy by a random sample of citizens implies that the politicians, who as elected representatives currently control policy decisions, relinquish decision making powers. Obviously, politicians may be less than

---

[1] "Deliberation is a particular kind of communication that ideally induces reflection about preferences, beliefs, and values in a non-coercive fashion, and that connects particular interests to more general principles. One of its key virtues is reciprocity: communicating in terms that others who do not share one's point of view or framework can accept. Deliberation is different from adversarial debate. The initial aim is not to win, but to understand. Deliberation allows that people are open to changing their minds. The Citizens' Parliament was designed to enable this kind of communication, and the facilitators were there to encourage that" (Dryzek, 2009).

enthusiastic and indeed outright hostile about this prospect.[2] Thence, the following stark question arises: Under what conditions, if any, will politicians voluntarily transfer decision making to a citizens' assembly? This is the focus of the present inquiry.

To pursue a meaningful analysis of this question we suppose that the mechanism of policy making is not enforced by an external party, nor is it a result of a violent conflict where the victor has imposed his will but is adopted by the voluntary agreement of the elected politicians. Assuming that politicians are rational actors, they will adopt the institution of policy making, either policy making by elected representatives or by a randomly drawn citizens' assembly, which maximises their expected payoffs.

Politicians derive two broad benefits from holding office: first, the ability to pursue their favourite policy and second, office rents, that is, monetary rewards, perks, patronage, glory, and personal satisfaction associated with occupying a public post. But to obtain these benefits, politicians have first to fight costly election contests whose outcomes are uncertain. On the other hand, when a randomly drawn citizens' assembly decides policy, politicians endure significant rent and policy losses, since they forgo the prestige and perks of office and may not have their favoured policy measures voted by the assembly, although they are also spared some of the expenses of the electoral contest. Thus, politicians will consent to a citizens' assembly decision on some public policy issues when they calculate that the expected benefit from transferring policy making power will be higher from fighting an election. Are there any circumstances that make this possible?

The paper unfolds as follows. Section 2 first describes historical and contemporary examples of the use of sortition. Section 3 reviews some of the scholarly research on the issue. Section 4 applies standard political economy methodology and sets up a formal model of the calculus of politicians under the institutions of elections and citizens' assemblies whose members are selected from the public by lot. We focus on the following context: for a given issue X, party leaders choose between (a) allocating decision making power to random citizens and avoid an immediate election on that issue and (b) calling an immediate election and letting the issue be decided by the elected representatives. We compare the payoffs of the politicians under the two systems and then specify the conditions under which they are better off with assembly-made policy. Section 5 concludes.

The aim here is not to argue for the adoption of a new political institution but to illustrate whether there are circumstances where institutional framers of different political persuasions may accept public policy making by randomly selected citizens and therefore make it more likely.

---

[2] "Matthew Taylor recalls that when he was the head of the prime minister's policy unit in Britain, he tried to get the two prime ministers he worked for, Tony Blair and Gordon Brown, interested in the idea of assemblies. "On both occasions both the politicians and officials loved the idea, up to the point at which I said, 'You can't control the outcome and you will have to respond to it positively. Not to implement it, but to respond to it positively'" *The Economist* 21-09-2020, accessed on 21-09-2020.

2 Recent Examples of Randomly Selected Citizens' Assemblies

Citizens' assemblies start from appointment to a decision making body by lot, a process known as sortition. Sortition has a long and distinguished pedigree going back to (at least) the direct democracy of ancient Athens, 507-322 BCE. The Athenians filled several public offices by lot. These included the Council of Five Hundred responsible for the day-to-day business of government, the 6000 jurors of the Athenian justice courts, and another 600 magistrates serving in administrative boards; see among others Hansen (1999), Tridimas (2012), and Lyttkens (2013) for extensive analysis. It bears noting that contrary to modern citizens' assemblies, in ancient Athens, sortition was used to fill public posts but such post holders did not choose policy; policy was decided directly by the Assembly (*Ecclesia*) of the Demos. The lot randomised appointment to office and consequently the distribution of office rents for offices discharging routine tasks that could be performed by any ordinary man.

Sortition was also used to select the Dodge of Venice, 697-1797 (see Molinari, 2020). Other famous examples of its use include Florence, 1328–1434 and again 1494–1512, and the Swiss *Landsgemeinden*, 1640–1837 (see Manin (1997) for details). Modern societies use random selection to appoint jurors in legal trials. Although its origin is disputed, by the fifteenth century, jury trial in England "became the established form of trial for both criminal and civil cases at common law" (https://www.britannica.com/topic/jury).[3]

The twenty-first century offers a multitude of examples of deliberative democracy and decision-making bodies whose members are citizens randomly selected from the electoral roll as a representative sample of the society stratified by sex, age, social class, and geographical region. Citizens' assemblies to deliberate electoral reform were set up in the Canadian provinces of British Columbia (2004) and Ontario (2007). In 2006 the Dutch government set up citizens' forum (BürgerForum Kiesstelsel) to consult the opinion of 140 randomly selected individuals on the electoral system; however, the government did not follow the advice of the Burger-forum. In 2009 the Australian Citizens' Parliament of randomly selected citizens was held in Canberra (funded as a research project) and looked at how the Australian government could be strengthened to better serve the people. In 2009 Iceland, a grassroots association gathered a random sample of 1200 citizens to discuss the fundamental values for the renewal of government in response to the deep financial and economic crisis. In 2010 this was followed by a government organised second gathering of 950 randomly selected individuals to discuss

---

[3] See also Mulgan (1984) for the rationale of choosing jurors by lot. Sortition is not used only for selecting juries. For example, in the primaries for the 2020 presidential election, faced with the impossibility of holding a presidential debate with twenty candidates, the Democratic Party held two debates; ten candidates would debate on the first night, ten on the second; the composition of the two groups was decided by drawing lots (The Economist 15-08-2020).

constitutional reform. It set in motion a process of constitutional amendment which involved the Supreme Court, a (non-binding) referendum, and the Parliament, but the draft constitutional proposals eventually failed as they were not adopted (see Landemore, 2014 for details). In Belgium, during 2011–2012 the G1000 project brought together a sample of citizens to deliberate on several policy issues including unemployment, pensions, health care, wealth taxes, and immigration.

France, the UK, and foremost the Republic of Ireland offer more recent examples. In October 2019, the French President set up the "citizens' climate convention" to propose measures *on* "*How* to reduce greenhouse gas emissions in France by at least 40% (in relations to 1990's levels) by 2030, in the spirit of social justice?" He has promised the 150 members of the convention that he would put 146 of their 149 proposed measures either to parliament or to a referendum. At the time of writing (January 2021), amid acrimony between the government and assembly members, it appears that the President will ignore the recommendations of the assembly. In the UK, a randomly selected 110-strong panel will try to make proposals on measures to tackle global warming and meet the government's target of net-zero emissions by 2050. The UK climate assembly differs from the French model in that it was commissioned by six select committees of the Parliament in 2019 rather than by the prime minister. There is no guarantee any of the proposals will be taken up by government.

On the other hand, Ireland has established a reputation as a leader of successful deliberative democracy where 100-member samples of randomly drawn citizens' assemblies address a range of controversial issues faced by the modern Irish society. During 2012–2014, the Convention on the Constitution considered (among various issues) gay marriage. Its recommendations paved the way for calling a Referendum in 2015 which approved that "marriage may be contracted in accordance with law by two persons without distinction as to their sex". In 2106–2018 the Citizens' Assembly deliberated the constitutional prohibition on abortions. The deliberations were followed by the 2018 Referendum which legalised abortions. Currently a new Citizens' Assembly is in place on gender equality.

We may then conclude that historical precedent and contemporary examples point to the potential of policy making by random samples of the citizenry, but currently its adoption is more often resisted and frustrated by elected politicians. This implies that the establishment of randomly selected citizens' assemblies with decision making responsibilities is a matter of institutional choice by elected politicians-legislators which can therefore be analysed by applying the usual tools of economic analysis.

3 Selective Review of the Theory of Sortition[4]

Use of the lot to make decisions denies the exercise of choice according to the preferences of the voters and is "a–rational" (Dowlen, 2008) as it implies a fixed probability of winning independent of personal effort and other characteristics of those contesting the election. The scholarly literature has explored a multitude of theoretical and practical questions. Mueller et al. (1972) saw randomised selection of legislators as offering a way to reduce incentives for pork barrel activities, achieving ex ante equality of voters, representing minorities proportionately and avoiding intransitive voting outcomes. Amar (1984) favoured lottery voting, a system where citizens vote for representatives, but the election winner is decided by a lottery of the ballots cast, so that a candidate who polls say x% of the vote has x % ex ante probability to be elected to office, rather than 100%. Frey (2017) argues that in so far as democracy is not tantamount with elections, random selection to fill public offices may improve democratic outcomes. Ackerman and Fishkin (2002) and Barnett and Carty (2008) examine different institutional ways to facilitate random selection. Fishkin (2009) looks at the effects of different types of deliberation on decision outcomes. In an echo of the Condorcet jury theorem, he shows that a randomly selected group of citizens when informed by experts on the various sides of an issue can judge it equally well to an elite body of judges. Dowlen (2008) and Stone (2011) analyse the normative properties of random selection of decision makers. Sutherland (2011) focuses on the difference between advocacy for factional interests, a role played by political parties, and decision-making for the public good, which opens the way for a deliberative legislature. He claims that a truly representative democracy would be one where parties winning elections are best suited only to initiate policy, while randomly drawn assemblies of citizens which are representative should determine the outcome of policy debates. In a similar vein, Pluchino et al. (2011) argue that adding randomly selected legislators to an elected parliament, which is composed of partisan legislators, increases the number of acts passed by the legislature and social welfare. Tierney (2012) views policy recommendations made by randomly drawn citizens' assemblies designed to represent the electorate as an exemplary case of popular deliberation through which ordinary citizens can engage directly in the democratic process.

Focusing on ancient Athens, Tridimas (2012) inquires if there are circumstances where a rational citizen seeking to benefit from public policy may prefer decision making by officeholders appointed through sortition rather than election. He concludes that since voting in elections requires that the citizen is informed about the policy issues (a costly undertaking), he will prefer sortition when the expected marginal benefit from casting an informed vote is smaller than the marginal cost of being informed. Tridimas (2018) evaluates the application of sortition in the

---

[4] A special blog "Equality-by-lot" (https://equalitybylot.com) by the self-styled "Kleroterians" (from the device used in Athens to pick lots) debates the deliberate use of randomness (lottery) in human affairs.

ancient Athenian direct democracy using the criteria of representativeness, equity, non-partisanship, rent seeking, resource economy, and suitability for office. He is sceptical on whether an institution which was successful in ancient Athens can be transplanted to contemporary representative democracies.

The present inquiry is close to the spirit of the empirical study of Jacquet et al. (2020). Using questionnaire data, they conclude that overall Belgian MPs are opposed to sortition as a method of appointment to public offices with decision-making powers, but left-wing MPs (socialist, green, and far-left) are more receptive to assemblies with elected and sortitioned members. Turning to the views of citizens, they find that citizens with a lower social status (as measured by income and educational achievement) and with left-wing leanings are favourably disposed to sortition and so are citizens disaffected with electoral politics. Older citizens tend not to support sortition, while there is no significant difference between the attitudes of men and women.

4 A Model of Policy Making by Elections and Randomly Chosen Citizens' Assembly

We postulate a setting of two players who are assumed to be rational politicians indexed by $i = A, B$ and whose joint agreement is needed to adopt a decision-making rule. Each politician chooses the institution of policy making which confers to him the highest expected payoff. We use a model of the two players as a short-cut to two sides with diverging interests. The players can be parts of a specially formed constitutional assembly or an ordinary parliament with the power to amend a constitution. They can be the government and the opposition when the unanimity rule applies, or two groups in a coalition government whose votes are needed to pass legislation, or two factions within a single ruling parliamentary party whose support is required to achieve the simple or qualified majority needed to introduce the new institution.

We posit that the status quo mechanism of policy making is elections, that is, rival politicians contest elections and the winner earns the right to decide public policy and reaps the office rents. We further assume that the status quo can change with the unanimous consent of both politicians. If one politician prefers policy making by a randomly selected assembly of citizens and the other by elected representatives, the status quo of deciding policy by elected representatives remains. Of course, the status quo remains when both politicians prefer elections. In a contemporary democracy where the government is formed upon winning competitive election, the premise is that politicians as winners of elections will be opposed to reforms which may weaken their position.[5]

4.1 Policy Making by Elected Politicians

To examine whether politicians are prepared to relinquish policy making power and transfer it to a randomly selected assembly, we employ a formal spatial model of single dimension decision making.[6]

The utility of each politician depends on two attributes, the public policy implemented and the rents from occupying office.[7] Let α and β denote the ideal policy points of A and B, respectively, and x the policy implemented. Each politician is assumed to have Euclidean preferences over policy. The utility losses of A and B from implementing policies that differ from their ideal points are written, respectively, as $-(x - \alpha)^2$ and $-(x - \beta)^2$. If A wins the election and implements his ideal policy, he sets public policy at his ideal point, $x = \alpha$ so that he suffers no utility loss. On the contrary, if he loses the election and B implements his ideal policy $x = \beta$, A utility is $-(\beta - \alpha)^2$. Analogously, if B wins the election, he suffers no policy utility loss, while if he loses the election, his utility is $-(\alpha - \beta)^2$. The difference $(\beta - \alpha)^2$ can be interpreted as the ideological or policy distance between $A's$ and B in the policy space, as, for example, in left-right scale; the larger their policy differences, the greater the size of $(\beta - \alpha)^2$. Let G denote the rents from office. As already said, these include monetary rewards from office, the attention received from being in the limelight, and other ego-rents and are not related to the policy dimension.

Let P be the probability that politician A wins the election and implements his preferred policy α; analogously, $1 - P$ is the probability that politician B wins the election and decides his preferred policy β, where $0 \leq P \leq 1$. As per standard practice, the utility function of each politician is assumed to be additive and separable in its attributes. It is further assumed that fighting an election is costly and the cost rises with the distance between the ideal policy points of A and B. Specifically, the election costs of A and B are expressed as $C_A = c(\beta - \alpha)^2$, $c > 0$, and $C_B = k(\beta - \alpha)^2$, $k > 0$. In general, we expect that the two different politicians confront different costs of fighting the election, because of differences in the appeals of their personalities, financial strength, and organisation of their parties,

---

[5] See Renwick (2011) and the literature therein for an analysis of the reform of electoral systems in Europe since the end of World War II and the changing roles of politicians and public opinion in this process.

[6] For a detailed analysis of the model employed here, see Tsebelis (2002) and Tridimas (2007) and the references therein.

[7] Although a politician may choose an institution for ideological reasons, that is, he may simply "like" or "dislike" decision making by a randomly drawn group of citizens, we abstract from the latter motivation, as it would bias the results of the theoretical inquiry.

effectiveness of their campaigns, and possible biases in the electoral system, so that $c \neq k$. We then write the expected utility from holding office and deciding policy of A and B as follows, where E denotes the expectations operator

$$U_A^R = -wE\left[P(\alpha-\alpha)^2 + (1-P)(\beta-\alpha)^2\right] + (1-w)E[PG] - c(\beta-\alpha)^2 \quad (1a)$$

$$U_B^R = -wE\left[P(\alpha-\beta)^2 + (1-P)(\beta-\beta)^2\right] + (1-w)E[(1-P)G]$$
$$- k(\beta-\alpha)^2 \quad (1b)$$

The first component in each one of the above sums denotes the expected (loss of) utility from the policy outcome; the second component captures the utility from winning office. The coefficient w shows the relative weight, or marginal utility, of the policy objective of the politician. The coefficient $1-w$ shows the relative weight of office rents. An opportunist politician, who does not care about policy, is characterised by $w = 0$; a purely ideological politician who is only interested in policy outcomes deriving no utility from office rents is characterised by $w = 1$. Rearranging, the election payoffs of A and B are written as

$$U_A^R = -(w(1-P)+c)(\beta-\alpha)^2 + (1-w)PG \quad (2a)$$

$$U_B^R = -(wP+k)(\beta-\alpha)^2 + (1-w)(1-P)G \quad (2b)$$

For A and B to participate in the policy making process the payoffs must be positive, that is, $U_A^R > 0$ and $U_B^R > 0$.

4.2 Policy Making by a Randomly Selected Assembly of Citizens

Policy making by a randomly selected assembly of citizens alters the previous model in four important ways. In the first instance, when public policy is decided by a randomly selected assembly, the probability that policy α favoured by politician A is implemented is assumed to be λ with $\lambda \neq P$, that is, in general λ differs from P. Analogously, the probability that policy β favoured by politician B is implemented is $1 - \lambda$. As before, λ is a random variable with $0 \leq \lambda \leq 1$.

The second important difference is that, from the standpoint of politicians who have lost control over the choice of policy, the policy decided by the assembly now becomes a stochastic variable whose outcome may differ from the ideal point of the politician. That is, in the calculations of the politicians, the policy choices of the random citizens' assembly are no longer α and β, but $\widehat{\alpha}$ and $\widehat{\beta}$. The latter are distributed with expected values $E(\widehat{\alpha}) = \alpha$ and $E(\widehat{\beta}) = \beta$ and variances σ_α^2 and σ_β^2, respectively. This is to recognise that after deliberation, the members of the assembly may reach decisions which diverge from the ideal points of the politicians. The reasons why from the viewpoints of the politicians the policy outcomes are stochastic relate to differences in the preferences of the politicians and the members of the assembly and/or lack of policy expertise of assembly members in comparison to politicians. Hence, even though the politicians expect that on average the assembly will pass the same policies as those that they would have chosen if they were in charge, there is in practice some deviation from α and β. In the special case where the decisions of the assembly vary equally around the ideal policy points α and β, we have $\sigma_\alpha^2 = \sigma_\beta^2$.

Third, when an assembly decides policy, a politician derives only a fraction η of office rents, with $0 \leq \eta < 1$, since his policy influence and prestige from decision making is now diminished.

Finally, it is reasonable to expect that when parts of public policy are decided by an assembly, politicians incur considerably fewer costs to secure passage of their ideal policies. Politicians will still argue their cases and try and convince the randomly selected assembly, but they no longer must secure the votes of the entire electorate. Further, a non-partisan citizens' assembly informed not only by political parties but by independent policy experts too alleviates the fear of a politician that by taking a side in a controversial issue may cost him popularity. Thus, the political contest costs of A and B are expressed as $C_A = s(\beta - \alpha)^2$, where $c > s > 0$, and $C_B = t(\beta - \alpha)^2$, where $k > t > 0$, and $s \neq t$. The expected utility functions of A and B are then written as

$$U_A^J = -wE\left[\lambda(\widehat{\alpha} - \alpha)^2 + (1-\lambda)\left(\widehat{\beta} - \alpha\right)^2\right] + (1-w)E[\lambda \eta G] - s(\beta - \alpha)^2 \quad (3a)$$

$$U_B^J = -wE\left[\lambda(\widehat{\alpha} - \beta)^2 + (1-\lambda)\left(\widehat{\beta} - \beta\right)^2\right] + (1-w)E[(1-\lambda)\eta G]$$
$$- t(\beta - \alpha)^2 \quad (3b)$$

Manipulating the latter and recalling that $E\left(\widehat{\alpha}^2\right) = \alpha^2 + \sigma_\alpha^2$ and $E\left(\widehat{\beta}^2\right) = \beta^2 + \sigma_\beta^2$, we have the following payoff functions:

$$U_A^J = -(w(1-\lambda) + s)(\beta - \alpha)^2 - w\left(\lambda \sigma_\alpha^2 + (1-\lambda)\sigma_\beta^2\right) + (1-w)\lambda \eta G$$
$$- s(\beta - \alpha)^2 \quad (4a)$$

$$U_B^J = -(w\lambda + t)(\beta - \alpha)^2 - w\left(\lambda \sigma_\alpha^2 + (1-\lambda)\sigma_\beta^2\right) + (1-w)(1-\lambda)\eta G$$
$$- t(\beta - \alpha)^2 \quad (4b)$$

The weighted sum $\lambda\sigma_\alpha^2 + (1-\lambda)\sigma_\beta^2$ indicates the average deviation of an assembly's policy from the ideal policies of the politicians, and the term $-w\left(\lambda\sigma_\alpha^2 + (1-\lambda)\sigma_\beta^2\right)$ reflects the disutility from this deviation.

4.3 The Choice of the Decision-Making Mechanism

Politician A chooses policy making by a randomly selected citizens' assembly when he gets a higher payoff from doing so instead of deciding policy after upon winning an election, formally $U_A^J > U_A^R$. Similarly, B chooses policy by a randomly selected assembly when $U_B^J > U_B^R$. Let $\rho \equiv \frac{G}{(\beta-\alpha)^2}$ denote the value of office rent relative to the utility derived from implementing one's ideal policy (instead of his rival's). Substituting from (4a) and (2a) and solving with respect to P, we find

$$U_A^J > U_A^R \quad \text{when}$$

$$P_A \equiv \lambda \frac{w + (1-w)\eta\rho}{w + (1-w)\rho} + \frac{c-s}{w + (1-w)\rho} - \frac{w\left(\lambda\sigma_\alpha^2 + (1-\lambda)\sigma_\beta^2\right)}{(w + (1-w)\rho)(\beta-\alpha)^2} > P \quad (5a)$$

That is, if the probability that A wins the election is less than the critical value P_A, then A is ex ante better off by letting policy to be decided by a randomly selected assembly instead of trying to win an election and then enact his ideal policy. The ratio $\frac{w+(1-w)\eta\rho}{w+(1-w)\rho} < 1$ shows the relative value conferred to a politician when his ideal policy is implemented by a randomly drawn assembly rather than after he wins the election. Thus, the product $\lambda\frac{w+(1-w)\eta\rho}{w+(1-w)\rho}$ represents A's expected value from winning the "lottery" of the assembly's decision. The ratio $\frac{c-s}{w+(1-w)\rho}$ shows the certain cost saved by A when his ideal policy is implemented by an assembly instead of winning the election contest. The third component in the right-hand-side $-\frac{w\left(\lambda\sigma_\alpha^2+(1-\lambda)\sigma_\beta^2\right)}{(w+(1-w)\rho)(\beta-\alpha)^2}$ captures the loss from the uncertainty generated when the politicians lose control of the policy process and the assembly may pass a policy that deviates from their ideal policies. Thence, analytically, expression (5a) shows that A chooses policy making by assembly if the probability of winning the election contest is smaller than the sum of the expected value of his ideal policy implemented by an assembly plus the cost saved from not campaigning for his ideal policy in an election adjusted for the loss incurred from the uncertainty about how far the decision of the assembly deviates from his ideal point. We further assume that $P_A \geq 0$, for otherwise the analysis does not make sense.

Working in a similar way with (4b) and (2b), we obtain

$$U_B^J > U_B^R \quad \text{when}$$

$$\Pi_B \equiv (1-\lambda)\frac{w+(1-w)\eta\rho}{w+(1-w)\rho} - \frac{w\left(\lambda\sigma_\alpha^2+(1-\lambda)\sigma_\beta^2\right)}{(w+(1-w)\rho)(\beta-\alpha)^2} + \frac{k-t}{w+(1-w)\rho}$$
$$> 1 - P \tag{5b}$$

That is, if the probability that B wins the election $1 - P$ is smaller than the critical value Π_B, then B is ex ante better off in by letting policy to be decided by a randomly selected assembly. As above, $(1-\lambda)\frac{w+(1-w)\eta\rho}{w+(1-w)\rho}$ represents B's expected value from winning the "lottery" of the assembly's decision. Again, the term $\frac{w\left(\lambda\sigma_\alpha^2+(1-\lambda)\sigma_\beta^2\right)}{(w+(1-w)\rho)(\beta-\alpha)^2}$ shows the uncertainty loss incurred from the possibility that the assembly passes policies that may differ from the ideal policies of the politicians. Analogously to P_A, the term $\frac{k-t}{w+(1-w)\rho}$ shows the certain cost saved by B when his ideal policy is implemented by an assembly instead of winning the election contest relative to the value of winning the election contest. Again, we assume that $\Pi_B > 0$. Rearranging, (5b) can be rewritten as

$$P > \lambda\frac{w+(1-w)\eta\rho}{w+(1-w)\rho} + \frac{(1-w)(1-\eta)\rho}{w+(1-w)\rho} + \frac{w\left(\lambda\sigma_\alpha^2+(1-\lambda)\sigma_\beta^2\right)}{(w+(1-w)\rho)(\beta-\alpha)^2}$$
$$- \frac{k-t}{w+(1-w)\rho}$$
$$\equiv P_B \tag{5c}$$

The latter implies that B chooses policy making by assembly if the probability of losing the election contest is greater than the critical value of P_B, the sum of the terms in (5c).

When both A and B are better off with policy decided by a randomly selected assembly, then they both willingly agree to give up policy making power and surrender it to the assembly. Formally, this is the case when inequalities (5a) and (5c) are simultaneously satisfied, that is,

$$P_A \equiv \frac{\lambda(w+(1-w)\eta\rho)+(c-s)}{w+(1-w)\rho} - \frac{w\left(\lambda\sigma_\alpha^2+(1-\lambda)\sigma_\beta^2\right)}{(w+(1-w)\rho)(\beta-\alpha)^2} > P >$$

$$\frac{\lambda(w+(1-w)\eta\rho)+(1-w)(1-\eta)\rho-(k-t)}{w+(1-w)\rho}+\frac{w\left(\lambda\sigma_\alpha^2+(1-\lambda)\sigma_\beta^2\right)}{(w+(1-w)\rho)(\beta-\alpha)^2}$$
$$\equiv P_B \tag{6}$$

That is, policy making by a citizens' assembly is established when the following conditions are simultaneously satisfied. First, the critical value of the probability that A wins the election, P_A, exceeds the critical value of the probability that B loses the election, P_B; $P_A > P_B$. Second, the actual probability that A wins (or equivalently B loses) the election contest is smaller than the critical value P_A. Third, the actual probability that A wins (or equivalently B loses) the election contest is greater than the critical level P_B. Each one of those conditions is necessary, and the three together are sufficient.

The theoretical circumstances where the two inequalities $P_A > P$ and $P > P_B$ are satisfied cannot be assessed at the present level of generality, where the determinants of P are not explicitly modelled. On the other hand, we can check under what theoretical circumstances, if any, the necessary inequality $P_A > P_B$ holds. Subtracting P_B from P_A, we have

$$P_A > P_B \quad \text{when} \quad (c-s)+(k-t)$$
$$> (1-w)(1-\eta)\rho + 2\frac{w\left(\lambda\sigma_\alpha^2+(1-\lambda)\sigma_\beta^2\right)}{(\beta-\alpha)^2} \tag{7}$$

The term $(c-s)+(k-t)$ is the sum of the election cost differentials of A and B; the term $(1-w)(1-\eta)\rho$ shows the value of the rents from office upon winning the election compared to the rents when the ideal policy is implemented by an assembly. Thus, when the sum of the election cost differentials of A and B is greater than the rent differential upon winning the election augmented by twice the loss from the uncertainty generated by the assembly decision making, it is $P_A > P_B$.

We then have that when P is outside the $[P_A, P_B]$ range, or when irrespective of the value of P, it is $P_A < P_B$, there is no agreement to grant authority to a randomly drawn assembly, and policy is decided by elected politicians. Hence, all in all, six combinations of values are possible as shown in Table 1. We can now see that in practice, differences in the adoption or rejection of decision making by randomly selected assemblies of citizens at different times correspond to the different cases illustrated in the entries of Table 1. Figure 1 shows graphically what is involved. It illustrates that policy making by an assembly is unanimously agreed for values of P to the right of P_B and to the left of P_A. In the context of the present inquiry, this is the most interesting case. The graph makes clear that, given P, an increase in the critical value of the probability that A wins the election P_A (depicted as a shift of P_A to the right in the upper panel of Fig. 1) increases the likelihood that A agrees to policy making by a randomly selected assembly of citizens, and the opposite is true for a decrease of P_A.

Table 1 The choice of public policy making mechanism

Probability range	Politician A chooses policy making by	Politician B chooses policy making by	Mechanism of policy making
$P_A > P > P_B$	Randomly selected assembly	Randomly selected assembly	Unanimously agreed assembly
$P > P_A > P_B$	Elected politicians	Randomly selected assembly	Status quo = election
$P_A > P_B > P$	Randomly selected assembly	Elected politicians	Status quo = election
$P_A < P < P_B$	Elected politicians	Elected politicians	Status quo = election
$P < P_A < P_B$	Randomly selected assembly	Elected politicians	Status quo = election
$P_A < P_B < P$	Elected politicians	Randomly selected assembly	Status quo = election

Notes: P = Probability that A wins the election = Probability that B loses the election $P_A \equiv$
$\frac{\lambda(w+(1-w)\eta\rho)+(c-s)}{w+(1-w)\rho} - \frac{w\left(\lambda\sigma_a^2+(1-\lambda)\sigma_\beta^2\right)}{(w+(1-w)\rho)(\beta-\alpha)^2}$; $P_B \equiv \frac{\lambda(w+(1-w)\eta\rho)+(1-w)(1-\eta)\rho-(k-t)}{w+(1-w)\rho} + \frac{w\left(\lambda\sigma_a^2+(1-\lambda)\sigma_\beta^2\right)}{(w+(1-w)\rho)(\beta-\alpha)^2}$; $\rho \equiv \frac{G}{(\beta-\alpha)^2}$

```
0                    P_B              P_A              1
+--------------------|----------------|----------------+
                     A chooses Assembly ← | → A chooses Election
                     ←-------------------|
          B chooses Election ← | → B chooses Assembly
          ------------------------------------→
```

(1) $P_A > P_B \Rightarrow$ Policy making by a *citizens assembly* when $P_A > P > P_B$

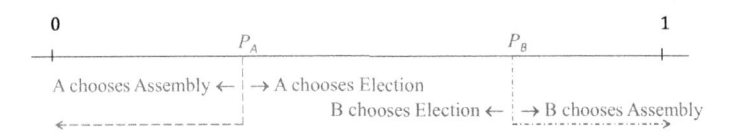

```
0           P_A              P_B                      1
+-----------|----------------|------------------------+
A chooses Assembly ← | → A chooses Election
                          B chooses Election ← | → B chooses Assembly
←-----------------------|
```

(2) $P_A < P_B \Rightarrow$ Policy making by elected representatives when $P_A < P < P_B$

Fig. 1 Politician choice of the mechanism of policy making

Similarly, a decrease in the P_B threshold (depicted by a shift of P_B to the left) increases the likelihood that B agrees to policy making by assembly and vice versa for an increase in P_B.

In this light, it is important to examine the comparative static properties of the two thresholds. The signs of the derivatives of P_A and P_B are shown in Table 2, while the full algebraic results are presented in the Appendix. We focus on the implications of the comparative statics when the necessary condition for accepting policy making by assembly $P_A > P_B$ is satisfied.

Table 2 Signs of the comparative statics of P_A and P_B

$P_A > P_B$	$\frac{dP_A}{dx} > 0 \Rightarrow$ A and B more likely to agree on policy by assembly										
	$\frac{dP_B}{dx} < 0 \Rightarrow$ A and B are more likely to agree on policy by assembly										
	Independent variable x										
	c	s	k	t	η	λ	G	w	$(\beta - \alpha)^2$	σ_α^2	σ_β^2
dP_A/dx	+	−			+	?	?	?	+	−	−
dP_B/dx			−	+	−	?	?	?	−	+	+

In accordance with intuition, the results show that P_A increases and P_B decreases, and consequently A and B are more likely to agree on policy making by a citizens' assembly under the following circumstances:

(a) The costs of the election contests increase (columns c and k) and the costs of the political contest under assembly-made policy fall (columns s and t), that is, when the two sides can avoid the costs of an expensive electoral contest by switching to decision by assembly.
(b) The difference in the ideal points of A and B, $(\beta - \alpha)^2$, increases which implies that the electoral contest becomes more expensive. As a result, other things being equal, the incentives of the politicians not to engage in an electoral fight increase.
(c) When the uncertainty regarding the deviations between assembly policy and the ideal points of A and B decreases (columns σ_α^2 and σ_β^2). That is, when the politicians are confident that the citizens' assembly decisions are close to those taken by the elected representatives, they have fewer reservations to accept policy making by assembly. This further implies that an assembly may be more palatable to the politicians if they have the right to propose policy and the assembly has only veto power on the proposals, so that it cannot amend.
(d) On the contrary, the effect of an increase of the marginal value of office rents under assembly η is ambiguous as the critical values P_A and P_B change in the same direction.

On the other hand, each one of the remaining determinants, that is, the probability that the assembly implements A's ideal policy λ, the size of rents G, and the marginal utility of the policy w, has an ambiguous effect on P_A and P_B, so that their outcomes cannot be signed at this level of generality. For example, the greater the probability that the assembly decides in accordance with A's view, λ, the more willing A is to chose policy by assembly, but this motive is mitigated by the possible deviation of the assembly's policy from A's ideal point σ_α^2; the inverse is true for B. If we further assume that the probability that A wins the election is equal to the probability that the assembly implements his ideal policy, $P = \lambda$, then upon substituting into (7), policy by assembly will be adopted for parameter values such that

$$\frac{(c-s)(\beta-\alpha)^2 - w\sigma_\beta^2}{(1-w)(1-\eta)G + w\left(\sigma_\alpha^2 + \sigma_\beta^2\right)} > P$$

$$> \frac{(1-w)(1-\eta)G - (k-t)(\beta-\alpha)^2 + w\sigma_\beta^2}{(1-w)(1-\eta)G + w\left(\sigma_\alpha^2 + \sigma_\beta^2\right)}$$
(8a)

The latter shows that even when the two mechanisms of policy making carry the same probability of success for the rival politicians, the politicians are not necessarily indifferent to which mechanism is used, because the two mechanisms are still characterised by different costs.

The greater the size of the office rent G, the more desirable office is which increases the incentive to win the election (since it offers the winner larger rents), but this effect is weakened the smaller the loss from the uncertainty of the assembly's policy.

A similar logic explains the ambiguity that characterises the effects of a change in the marginal utility of policy w (equivalently, fall of marginal utility of rents). Nevertheless, two special cases are of interest here. First, when both politicians are opportunists $w = 0$, that is, they are only interested in office rents. Substituting into (7) we have, a randomly citizens' assembly will be agreed for parameter values such that

$$\lambda\eta + \frac{c-s}{\rho} > P > 1 - \eta(1-\lambda) - \frac{k-t}{\rho}$$
(8b)

The somehow surprising result here is that even in this "cynical" case where politicians are only interested in office rents, the necessary condition for politicians to accept a citizens' assembly may still be satisfied. The reason is that there may be parameter values such that A's winning probability is still smaller than the relevant critical threshold and simultaneously bigger than B's losing threshold. It bears noting that in the present case the deviation of assembly decision from the ideal policies of the politicians, σ_α^2 and σ_β^2 no longer features.

Second, the opposite extreme is when the politicians are only motivated by policy $w = 1$; thence, the necessary condition (7) yields

$$c + k > s + t + 2\frac{w\left(\lambda\sigma_\alpha^2 + (1-\lambda)\sigma_\beta^2\right)}{(\beta-\alpha)^2}$$
(8c)

The latter implies that the necessary condition for the politicians to adopt policy making by a random assembly is that the election costs exceed the sortition costs augmented by twice the uncertainty loss from policy by the assembly. Once more, the theoretical result suggests that we cannot rule out that with purely policy motivated politicians the necessary condition for introducing policy making by citizens' assembly, $P_A > P_B$, is satisfied.

5 Conclusions

A priori, it may be thought that rational self-interested politicians, whose expected utility from competing for public office (a contest whose outcome is uncertain) depends on the gains from pursuing their ideal policies and the rents from office, will never give up policy making power to a randomly selected assembly of citizens drawn to represent the citizenry. The present analysis warns that a more nuanced view is more appropriate. The key to explain this result is how the expected probability that each politician wins an election (which allows him to obtain office rents and apply his preferred policy) compares to a threshold value depending on the probability that the random assembly passes a similar policy adjusted for reduced net cost of avoiding an election fight. Solving the model identified necessary and sufficient conditions for politicians to adopt sortition for the selection of legislators. We showed that under conditions of (a) low rather than high uncertainty characterising policy outcomes from random citizens, (b) high rather than low costs of attracting electoral support, and (c) low costs of attracting assembly support (albeit with a certain loss of office rents), transferring policy making to an assembly may present an attractive alternative to an election. Whether the theoretical conditions hold in practice is a question for empirical research. The recent examples of British Columbia, Ontario, and Ireland show that politicians are not necessarily averse to deferring to randomly drawn citizens' assemblies. On the other hand, the Netherlands, the UK, and France reveal that politicians are hostile to such reforms of the institutional framework.

Appendix 1 Comparative static properties of P_A and P_B

$$P_A \equiv \frac{\lambda(w + (1-w)\eta\rho) + (c-s)}{w + (1-w)\rho} - \frac{w\left(\lambda\sigma_\alpha^2 + (1-\lambda)\sigma_\beta^2\right)}{(w + (1-w)\rho)(\beta - \alpha)^2}; \quad \rho \equiv \frac{G}{(\beta - \alpha)^2}$$

$$\frac{dP_A}{dc} = \frac{1}{w + (1-w)\rho} > 0; \quad \frac{dP_A}{ds} = \frac{-1}{w + (1-w)\rho} < 0; \quad \frac{dP_A}{d\eta} = \frac{\lambda(1-w)\rho}{w + (1-w)\rho}$$
$$> 0$$

$$\frac{dP_A}{d\lambda} = \frac{w+(1-w)\eta\rho}{w+(1-w)\rho} - \frac{w}{w+(1-w)\rho}\frac{\sigma_\alpha^2 - \sigma_\beta^2}{(\beta-\alpha)^2} > 0 \text{ for } \sigma_\alpha^2$$

$\leq \sigma_\beta^2$; otherwise ambiguous

$$\frac{dP_A}{dG} = \frac{(1-w)\left(-(\lambda w(1-\eta)+c-s)+w\left(\lambda\sigma_\alpha^2+(1-\lambda)\sigma_\beta^2\right)\right)}{(w+(1-w)\rho)^2(\beta-\alpha)^2} = ?$$

$$\frac{dP_A}{d(\beta-\alpha)^2} = \frac{(1-w)(w\lambda(1-\eta)+c-s)G + w^2\left(\lambda\sigma_\alpha^2+(1-\lambda)\sigma_\beta^2\right)}{(w+(1-w)\rho)^2(\beta-\alpha)^4} > 0$$

$$\frac{dP_A}{dw} = \frac{1}{(w+(1-w)\rho)^2}\left(\lambda(1-\eta)\rho - (1-\rho)(c-s) - \frac{\rho\left(\lambda\sigma_\alpha^2+(1-\lambda)\sigma_\beta^2\right)}{(\beta-\alpha)^2}\right)$$

$= ?$

$$\frac{dP_A}{d\sigma_\alpha^2} = \frac{-w\lambda}{(w+(1-w)\rho)(\beta-\alpha)^2} < 0; \quad \frac{dP_A}{d\sigma_\beta^2} = \frac{-w(1-\lambda)}{(w+(1-w)\rho)(\beta-\alpha)^2} < 0$$

$$P_B \equiv \frac{\lambda(w+(1-w)\eta\rho)+(1-w)(1-\eta)\rho-(k-t)}{w+(1-w)\rho}$$

$$+ \frac{w\left(\lambda\sigma_\alpha^2+(1-\lambda)\sigma_\beta^2\right)}{(w+(1-w)\rho)(\beta-\alpha)^2}; \quad \rho$$

$$\equiv \frac{G}{(\beta-\alpha)^2}$$

$$\frac{dP_B}{dk} = \frac{-1}{w+(1-w)\rho} < 0; \quad \frac{dP_B}{dt} = \frac{-1}{w+(1-w)\rho} > 0; \quad \frac{dP_B}{d\eta}$$

$$= \frac{-(1-w)\rho(1-\lambda)}{w+(1-w)\rho} < 0$$

$$\frac{dP_B}{d\lambda} = \frac{w+(1-w)\eta\rho}{w+(1-w)\rho} + \frac{w\left(\sigma_\alpha^2-\sigma_\beta^2\right)}{w+(1-w)\rho} > 0 \text{ for } \sigma_\alpha^2 \geq \sigma_\beta^2; \text{otherwise ambiguous}$$

$$\frac{dP_B}{dG} = \frac{(1-w)\left((w(1-\lambda)(1-\eta)+k-t)-w\left(\lambda\sigma_\alpha^2+(1-\lambda)\sigma_\beta^2\right)\right)}{(w+(1-w)\rho)^2(\beta-\alpha)^2} = ?$$

$$\frac{dP_B}{d(\beta-\alpha)^2} = -\frac{(1-w)(w(1-\lambda)(1-\eta)+(k-t))G + w^2\left(\lambda\sigma_\alpha^2+(1-\lambda)\sigma_\beta^2\right)}{(w+(1-w)\rho)^2(\beta-\alpha)^4} < 0$$

$$\frac{dP_B}{dw} = \frac{1}{(w+(1-w)\rho)^2}$$
$$\times \left(-(1-\lambda)\rho(1-\eta) + (1-\rho)(k-t) + \frac{\rho\left(\lambda\sigma_\alpha^2 + (1-\lambda)\sigma_\beta^2\right)}{(\beta-\alpha)^2} \right)$$
$$= ?$$

$$\frac{dP_B}{d\sigma_\alpha^2} = \frac{w\lambda}{(w+(1-w)\rho)(\beta-\alpha)^2} > 0; \quad \frac{dP_B}{d\sigma_\beta^2} = \frac{w(1-\lambda)}{(w+(1-w)\rho)(\beta-\alpha)^2} > 0$$

References

Ackerman, B., & Fishkin, J. (2002). Deliberation day. *Journal of Political Philosophy, 10*, 129–152.

Amar, A. R. (1984). Choosing representatives by lottery voting. *Yale Law Journal, 93*, 1283–1308.

Barnett, A., & Carty, P. (2008). *The Athenian option: Radical reform for the House of Lords* (2nd ed.). Imprint Academic.

Dowlen, O. (2008). *The potential of sortition. A study of the random selection of citizens for public office*. Imprint Academic.

Dryzek, J. (2009). The Australian Citizens' Parliament: A world first. *Papers on Parliament 51*, Parliament of Australia. Retrieved September 10, 2020, from https://www.aph.gov.au/~/~/link.aspx?_id=E03B9D7AA31049C2AD126EBD7AC3247E&_z=z

Fishkin, J. S. (2009). *When the people speak: Deliberative democracy and public consultation*. Oxford University Press.

Frey, B. S. (2017). Proposals for a democracy of the future. *Homo Oeconomicus, 34*, 1–9.

Hansen, M. H. (1999). *The Athenian democracy in the age of demosthenes. Structure, principles and ideology*. Bristol Classical Press.

Jacquet, V., Niessen, C., & Reuchamps, M. (2020). Sortition, its advocates and its critics: An empirical analysis of citizens' and MPs' support for random selection as a democratic reform proposal. *International Political Science Review*. Retrieved September 10, 2020, from https://journals.sagepub.com/doi/full/10.1177/0192512120949958

Landemore, H. (2014). Inclusive constitution-making: The Icelandic experiment. *Journal of Political Philosophy, 23*, 166–191.

Lyttkens, C. H. (2013). *Economic analysis of institutional change in Ancient Greece. Politics, taxation and rational behaviour*. Routledge.

Manin, B. (1997). *The principles of representative government*. Cambridge University Press.

Molinari, C. M. (2020). How the Republic of Venice chose its Dodge: lot-based elections and supermajority rule. *Constitutional Political Economy, 31*, 169–187.

Mueller, D. C., Tollison, R. D., & Willet, T. D. (1972). Representative democracy via random selection. *Public Choice, 12*, 57–69.

Mulgan, R. G. (1984). Lot as a democratic device of selection. *Review of Politics, 46*, 539–560.

Pluchino, A., Garofalo, C., Rapisarda, A. Spagano, S. & Caserta, M. (2011). *Accidental politicians: How randomly selected legislators can improve parliament efficiency*. Available at: http://arxiv.org/pdf/1103.1224v2.pdf

Renwick, A. (2011). Electoral reform in Europe since 1945. *West European Politics, 34*, 456–477.

Stone, P. (2011). *The luck of the draw*. Oxford University Press.

Sutherland, K. (2011). The two sides of the representative coin. *Studies in Social Justice, 5*, 197–211.
Tierney, S. (2012). *Constitutional referendums. The theory and practice of Republican deliberation*. Oxford University Press.
Tridimas, G. (2007). Ratification through referendum or parliamentary vote: When to call a non required referendum? *European Journal of Political Economy, 23*, 674–692.
Tridimas, G. (2012). Constitutional choice in ancient Athens: the rationality of selection to office by lot. *Constitutional Political Economy, 23*, 1–21.
Tridimas, G. (2018). On sortition. Comment on "Proposals for a democracy of the future" by Bruno Frey. *Homo Oeconomicus, 35*, 91–100.
Tsebelis, G. (2002). *Veto players: How political institutions work*. Princeton University Press.

George Tridimas is Professor of Political Economy at the Business School of Ulster University. He obtained a BA in Economics from the University of Athens and an MPhil and a DPhil in Economics from the University of Oxford. He had held positions at the University of the Witwatersrand in South Africa and the University of Reading in England. His research interests are in political economy, public economics, and law and economics. He has published widely in topics such as mechanisms of collective decision-making, including elections, referendums, power-sharing arrangements, choice of constitutional orders and randomly selected politicians, the size of government, publicly provided goods and the economic behaviour of agents, the economic analysis of the judiciary, and the dynamics of European judicial integration. His current research focuses on the direct democracy of ancient Athens, its emergence, policy making processes, economic performance, and fall. His work combines theory, analysis of policy, and applied econometrics and has a strong interdisciplinary element borrowing from history, political science, and law. He has held various visiting fellowships in Canada, the Czech Republic, Romania, and the USA. He is co-founder and managing co-editor of the German-Greek Yearbook of Political Economy. He is a member of the editorial boards of a number of academic journals.

Legislature by Lot: A Way Out of the Problems of Modern Democracy or Just Another Unrealistic Approach?

Spyridon Vlachopoulos

Abstract What is the connection between sortition parliament and modern democracy? Debate on what democracy means and how it should be implemented has been, and still continues to be, broad. The roots of the sortition parliament notion are already found in the Homeric epics and in ancient Greece. Moving to the present, several movements in favor of sortition parliaments have appeared in Europe, Canada, and the USA. Furthermore, the idea of public officers selected by lot, as part of reworking the state, has been elaborated in the political theory. After all these, we have to answer the question: Should we introduce a sortition parliament in modern democracy? Of course, like in every topic, there are arguments in favor and against it. What would be the conclusion that follows after pointing out the advantages and the disadvantages of legislature by lot? Perhaps the time has come to think "out of the box" and combine the advantages of the traditional representative democracy with elements of alternative models.

Keywords Sortition · Lot · Parliament · Ancient Greece · Modern democracy · Political parties · Representative democracy · Accountability

A. The subject of this presentation may surprise at first sight. What is the connection between sortition parliament[1] and modern democracy? The use of sortition accompanies the renewal of debates on democracy. Debate on what democracy means and how it should be implemented has been, and still continues to be, broad in the area of theory, philosophy, and political science and is also a core concern of many progressive social movements. First of all and as we do in every topic, also in this field, we have to examine the roots. In the Homeric epics, our earliest surviving texts,

---

[1] The selection by lot as a way to staff state organs reflects a more general political theory and does not refer only to the idea of a sortition parliament (see, e.g., the jurors of the criminal courts in many legal orders). Nevertheless, this presentation is limited only to the problematic of a legislative body, the members of which are randomly selected among the citizens ("sortition parliament").

S. Vlachopoulos (✉)
School of Law, National and Kapodistrian University of Athens, Athens, Greece
e-mail: svlacho@law.uoa.gr

allotment is illustrated in the selection of which young people to send off to war or to found a colony, in accordance with a practice that was common in all times and places. It appears again, during war, in the choice of a champion to do battle in the name of everyone. At Troy, in the absence of Achilles, withdrawn to his tent, how could the most valorous Greek be chosen to meet Hector in single combat? By tossing name-inscribed lots into a helmet and shaking it (Demont, 2010).

There is a vast literature of reflection upon sortition as a democratic procedure of distribution of political posts. Election by lot, or sortition, frequently used in plenty of ancient democracies and in Renaissance republics (Venice and Florence, among others), represents a challenge for the thesis that claims that politics requires a type of specialized knowledge. However, election by lot was never presented in a pure state, but rather combined with elective procedures, reserving the latter for the distribution of posts that were considered to require a certain qualification.

In ancient Greece, the "birth giver" of democracy, the members of the governmental (parliamentary and judicial) bodies were not elected, but selected by lot (James, 1956). More precisely, in ancient Athens not only the 5.000 judges of "Iliaia" (the highest Court), but also the 500 members of the Parliament were designated by lot. One-third of all Athenian citizens above 30 years of age had served in the Parliament at least once in their lifetime during the 25 years before the Peloponnesian war, and no one could be chosen for more than two times in their lifetime (Marangudakis, 2016).

Only the Generals and the Clerks were elected by the general assembly of the Athenians (the so called Ecclesia touDimou). As far as ancient political theory is concerned, Aristotle in his *"The Politics (Politica)"* insisted that:

> It is accepted as democratic when public offices are allocated by lot; and as oligarchic when they are filled by election. (Demont, 2010; Gastil & Wright, 2019, p. 47)

Lot, almost unconceivable in modern democracies, verified the equality of all citizens as it did not allow favoritism. It nullified electoral campaigns as well as the privilege of wealth, eloquence, or charisma.

Democracy was run by ordinary citizens that represented the will of the whole body of citizens. Also Herodotus advocates in favor of the random selection for public offices and sees a very strong affiliation between democracy and selection by lot:

> The rule of the people has the fairest name of all, equality, and does none of the things that a monarch does. The lot determines offices, power is held accountable, and deliberation is conducted in public. (Herodotus, *Histories*, 3.80)

Furthermore, according to Plato:

> Democracy arises after the poor are victorious over their adversaries . . ., then they share out equally with the rest of the population political offices and burdens; and in this regime public offices are usually allocated by lot (Plato, *Republic*, 8.557a)

Procedures of various forms, through which public officers were selected by lot, can also be found in several places and historic periods, e.g., in Italy (Lombardy, Venice, and Florence) in the Middle Ages. Also, in Switzerland, because financial gain could be achieved through the position of the mayor, some parts of the country used random selection, during the years between 1640 and 1837, in order to prevent corruption (Carson & Martin, 1999, p. 33).

Let's now move to the present: the former United Nations Secretary General, Kofi Annan, has called the States to:

reintroduce the ancient Greek practice of selecting parliaments by lot instead of selection[2]

In his view, such a system:

would prevent the formation of self – serving and self – perpetuating political classes disconnected from their electorates.

Moreover, several movements in favor of sortition parliaments have appeared, inter alia, in the United Kingdom, the United States, and Canada. There is also a "sortition foundation," following the motto: "Let's do democracy differently. Let's do democracy better".[3]

Especially after the recent economic crisis, the movement demanding a "sortition" democracy has increased. The concept of democracy and the different ways of implementing it is a central theme of discussion in social movements. In Iceland, in 2009 there was an unsuccessful attempt to draft the new Constitution by Assemblies, the members of which were not elected but selected by lot (Gastil & Wright, 2019, p. 59).

Nevertheless, the same attempt in Ireland was more successful: In 2012, 67% of the members of the Constitutional Convention were citizens randomly selected from the electoral register. This Constitutional Assembly is considered as successful and progressive, and one of its proposals, the legalization of same-sex marriage, was adopted by a referendum some years after. The same "experiment," this time in a more "revolutionary" form, was repeated in Ireland in 2017–2018, and the Constitutional Convention was entirely selected by lot (Gastil & Wright, *ibid.*, p. 60).

Finally, it must be pointed out that the idea of public officers selected by lot, as part of reworking the state, of replacing elected legislative bodies or an appointed upper house, of choosing legislative juries, and supplementing or replacing some of the legislators, has been further elaborated in the political theory and incorporated in more general political theories. For instance, one should mention the "demarchy" of John Burnheim (Martin, 1992), where he describes a political system in which many small "citizen's juries" would deliberate and make decisions about public policies and the "Lottocracy" of L. León, where he describes a sortition procedure that is somewhat different from Burnheim's demarchy. More precisely, while Burnheim "insists that the random selection be made only from volunteers," León states "that first of all, the job must not be liked." Even the random selection of the members of the House of Lords in the United Kingdom and the House of Representatives in the

---

[2] Speech given at the 2017 *The New York Times* Athens Democracy Forum, found in https://equalitybylot.com/2017/09/22/kofi-annan-endorses-sortition/; see also https://www.athensdemocracyforum.com/gallery/2017.

[3] https://www.sortitionfoundation.org/history.

United States was proposed in the legal theory (Callenbach & Phillips, 1985; Barnett & Carty, 1998). Furthermore, a number of modern advocates of deliberative democracy have proposed a variety of sortition schemes (Bouricius, 2013).

After all these we have to face the problematic and answer the question that arises: Should we follow the model of ancient Greece? Should we introduce a sortition parliament? Of course, like in every topic, there are arguments in favor and against it. Let's, first, examine the possible advantages of a parliament, the members of which are not elected by people but designated by lot.

B. People in the modern democracies, especially after the economic and pandemic crises of the last decade, need something "new." Everything new seems to be good, at least at the beginning. This is of great importance, because of the skepticism and disbelief of the citizens against the classic parliamentary system (Dunlop, 2018). One could argue that people are tired of the representative system, and they need a new element in the state organization, which will strengthen their democratic consciousness.

Moreover, by the eventual introduction of a sortition parliament, some people who don't actually have the opportunity to become members of the elected parliament could obtain opportunity to become parliamentarians in the future (Dowlen, 2009).

This point is also very important, because there are efficient people who are willing to participate in the political life but, because they cannot finance an electoral campaign or because they are not affiliated to a political party, don't have the chance to be elected. It is commonly known that the independent members of the Parliament who do not belong to a political party are very few and in some parliaments do not even exist.[4] Consequently, the introduction of a sortition parliament can be seen also as a matter of enforcement of the equality principle: All citizens will have the same chance to become members of the legislative body.[5] At the same time, the selection by lot increases the diversity and the representativeness of the legislative body.

In this context, one could also argue that the sortition parliament is composed by people, who feel that they are executing a public service/duty in the genuine sense of the word and they are not acting as professionals. The fact also that they are not interested to be reelected means that they are willing to take the "difficult" but necessary decisions in favor of the public good, even against the will of the voters. Members of the parliament selected by lot are also more probable to think and act "out of the box" and less traditionally, finding new solutions for old problems. In this

---

[4] In 2005 there were only three independent MPs so that 99.5% of all UK MPs belonged to a political party. See https://en.wikipedia.org/wiki/List_of_UK_minor_party_and_independent_MPs_elected.

[5] Compared to a voting system—even one that is open to all citizens—a citizen-wide lottery scheme for public office lowers the threshold to office. This is because ordinary citizens do not have to compete against more powerful or influential adversaries in order to take office and because the selection procedure does not favor those who have pre-existing advantages or connections—as invariably happens with election by preference (Dowlen, 2009). See also Gastil and Wright (2019, p. 237) et seq (contribution by Dimitri Courant).

sense, the sortition parliament could also act as an "antidote" to populism. After all these arguments, it is not surprising that, according to an analysis of Italian researchers, the sortition parliament is more effective than the elected parliament (Pluchino et al., 2011; Soufleri, 2011).

Apart from that, the selection by lot can be seen as a contribution to the rational governance, given that popular mandate and powerful legitimation resulting in public vote increase the danger of power's abuse and misconduct.[6,7]

The said major effectiveness of the sortition parliament can be also explained with the abolishment of the affiliation of its members to a political party. The members of the elected parliament have to be "loyal" to the party and especially to its leader, if they want to participate to the next elections as candidates of the party's ballot. As far as the members of the parliament of the governing party are concerned, they have to "obey" the will of the Prime Minister if they want to have a chance to become ministers. After all that, it is evident that the members of the parliament are not actually free and that constitutional provisions like Art. 60 par. 1 of the Greek Constitution ("Members of Parliament enjoy unrestricted freedom of opinion and right to vote according to their conscience") do not represent the political reality.

The contra argument, that the essence of the representative democracy through the sortition parliament is lost and replaced by pure luck, can be refuted by observing that the modern democracy was never really representative. Only the wealthiest and the most educated people normally had the opportunity to become members of the parliament (Gastil & Wright, 2019, p. 251 et. seq contribution by Arash Abizadeh).

Moreover, it is well-known that some professions (e.g., lawyers, engineers, medical doctors) are overrepresented in the modern parliaments, while other professions (e.g., farmers) are underrepresented. It is also important to note that, even today, in some countries women are underrepresented in the national parliaments. A very characteristic example may be concluded from the Greek Parliament elected in July 2019: only 63 of its 300 members are women.[8]

C. On the other hand, the withdrawal of the representative parliamentary democracy may have serious negative effects.

---

[6] Aristotle (*Constitution of Athens*, 48. 3) notes the use of sortition in Athens as an instrument of constraint against the traffic of influences: a tribunal elected by lot is less corruptible, because it is difficult to foresee who its members will be.

[7] The Athenians used an intricate machine, a kleroterion, to allot officers. Headlam (1891) explains that:

> the Athenians felt no distrust of the lot, but regarded it as the most natural and the simplest way of appointment.

See also https://www.themata-archaiologias.gr/%CE%B1%CE%B8%CE%B7%CE%BD%CE%B1%CF%8A%CE%BA%CE%AE-%CE%B4%CE%B7%CE%BC%CE%BF%CE%BA%CF%81%CE%B1%CF%84%CE%AF%CE%B1-%CE%BA%CE%BB%CE%B7%CF%81%CF%89%CF%84%CE%AE%CF%81%CE%B9%CE%BF%CE%BD-%CE%BA%CE%B1%CE%B9/.

[8] https://www.hellenicparliament.gr/Vouleftes/Statistika-Stoicheia/Statistika-Stoicheia-IE-Periodou/.

The main disadvantage of the sortition parliament is the lack of accountability (Manin, 1997). The members of such a parliament are not obliged to account for their actions/omissions, like the members of the elected parliament to their voters. Consequently, the only limit to the behavior of the members of the sortition parliament is the law. The members of such a parliament would be allowed to do anything they wanted without any, even political, consequences. Of course, they would not be allowed to breach the law. The other limitations which exist in the modern representative democracies and decrease the danger of the abuse of power (e.g., mass media, public opinion, other political parties) do not fit into the scheme of the sortition parliament. Also, just as in elected legislatures, citizens in a sortition legislature are vulnerable to bribes when important legislation is being considered, and some mechanism of accountability needs to be in place to deal with this (Gastil & Wright, 2019, p. 15).

Furthermore, because the selection as a member of a sortition parliament is a pure matter of luck, it is probable that the sortition parliament would be composed by totally indifferent/inefficient people or by citizens who do not possess the necessary skills in order to perform the duty of a parliamentarian.[9] It is very characteristic that even in ancient Greece, the officials selected by lot had to undergo an examination (called "dokimasia"), in order to reaffirm that the randomly selected lot was not incapable to become a public officer. But if we introduced such an examination as a corrective, then the essence of the system of selecting officials by lot would be lost.[10] Apart from that, such an examination opens a wide range of questions, concerning, e.g., the content of the examination and the person who is going to conduct it. It is also well-known that in ancient Greece, some of the most important public offices (e.g., military commanders, clerks) were excluded by the sortition procedure. According to Xenophon, Socrates:

> taught his companions to despise the established laws by insisting on the folly of appointing public officials by lot, when none would choose a pilot or builder or flautist by lot, nor any other craftsman for work in which mistakes are far less disastrous than mistakes in statecraft. (Martin, 1992)

The modern parliaments have decisive powers over vital public matters, like their power to declare the country under martial law. Is this compatible with the selection of the members of the parliament through pure luck, which can lead to the nomination of eventually inefficient/indifferent people?

---

[9] According to Xenophon (*Memorabilia*, Book 3, chapter 10, section 9), Socrates used to say (and Plato greatly elaborated this demand for knowledge in political affairs):

> The true kings, the true magistrates, (...) are not those who wear crowns, those who have been elected by just anyone, those who have been chosen by lot, nor those who have used force or fraud, but those who know how to rule.

[10] A generally accepted point of view is that training and staff support programs should be introduced and would be of great service to the sortition legislature. See Gastil and Wright (2019, pp. 21–22).

Under a more general point of view, it can be argued that the replacement of the classic elected parliament through a sortition parliament can decrease the interest of the public for political life, since the possibilities for a citizen to be selected by lot are nowadays negligible (contrary to the situation in ancient Greece with a remarkable smaller number of citizens).

Moreover, the sortition parliament would lead to the end of the political parties and of the ideologies which are presented by them. Our modern parliamentary democracy is based on the political parties, which are quite often the object of a very strong critic, like in the interwar period, as well as in the modern times the political parties are accused for every negative symptom of the governmental system. Nevertheless, nothing else is presented until now as a real alternative to the political parties (Georgakopoulos, 2016). Despite the disadvantages of the political parties and the problem of the democratic deficit concerning their organization, it cannot be denied that the political parties, by uniting people with the same ideology or interests, strengthen the political homogeneity. On the contrary, heterogeneity and difficulty in the composition of different attitudes and interests represent a main disadvantage of a randomly selected and in its variety "chaotic" parliament. This will possibly lead to the serious possibility of governmental instability, which will eventually turn to instability of the whole political system. More generally, the introduction of a sortition parliament could lead to the farewell of the main features and advantages of the parliamentary system, as this was formed in the modern times.

The main problematic point of the sortition parliament has to do with the notion of democracy. It can be quite controversial if the system where the legislators are selected by lot and not elected by the people is compatible with the modern notion of democracy. Democracy means the political system, according to which people, or at least the majority of them, rule. In a system of sortition parliament, the will of the people does not rule. Luck is the only decisive factor. Already in the ancient times, Isocrates (*Areopagiticus*, 23) had pointed out that appointing magistrates through elections:

> was also more democratic than the casting of lots, since under the plan of election by lot chance would decide the issue and the partisans of oligarchy would often get the offices; whereas under the plan of selecting the worthiest men, the people would have in their hands the power to choose those who were more attached to the existing constitution.

D. What is the conclusion that follows from the above list of arguments in favor and against a sortition parliament?

Perhaps the time has come to think "out of the box." Not in the meaning that we should abolish the representative democracy and substitute it by a "random" democracy, where the members of the one and only parliament will be designated by lot. But in the meaning that we could perhaps combine the advantages of the traditional representative democracy with "small" and "gradual" doses of alternative models, e.g., with a second legislative body, the members of which will be chosen by lot and will have advisory competencies. After all, perhaps it would not be a bad idea to introduce a system, which would combine the advantages of both parliaments (elected and sortition parliament).

References

Barnett, A., & Carty, P. ([1998] 2008). *The Athenian option: Radical reform for the House of Lords.* Exeter: Imprint Academic.

Bouricius, T. (2013). Democracy through multi-body sortition: Athenian lessons for the modern day. *Journal of Public Deliberation, 9*(1). https://doi.org/10.16997/jdd.156. https://delibdemjournal.org/article/id/428/

Callenbach, E., & Phillips, M. (1985). *A citizen legislature.* Berkeley/Bodega California: Banyan Tree Books/Clear Glass. Retrieved at: https://people.well.com/user/mp/citleg.html

Carson, L., & Martin, B. (1999). *Random selection in politics.* Westport, CT: Praeger Publishers. Available at: https://www.bmartin.cc/pubs/99rsip.pdf

Demont, P. (2010). *Allotment and democracy in ancient Greece.* Available at: https://booksandideas.net/Allotment-and-Democracy-in-Ancient.html

Dowlen, O. (2009). Sorting out sortition: A perspective on the random selection of political officers. *Political Studies, 57,* 298–315.

Dunlop, T. (2018). Voting undermines the will of the people – it's time to replace it with sortition. *The Guardian.* 14-10-2018. Available at: https://www.theguardian.com/australia-news/2018/oct/14/voting-undermines-the-will-of-the-people-its-time-to-replace-it-with-sortition

Gastil, J., & Wright, E. O. (2019). *The real utopias project – Legislature by lot. Transformative designs for deliberative governance.* New York: Verso (contributions by Abizadeh A., Arnold T., Bouricius T., Burks D. et al.).

Georgakopoulos, T. (2016). The electoral system that Greece needs, *Kathimerini,* 19-02-2016. Available at: https://www.kathimerini.gr/opinion/850091/to-eklogiko-systima-poy-chreiazetai-i-ellada/

Headlam, J. W. (1891). *Election by lot at Athens.* Cambridge University Press.

James, C. L. R. (1956). Every cook can govern, transcribed: by David Harvie, 2003. Available at: https://www.marxists.org/archive/james-clr/works/1956/06/every-cook.htm

Manin, B. (1997). *The principles of representative government.* Cambridge University Press.

Marangudakis, M. (2016). Visions of brotherhood. A comparative analysis of direct democracy in ancient and modern Greece. *Política y Sociedad, 53*(3), 773–793.

Martin, B. (1992). Demarchy: A democratic alternative to electoral politics. Published in Kick It Over. No. 30, pp. 11–13. Available at: https://documents.uow.edu.au/~/bmartin/pubs/92kio/

Pluchino, A., Garofalo, C., Rapisarda, A., Spagano, S., & Caserta, M. (2011). Accidental politicians: How randomly selected legislators can improve parliament efficiency. *Physica A: Statistical Mechanics and its Applications, 390*(21–22), 3944–3954.

Soufleri, I. (2011). Elected in the Parliament, *To Vima, 26-05-2011.* Available at: https://www.tovima.gr/2011/05/26/science/klirwtoi-sti-boyli/

Spyridon Vlachopoulos graduated from Law School of National and Kapodistrian University of Athens (1990) and was awarded a PhD by the Faculty of Law of the University of Munich (1995) for a thesis on "The relationship of freedom of art and the protection of youth." In 2003 he was elected Lecturer of Public Law, specialized in Constitutional Law, in 2007 Assistant Professor, in 2012 Associate Professor, and in 2016 Professor of the First Grade in the Faculty of Law of National and Kapodistrian University of Athens. He teaches at the National School of Judges, and he has authored a major number of books and articles, mainly for issues concerning constitutional history, interpretation of the Constitution, and the protection of the human rights. Indicatively, some of his works are "The right of petition under Greek and European Community Law" (1998), "Aspects of the right of judicial protection before the Council of State" (1998), "Privatization: the constitutional framework of a political decision" (1999), "Cloning in the Greek legal order" (2000), "Transparency of the state action and protection of personal data" (2007), "The crisis of Parliamentarism in the interwar period and the end of the Second Hellenic Republic in 1935. The institutional aspects of an economic crisis?" (2012), "Fundamental Rights" (Collective work, 2017),

"Dilemmas of the Greek constitutional history: 20th century" (together with Evanthis Hatzivasileiou, 2018), "The constitutional dimensions of the change in jurisprudence" (2019), and "Constitutional Mithridatism" (2020). He is a practicing lawyer before the Greek Council of the State and the second instance Administrative Courts, especially for cases of public law. He is the President of the Committee for the Evaluation of the Law-Making Process and a member of the Hellenic Data Protection Authority.

Asymmetric Information, Social Choices, and Democracy

Emmanouil M. L. Economou and Nicholas C. Kyriazis

Abstract A crucial premise of most neoclassical models is that perfect markets (e.g., in microeconomics) cannot function unless all the involved have perfect and *symmetrical* information. This premise has been challenged and modified by the research of George Akerlof, Jean Tirole, and many others. A similar problem applies in the political sphere concerning the *asymmetric information* of ordinary citizen-voters as against "experts" or politicians in modern representative democracies. This inhibits their smooth functioning and facilitates the rise of populist parties on the right and left, as well as bringing about wrong decisions in referenda (e.g., the Brexit in 2016). We analyze the issue of asymmetric information in representative democracies and compare it to ancient Greek direct democracies, especially Athens. We show that the institutional setup of the Athenian Assembly of citizens disseminates the knowledge of the expert to all participating citizens, thus providing common and shared symmetric information as a basis for decision-making. Then we present our proposals to ameliorate the present situation.

Keywords Asymmetric information · Arrow's impossibility theorem · Social choice · Democracy

1 Introduction

One of the major problems for the functioning of representative democracies is the *asymmetric information* between the agent (government and agents, f.e. Central Banks) and the principal, the citizen-voters. This asymmetric information leads to fake news, populism, and wrong decisions, as in referenda like Brexit. The existence of asymmetric information is well known and has been analyzed by many economists (see, among others, Akerlof, 1970; Stiglitz & Weiss, 1982; Tirole, 2017, pp. 117, 120–121) as one of the main problems of the functioning of markets and

---

E. M. L. Economou · N. C. Kyriazis (✉)
Department of Economics, University of Thessaly, Volos, Greece
e-mail: emmoikon@uth.gr; nkyr@uth.gr; nkyr@ergoman.net

© The Author(s), under exclusive license to Springer Nature Switzerland AG 2022
E. M. L. Economou et al. (eds.), *Democracy in Times of Crises*,
https://doi.org/10.1007/978-3-030-97295-0_8

by political scientists as the main problem of the "political market" (Levitsky & Ziblatt, 2018, p. 199).

In representative democracies it is difficult to effectively motivate citizens in mass democracy to become informed, because the cost of becoming informed (in terms of time and effort devoted to this) outweighs the benefit of better information in decision-making. Thus, citizens tended to be informatively myopic (Achen & Bartels, 2017, pp. 187, 198, 199). On the other hand, becoming informed on the issues permits change in the policy outcome and leads to better decisions. Linked to this is the issue of deciding on the "common good." As Tirole (2017, p. 12) writes:

> The problem of limited (or "asymmetric") information is everywhere at the heart of our institutional structures and our political choices and at the heart of the economies of the common good.

In the present essay, we first discuss briefly the issue of the definition of the "common good" in relation to Kenneth Arrow's *possibility theorem* (better known as "*impossibility*"), and then we discuss, with examples, how the common good was established under the Athenian direct democracy. Contrary to the current problems of asymmetrical information in modern societies, we show that the institutional setup of the Athenian Assembly of citizens disseminated the knowledge of the expert to all participating citizens, thus providing common and shared symmetric information as a basis for decision-making.

We then present an analysis of decision-making for the common good under direct and representative democracy, followed by our conclusions and proposals to ameliorate the present situation. The proposals include, among others, three institutional arrangements: (i) *citizens' initiatives* as a specific procedure for submitting proposals to the state for adopting specific laws addressing social and other local, regional, or national issues; (ii) *bottom-up referenda* on specific issues that are decided by the citizens themselves (contrary to *top-down referenda* decided by governments) through the introduction of *popular initiatives* (which become more and more common all over the world); and (iii) the implementation of the so-called *recall* procedure.[1]

---

[1] A *recall* is a procedure by which, in certain cases, voters can remove an elected official from office through a direct vote before that official's term has ended. See, among others, Cronin (1999) and Economou and Kyriazis (2019).

2 Arrow's Impossibility Theorem

The first issue in our analysis is to define the "common good," something that may appear straightforward but is not so. What is the "common good," and who decides what it is?[2] Under non-democratic regimes, the answer to the question is simple (although not satisfactory for the majority presumably): The decision maker is the autocrat, a king, emperor, and dictator (or in Plato's *Republic*, the guardians-philosophers), and he decides what the "common good" is. In democracies, the situation is more complex. Here, the citizens-voters have to decide and define the "common good." Social choice theory, beginning with Arrow's *possibility theorem* ([1951], 1963), concludes that one cannot devise a mechanism for making decisions on the "common good" which simultaneously meets a number of reasonably sounding conditions that we might want to impose, such as monotonicity or the requirement that if a voter raises the position of one option in his own personal ranking, this cannot have the effect of lowering it in the social ranking. Simply put, there is no fair and rational way of aggregating voters' preferences to reach a social decision. Also, the circularity of decision-making is possible.[3]

This has triggered an ongoing discussion and attempts to circumvent and solve the problem. Sen (2006), for example, proposed that the issue of freedom is fundamental, thus choosing not among alternatives but among valuations and preferences and attaching importance to the liberty of people and to their minds on the basis of conscious reflection and decision. This, as we will analyze further on, is how *direct* (and, in part, *deliberative*) democracy work,[4] but as Sen puts it, it does not solve the *impossibility theorem*. It just introduces new elements in the social function.

Buchanan (1954a, b) argued that rationality or irrationality as an attribute of the social group implies the importation to that group of an organic existence apart from that of its individual components, a kind of collective will. Buchanan thus criticizes Arrow's theorem as a mistaken attempt to impose the logic of welfare maximization on the procedures of collective choice. According to Sen's (1995) interpretation, this would lead to abandoning consequence-based evaluation of social happenings, opting instead for a procedural approach, looking for "right" institutions rather than "good" outcomes.

Related to this is the role of social interactions and the connection between value formation and the decision-making processes. Arrow (1951, p. 7) assumed (strongly)

---

[2] The fact that the definition is not simple is illustrated, for example, in J. Tirole's (2017) book which has its title *Economics for the Common Good*. Nowhere in the book is given a specific definition of what the "common good" is.

[3] In technical terms, the social choice function is not single-peaked (it has no unique maximum).

[4] *Deliberative democracy*, school of thought in political theory, claims that political decisions should be the product of fair and reasonable discussion and debate among citizens. In *deliberation*, citizens exchange arguments and consider different claims that are designed to secure the public good. For a detailed analysis, see Fishkin (2011) and Neblo (2015).

that individual values are taken as data and are not capable of being altered by the nature of the decision process itself. Buchanan criticizes this by writing (1954a, p. 120) "the definition of democracy as government by discussion" implies "that individual values can and do change in the process of decision making." In our discussion of the working of ancient direct democracy below, we will analyze how, under its procedures, information is acquired and diffused, becoming more symmetric, and common knowledge for all participants, thus permitting a better understanding and definition of the "common good."[5]

Another problem related to this is how individual preferences are revealed correctly, because in some cases persons may have an incentive not to reveal their true preferences (Sen, 1977). Thus, this is an additional problem arising before Arrow's *possibility theorem*. Before even discussing if preferences can be aggregated, we must know what these preferences truly are! In attempting to find a solution to the *impossibility theorem*, Sen (1995, p. 8) writes:

> Once interpersonal comparisons are introduced, the impossibility problem, in the appropriately redefined framework, vanishes

but further on accepts that mechanisms which must rely on some standard expressions of individual preference (such as voting) do not readily lend themselves to interpersonal comparisons (p. 9). So, in practice, the problem remains. Arrow (1999) in evaluating Sen's contribution states that making pairwise choices by majority voting determines a social ordering if the social alternatives can be thought of as arranged along one dimension and if each individual's preference ordering over this array is single peaked. He however does not suggest how such a pairwise system can be implemented in practice. As we will show further on, this is exactly the way ancient direct democracy worked.[6]

Sen (1999) discusses social welfare judgments through variants of voting systems, emphasizing the advantages and limitations of voting. Thus, through voting each person can have different alternatives, but there is no direct way of getting interpersonal comparison of different person's well-being from voting data. Sen emphasizes this shortcoming in his attempt to solve the *impossibility theorem* through interpersonal comparisons, as stated above, and continues by discussing the informational basis of interpersonal comparisons. Akerlof and Dickens (1982) discuss a related issue, the role of information in shaping people's beliefs and values, using *cognitive dissonance* theory adopted from psychology.[7] Within this,

---

[5]This arises, for example, in the case of subscription schemes where a person is charged according to benefits received. It is to the person's interest to understate the expected benefits because thus he would have to pay less, but this may lead to a rejection of a public project, which would have been justified if true benefits were known (Sen, 1977, p. 331).

[6]This goes actually back to Condorcet's rule that any option which beats all the others in a series of binary choices should be the social choice.

[7]*Cognitive dissonance* is the mental stress or discomfort experienced when holding two conflicting thoughts. It occurs in situations where a person is presented with facts that contradict that person's self-image, attitudes, beliefs, or behaviors.

reputation is important as a shortcut of acquiring information (p. 315).[8] As we will analyze in the next section, reputation of proposers in the Athenian Assembly was an important element in decision-making.

We have reviewed here briefly some of the problems of social choice and the definition of the "common good" (or public good) out of a vast literature. We conclude, according to Achen and Bartels (2017, p. 14):

> The populist ideal of electoral (e.g., representative) democracy... is largely irrelevant in practice, leaving elected officials mostly free to pursue their own motions of the public good or to respond to party and interest groups pressure.

In the next section, we analyze the practice of direct democracy in Classical Athens, in order to show how the citizens solved the issue of defining the common good and thus arriving to a solution of Arrow's *impossibility theorem*.

3 Defining the Common Good Under Direct Democracy

The supreme decision-making body in Classical Athens was the citizen's *assembly* which met 40 days or even more sometimes per year during the fourth century BC. The *Council of the Five Hundred* members was elected by lot among the citizens and was responsible, among others, for setting the agenda to be discussed in the assembly and divided into 50 acting government members per month, known as *prytaneis*. This political body (*prytany*) was responsible for the actual functioning of the state (Thorley, 1996; Ober, 2008; Economou & Kyriazis, 2019; Bitros et al., 2020).

Every Athenian was free, under the principle of *isegoria* (the right to propose) to propose measures and actions on any subject, ranging from foreign relations (alliances, war, peace) to economic and monetary subjects. In fact, few Athenians did propose, called *initiators*. They were kin to today's expects in various fields, such as Themistocles on foreign relations and defense, Pericles on general political issues and in particular cultural (the Parthenon building program), and Nicophon on monetary and trade issues.[9]

Two elements were essential for the smooth functioning of democracy: listening to the experts and acquiring symmetrical information. The expert–initiator called *ho boulomenos* (meaning, "he, who wished to propose") had to convince his fellow citizens on the correctness of his proposal, in general in opposition to a counter

---

[8]This again may be interpreted as a manifestation of *bounded rationality*, the theroretical concept developed by Simon (1978, 1982, 1991).

[9]For a detailed analysis regarding functioning of institutions and the working of direct democracy in practice in Classical Athens, see, among others, Ober (2008, 2017) and Economou and Kyriazis (2019). For Nicophon's law which ensured the circulation of reliable currency within the Athenian economy, see Figueira (1998), Ober (2008), Bitros et al. (2020), Economou et al. (2021a, b), and Halkos et al. (2021).

proposal by another expert. So, in general the proposals were well argued, and in case a proposal was linked to public expenditure, the expenditure and the source of the revenue had to be exactly quantified. Since usually for longer periods of times the same persons came forward as initiators (such as Themistocles, Ephialtes, and Pericles during the fifth and Demosthenes and Phocion during the fourth centuries), the citizens could judge the effects of new proposals by the same initiator out of their experience of the past proposals.

If the initiator's past proposals were deemed to have been to the benefit of the citizens, the citizens were more prone to accept new ones by him. Thus, successful initiators build credibility and mutual trust between them, being the experts, and their fellow citizens, which is a way to reduce information transaction costs.[10]

Credibility and trust generate information both on the initiator's character (honest, truthful, etc.) and on the expected outcome of his proposals (Kyriazis & Economou, 2015). Since the proposals (and counter proposals) were debated in front of the assembly with arguments in favor and against them, at the end of the day, all citizens present, who were to vote, had acquired symmetrical information on the issue. They had then to decide by voting on the best proposal, which corresponded to the "common good" according to their perception (Economou & Kyriazis, 2019, 2022).

Let us illustrate the procedure through a well-known historical case. In 483–482 BC, the then leading politician of Athens, Themistocles, perceived the danger of a renewed Persian invasion of Greece, although the Athenians and Plataeans had defeated the first Persian invasion at the Battle of Marathon in 490 BC. He proposed a double strategy, to combat the Persians in a sort of combined operations on land and sea. For this strategy to succeed, Athens needed a strong navy which it lacked till then. So, Themistocles proposed to build a new fleet of 200 *trireme* types of warships[11] (100 each year for a 2-year period). The cost of constructing each ship was calculated equal to one *talent* (equivalent to 6.000 *drachmae*). The revenue would come from the proceeds of the Laurion silver mines. He further elaborated the proposal giving details as to how the ships would be built (possibly, the first public-private partnership ever); the benefits of victory, both short run (repel the invasion) and long run (turn to the sea), transform Athens into Greece's foremost sea power and deepen democracy by granting full citizen rights also to the poorest and most numerous class of citizens, the low-income *thetes*, who would be employed as rowers in the fleet (Kyriazis & Zouboulakis, 2004; Halkos & Kyriazis, 2010; Tridimas, 2013; Economou & Kyriazis, 2019). But, as usual, there was a counter proposal to use the silver proceeds to be distributed equally to each citizen, to the amount of 10 *drachmae*[12] (about half a month's income for an artisan).

---

[10] For further analysis regarding how this was actually taking place, see our own contributions, in Kyriazis and Economou (2015) and Economou and Kyriazis (2019, 2022 forthcoming).

[11] For *triremes* and their finance, a detailed analysis is provided by Gabrielsen (1994), among others.

[12] *Drachma* (in plural, *drachmae*) was the main currency unit of the Athenian democracy and the rest of the Greek world in Classical (508–323 BC) and Hellenistic (322–146 BCE) times.

So, in this case, the binary choice under the logic of the Condorcet method would be to choose either the public good ships defense or the private good consumption. Athenians voted for defense, which became Themistocles Naval Decree (Economou et al., 2017). The ships were built and contributed decisively to the naval victory of Salamis in September 480 BC, thus saving Greece, democracy, and shaping the future of the western world (Strauss, 2004). Through this vote, the "common good" was established: It was defense, as against consumption.

We now turn to the presentation of a simple theoretical model that contrasts decision-making under direct and representative democracy and the establishment of a social welfare function.

4 Outline of the Theoretical Model

The institutional and procedural setup in representative and direct democracy differs, and this leads to different choice outcomes. In representative democracies, citizens have to choose among a limited set of alternatives, offered by the political parties participating in the elections. Each party, through its program, offers its estimation of the "common good" in an aggregation of all policy options, such as economic measures (taxation, etc.), education, public health, public safety, immigration, defense, etc., in the form of a "practical" welfare social function. So, there are as many proposals on welfare functions, as the number of parties participating in the elections.

The main problems that arise here are the following: First, we have a top-down offer of policy choices (not like in Arrow's theorem) to be seen as individual preferences, and, second, the citizens are offered bundles out of which they have to choose. They do not have the possibility, say, to choose one option (e.g., the education proposal of party A) and at the same time to choose another option contained in a different proposed social welfare function (e.g., the defense proposal of party B or the agricultural policy of party C, etc.). Thus, what the citizens do is to set a ranking to the alternatives within each proposed social welfare function and choose the one that maximizes their utility. The social welfare function that gets the majority of voters is the chosen one, and the party that proposed it gets elected. The type of choice corresponds more or less to the *Borda Rule*[13] of ranking. But if each citizen could unbundle the choices, e.g., choose the preferred alternative for each issue out of the different functions offered, this outcome would be for him superior in terms of utility maximization at the personal level. This again would apply for almost

---

[13] The *Borda Rule* is used in elections and decision-making in various contemporary situations. Each candidate is given a number of points, and once all votes have been counted, the option with the most points is considered the best and therefore the winner. The *Borda Rule* is intended to be able to choose different options and candidates, rather than the option that is preferred by the majority (Darmann & Klamler, 2019).

all citizens.[14] Thus, the outcome under representative democracy is inferior to a possible alternative of unbundling.

Under direct democracy procedures and practice, the situation is different. Here the citizens-voters face a disaggregation of issues (policies) and decide by voting case by case. Each voter maximizes his utility for each issue separately, choosing either defense or consumption in Themistocles' Decree, for example, as analyzed in the previous section or between generating electricity by coal, gas oil, or nuclear fuel. This happens for all policy issues. By the end of the voting procedure on all issues, the citizen would have established and revealed his preference on each of them. His individual welfare function would thus contain all his choices on the issues. In the assembly's voting procedure, a majority is required for the proposals on each issue, for example, a majority has voted for generating electricity using gas. Thus, winning proposals are established for each issue. This procedure corresponds more or less to a Condorcet rule. The last step is the integration of the winning choices (those which have gotten the majority of votes) into a single welfare function. This function reflects the "common good" as perceived by the majority of the citizens.

In the case of direct democracy, we have a bottom-up aggregation of preferences which avoids cyclicity, one of the main problems of Arrow's theorem. In concluding, what the direct democracy procedure does is to break the decisions down among its several elements (policy options on the various issues) on each of which a winning position is found. Putting these winning positions together, we end up in an overall result which represents the majority's will and the majority's perception of the "common good," since it follows the majority's judgment on each dimension of policy choice.[15]

5 Further Considerations Regarding Direct Democracy Procedures in Decision-Making

A further procedural advantage of direct democracy is that the social welfare function is open; in other words, it has an unrestricted domain. It may be enriched at any time through a new proposal by an initiator, which may reflect either a change in preferences or the perception of a new danger or opportunity, as in the cases of Themistocles and Nicophon. In modern states which implement elements of direct democracy such as in Switzerland, Uruguay, and some US and German states at the federal level, this enrichment of the choice set is done through *popular initiatives*

---

[14]The exception would be citizens who would choose, even if they have the possibility of unbundling, only the choices on the various issues, of one party, and, for example, on ideological grounds.

[15]Fishkin (2011, p. 7) points out for *deliberative democracy* that it breaks the voting cycle and that the function is single peaked. This holds even more for direct democracy.

that lead, if they receive a sufficient number of signatures,[16] to a referendum, with a binding result, concerning also monetary or fiscal issues, as was the case in Classical Athens.

The most characteristic example of a modern state which practices direct democratic procedures in decision-making both at the federal and at each state's level (we mean the *cantons*) is Switzerland where a series of referendums take place every year. The following three referenda cases on economic issues provide only a small proof of this.[17]

Firstly, an *initiative* was voted upon (and rejected) concerning the decision of the governor of the Swiss National Bank to increase gold reserves. In this referendum that took place on November 30, 2014, the result was no (78% voted against expanding central bank gold reserves to 20% of central bank assets). If a yes vote had passed, then the Swiss National Bank (SNB) (i) would have been obliged to hold at least a fifth of its assets in gold within 5 years, (ii) would have been required to repatriate all Swiss gold held abroad, and (iii) would have been banned from selling any of its gold holdings in the future.[18] Under the democratic procedures' perspective here, the initiative proposed that the central bank should not have done this without asking the citizens (to whom ultimately the gold belonged) and it should buy it back.

Secondly, in a recent referendum held on March 4, 2018, 84% of the Swiss citizens approved a federal decree on the new *Financial Regulation 2021*, which would extend the right of the federal government to levy VAT and direct federal tax until 2035.[19]

Thirdly, in a characteristic case, on June 10, 2018, Swiss citizens, through a referendum known as the *Vollgeld*, decided that they do not wish to give the Swiss National Bank the sole authority to create money (75.7% of the voters rejected the initiative proposal as against only 24.28% who voted to grant that authority).[20] The "sovereign money" initiative, if having been accepted, could have led to a radical overhaul of the Swiss financial system. The initiative called on the central bank to take total control of money supply, which would have imposed much tighter controls on commercial bank lending. The fact that the initiative was defeated in the vote,

---

[16] Usually, 8–10% of those who have voted for the same level (national, state-canton, county city) at the previous elections.

[17] For direct democratic procedures in Switzerland, see, among others, Feld and Savioz (1997), Feld et al. (2010), and our own Economou and Kyriazis (2019, Chapter 11).

[18] https://www.forbes.com/sites/jonhartley/2014/11/30/swiss-voters-reject-increasing-gold-reserves-in-referendum/#54bed76e4553 and https://www.ccn.com/voters-fail-to-pass-swiss-gold-reserves-referendum/.

https://snbchf.com/swissgold/referendum/swiss-gold-referendum-latest-news/.

[19] https://www.admin.ch/gov/de/start/dokumentation/abstimmungen/20180304.html.

[20] https://www.admin.ch/gov/fr/accueil/documentation/votations/20180610/initiativemonnaie-pleine.html.

with 76% of voters rejecting, means that three out of four of the Swiss people are in favor of alternative money issuing practices, such as cryptocurrencies.[21]

Direct democracy relies upon a person's capacity to be convinced by national argument and to lay aside particular and personal interests in deference to overall fairness and the common interest of the collectivity. Deliberation and argumentation in front of the assembly, by offering rational arguments and disseminating a common base of information, had exactly this purpose, as in the case of Themistocles Naval Decree. The discussion generated common knowledge (as in that case, the danger of Persian aggression), and the necessary means to combat it. Discussion and direct decision-making may also create common norms and values.

The institutional and procedural setup of direct democracy was a good way of establishing trust and a "common purpose," or even a sense of belonging and common destiny, which was very strong among Ancient Athenians and the other Greek democratic city-states and federations.[22] This sense of belonging is persuasively analyzed and described by Manville and Ober (2003) who characterize Athens as a "company of citizens" because it expanded and enhanced this meaning of "belonging" to a community—making membership available, real, practical, and emotionally satisfying. On pages 82–83, they explain why the Athenian political model of direct participation was successful. They write:

> Cleisthenes and his colleagues transformed the existing status of "being an Athenian." They gave it deeper meaning, with language and passionate rhetoric celebrating the values of freedom and equality. They also made citizenship more reliable by formalising the procedure of membership enrollment and certification........Now it was not some elite ruler but your fellow citizens as a community who guaranteed for you your status of citizenship. You became a citizen through a vote by the citizens, and no one but your fellow citizens could ever take citizenship away from you. The formalization of that status created a new and stronger sense of individual security. That in turn allowed for the growth of the deep mutual trust on which a true company of citizens must be built.

Using modern language, direct democracy transformed politics in a cooperation and coordination game. So, Buchanan's emphasis of the role of public discussion in the formation of preferences and values is fully pertinent for direct democracy (Buchanan, 1954a, b) as recognized also by Knight ([1947], 1982, p. 280). The institutional setup helps participants, as stated above, gain knowledge on the initiators' character and capabilities (see also Kyriazis and Economou (2015) and Economou and Kyriazis (2019, 2022) on this). Initiators who were proven continuously wrong or promise unattainable outcomes (as by populist leaders in some of today's countries) would be mistrusted, becoming political outcasts, or, to use metaphorically Akerlof's (1970) terminology, are recognized as "political

---

[21] https://country.eiu.com/article.aspx?articleid=436814627&Country=Switzerland&topic=Politics&subtopic=Forecast&subsubtopic=Election+watch.
https://www.swissinfo.ch/eng/vote-june-10%2D%2D2018_swiss-unlikely-to-buy%2D%2Dsovereign-money%2D%2Dproposal-/44174184.

[22] For federalism in Ancient Greece, see, among others, Economou et al. (2015) and Economou (2020).

lemons."[23] The production of informed, considered opinion, as generated through the working of direct democracy, is a public good itself, as Fishkin (2011, p. 7) argues for *deliberative democracy*.

At the beginning of this third decade of the twenty-first century, it appears that democracy's prestige worldwide faces many and strong challenges for a variety of different reasons (Levitsky & Ziblatt, 2018). We believe that what is of major importance is the legitimization of democracy itself in the eyes of the people themselves. In other words, what is important is to achieve the people's willingness to "defend the system" according to Weingast (1997). Based on the above analysis as well as the writings of authors such as Barber (2003) and Fishkin (2011), we believe that this can happen if the institutional setup of modern democracy favors participatory procedures in decision-making. Three important elements toward this direction are *citizens' initiatives*, *referendums*, and the *recall* procedure.[24]

A *citizens' initiative* is a specific procedure for submitting proposals to the state for adopting specific laws addressing social and other local, regional, or national issues. A *referendum* is the practice of submitting to popular vote a measure proposed by a legislative body or by popular initiative. In other words, it is a vote in which all the people in a country, a region, or a municipality are asked to give their opinion about or decide on an important political or social question.

A citizens' *recall* is practiced in Switzerland and more and more states of the USA and Canada, in Bavaria in Germany, and in various forms that is included in the constitutions of Latvia, Peru, Uruguay, the Philippines, Taiwan, Ukraine, etc. It refers to a procedure whereby an elected representative, a municipal councilmember, school board officer, mayor, congressional representative, or even a state governor, if shown to be performing inadequately (incompetent, corrupt, unjust, etc.), can be removed from office before the end of the individual's term. *Recalls*, which are initiated when sufficient voters sign a petition, have a history dating back to ancient Athenian democracy (Economou and Kyriazis 2019).

The process begins with an *initiative* whereby any citizen, or group thereof, gathers signatures to petition. If a minimum number is collected (usually 8–10% of the number of voters in the last elections), then it is put to a vote, and if it receives a majority, the individual is removed from office. In a wider context, this procedure favors transparency in decision-making regarding the issue of achieving good administration by elected magistrates and civil servants (Cronin, 1999; Economou & Kyriazis, 2019).

---

[23] "Lemons" are used cars of bad quality in Akerlof's paper.

[24] In Economou and Kyriazis (2019, chapter 11) we analyze in detail various cases of citizen's initiatives, referendums worldwide and the recall procedure in the US. A detailed analysis with an analytical catalogue of such cases and their outcome exceeds the scope of this essay.

6 Conclusion

We have argued that under the institutional procedural setup of direct democracy, a solution to Arrow's *possibility theorem* may be found. This is a fundamental advantage of direct versus representative democracy, which is a crucial addition to its other's advantages. In more recent decades, numerous studies, such as those of Matsusaka (2005a, b), Blume et al. (2009), Feld et al. (2010), LeDuc (2011), and Blume and Voigt (2012), using data from isolated incidences of direct democracy in the USA, Switzerland, and the rest of the world, have assessed the advantages of direct in comparison to those of representative democracy and have shown the superiority of the former over the latter in various key economic issues.

Direct democracy is potentially a "school of public spirit," as Pericles recognized implicitly when in the *Funeral Oration* (Thucydides, 1910) he argued that Athens (a direct democracy, in contrast to other city-states like Sparta) was the "school of Greece" (Thuc. *History* 2.41). He wrote that:

> In short, I say that as a city we are the school of Hellas; while I doubt if the world can produce a man, who where he has only himself to depend upon, is equal to so many emergencies, and graced by so happy a versatility as the Athenian.

Further, direct democracy solves the principal-agent problem, since decision-makers are the principals themselves.[25] We accept the following quote of Kant (2012, p. 46):

> In the kingdom of ends, everything has either a price, or a dignity. What has a price can be replaced with something else, as its equivalent, whereas what is elevated above any price, and hence allows of an equivalent, has a dignity.

Direct democracy provides persons with the dignity to decide for themselves on the issues that concern them.

References

Achen, C. H., & Bartels, L. M. (2017). *Democracy for realists. Why elections do not produce responsive dovernment*. Princeton University Press.
Akerlof, G. A. (1970). The market for "lemons": Quality uncertainty and the market mechanism. *The Quarterly Journal of Economics, 84*(3), 488–500.
Akerlof, G. A., & Dickens, W. T. (1982). The economic consequences of cognitive dissonance. *The American Economic Review, 72*(3), 307–319.
Arrow, K. J. ([1951], 1963). *Social choice and individual values*. New York: Wiley.
Arrow, K. J. (1999). Amartya K. Sen's contributions to the study of Social Welfare. *The Scandinavian Journal of Economics, 101*(2), 163–172.
Barber, B. R. (2003). *Strong democracy: Participatory politics for a New Age*. MacMillan Press.
Bitros, G. C., Economou, E. M. L., & Kyriazis, N. C. (2020). *Democracy and money. Lessons for today from Athens in Classical times*. Routledge.

---

[25] For a discussion of shortcomings of representative democracy, see Tirole (2017, pp. 162, 169).

Blume, L., & Voigt, S. (2012). Institutional details matter - More economic effects of direct democracy. *Economics of Governance, 13*, 287–310.
Blume, L. J., Muller, J., & Voigt, S. (2009). The economic effects of direct democrat – A first Global Assessment. *Public Choice, 140*, 431–461.
Buchanan, J. (1954a). Social choice, democracy and free markets. *Journal of Political Economy, 62*, 114–123.
Buchanan, J. (1954b). Individual choice in voting and the market. *Journal of Political Economy, 62*(3), 114–123.
Cronin, E. T. (1999). *Direct democracy. The politics of initiative, referendum, and recall*. Harvard University Press.
Darmann, A., & Klamler, C. (2019). Using the Borda rule for ranking sets of objects. *Social Choice and Welfare, 53*, 399–414.
Economou, E. M. L. (2020). *The Achaean federation in Ancient Greece. History, political and economic organization, warfare and strategy*. Springer Verlag.
Economou, E. M. L., & Kyriazis, N. C. (2019). *Democracy and economy. An inseparable relationship since ancient times to today*. Cambridge Scholars Publishing.
Economou, E. M. L., & Kyriazis, N. C. (2022). The emergence of democracy: A behavioural perspective. In E. M. L. Economou, N. C. Kyriazis, & A. Platias (Eds.), *Democracy and Salamis. 2500 years after the battle that saved Greece and the Western World*. Springer Verlag.
Economou, E. M. L., Kyriazis, N., & Metaxas, T. (2015). The institutional and economic foundations of regional proto-federations. *Economics of Governance, 16*(3), 251–271.
Economou, E. M. L., Kyriazis, N. C., & Kyriazis, N. A. (2021a). Money decentralization under direct democracy procedures. The case of Classical Athens. *Journal of Risk and Financial Management, 14*(1), 30. https://doi.org/10.3390/jrfm14010030
Economou, E. M. L., Kyriazis, N. C., & Kyriazis, N. A. (2021b). Managing financial risk while performing international commercial transactions. Intertemporal lessons from Athens in Classical times. *Journal of Risk and Financial Management, 14*(11), 509. https://doi.org/10.3390/jrfm14110509
Economou, E. M. L., Kyriazis, N. C., & Metaxas, T. (2017). Athenians, Californians and modern Greeks: A comparative analysis of choice under direct democratic procedures. *Homo Oeconomicus, 34*, 47–65.
Feld, P. L., Kirchgässner, G., & Fischer, A. V. J. (2010). The effect of direct democracy on income redistribution: Evidence for Switzerland. *Economic Inquiry, 48*(4), 817–840.
Feld, P. L., & Savioz, M. R. (1997). Direct democracy matters for economic performance: An empirical investigation. *Kyklos, 50*, 507–538.
Figueira, T. J. (1998). *The power of money: Coinage and politics in the Athenian Empire*. University of Pensylvania Press.
Fishkin, J. S. (2011). *When the people speak: Deliberative democracy and public consultation*. Oxford University Press.
Gabrielsen, V. (1994). *Financing the Athenian fleet: Public taxation and social relations*. John Hopkins University Press.
Halkos, G., & Kyriazis, N. (2010). The Athenian economy in the Age of Demosthenes. *European Journal of Law and Economics, 29*, 255–277.
Halkos, G., Kyriazis, N. C., & Economou, E. M. L. (2021). Plato as a game theorist towards an international trade policy. *Journal of Risk and Financial Management, 14*, 115. https://doi.org/10.3390/jrfm14030115
Kant, I. (2012). *Groundwork of the metaphysics of morals*. Cambridge University Press.
Knight, F. ([1947] 1982). *Freedom and reform: Essays in economic and social philosophy*. Indianapolis: Harper and Liberty Publishers.
Kyriazis, N. C., & Economou, E. M. L. (2015). Macroculture, sports and democracy in Classical Greece. *European Journal of Law and Economics, 40*, 431–455.

Kyriazis, N. C., & Zouboulakis, M. (2004). Democracy, sea power and institutional change: An economic analysis of the Athenian naval law. *European Journal of Law and Economics, 17*, 117–132.

LeDuc, L. (2011). Electoral reform and direct democracy in Canada: When citizens become involved. *West European Politics, 34*(3), 551–567.

Levitsky, S., & Ziblatt, D. (2018). *How Democracies Die*. Crown.

Manville, B., & Ober, J. (2003). *The company of citizens. What the world's first democracy teaches leaders about creating great organizations*. Harvard Business Review Press.

Matsusaka, G. J. (2005a). Direct democracy works. *Journal of Economic Perspectives, 19*, 185–206.

Matsusaka, G. J. (2005b). The eclipse of legislatures: Direct democracy in the 21st century. *Public Choice, 124*, 157–177.

Neblo, M. A. (2015). *Deliberative democracy between theory and practice*. Cambridge University Press.

Ober, J. (2008). *Democracy and knowledge. Innovation and learning in Classical Athens*. Princeton University Press.

Ober, J. (2017). *Demopolis: Democracy before liberalism in theory and practice*. Cambridge University Press.

Sen, A. (1977). Rational fools: A critique of the behavioral foundations of economic theory. *Philosophy & Public Affairs, 6*(4), 317–344.

Sen, A. (1995). Rationality and social choice. *The American Economic Review, 85*(1), 1–24.

Sen, A. (1999). The possibility of social choice. *The American Economic Review, 89*(3), 349–378.

Sen, A. (2006). Reason, freedom and well-being. *Utilitas, 18*(1), 80–96.

Simon, H. A. (1991). Bounded rationality and organizational learning. *Organisation Science, 2*(1), 125–134.

Simon, H. A. (1978). Rationality as a process and a product of thought. *American Economic Review, 68*, 1–16.

Simon, H. A. (1982). *Models of bounded rationality* (Vols. 1 and 2). Cambridge, MA: MIT Press.

Stiglitz, J. E., & Weiss, A. (1982). Asymmetric information in credit markets and its implications for macro-economics. *Oxford Economic Papers, New Series, 44*(4), 694–724.

Strauss, B. (2004). *The Battle of Salamis: The naval encounter that saved Greece-and western civilization*. Simon and Schuster.

Thorley, J. (1996). *Athenian democracy*. Routledge.

Thucydides. (1910). *The Peloponnesian War*. London, J. M. Dent; New York, E. P. Dutton. The Perseus Digital Library.

Tirole, J. (2017). *Economics for the common good*. Princeton University Press.

Tridimas, G. (2013). Homo Oeconomicus in ancient Athens: Silver bonanza and the choice to build a navy. *Homo Oeconomicus, 30*(4), 435–458.

Weingast, B. R. (1997). The political foundations of democracy and the rule of law. *The American Political Science Review, 91*(2), 254–263.

Emmanouil M. L. Economou is currently an Adjunct Assistant Professor at the Department of Economics, University of Thessaly (Greece). He is a member of the Laboratory of Economic Policy and Strategic Planning (L.E.P.S.PLAN) at the same. He is also a Member of the Laboratory of Intelligence and Cyber-Security, Department of International and European Studies, University of Piraeus (Greece). His research focuses on Economic History, Institutional Economics, International Political Economy, and Defense Economics. He is an author of eight books (three in English and five in Greek) published in acclaimed publishing houses such as Springer, Routledge, and Cambridge Scholars Publishing.

He has contributed to the international academic bibliography with 38 papers in peer review quality academic journals, such as the *Journal of Institutional Economics* (2); *Defence and Peace Economics* (2); *Sustainability, European Journal of Law and Economics*, and *Journal of Risk and*

Financial Management (3); *Peace Economics, Peace Science and Public Policy* (2); *European Journal of Law and Economics, Economics of Governance, Evolutionary and Institutional Economics Review*, and *Homo Oeconomicus*; etc.

He has contributed to the international academic bibliography with 24 papers in English and Greek collective volumes. Furthermore, he has published 79 papers as Discussion Papers (64 in English, in the IDEAS RePec—Munich International Library and 15 as "ΚΟΙΔΑ" Discussion papers published by the Laboratory of Economic Policy and Strategic Planning (ERGOPOLIS) of the Department of Economics, University of Thessaly, in Greek). He has participated in 42 International and Greek conferences.

Nicholas C. Kyriazis combines academic and business experience. He took his diploma and PhD degree in economics in Bonn University in Germany in 1979 and has been a visiting Professor at Harvard University with a Fulbright grant and a visiting Professor at Trier University. He is Professor Emeritus at the Department of Economics, University of Thessaly, Greece, where he also served as a Dean during the period of 2013–2015. He has published 14 academic books in English or Greek language, 60 papers in international-referred academic journals such as the *European Journal of Law and Economics* and the *Journal of Institutional Economics*, and 26 papers in book chapters (collective volumes).

In 2005, the President of the French Republic honored him with the France's highest decoration, the Knight of the Legion of Honour (*Chevalier de la Legion d'Honneur*) for his contribution to European integration and the preparation for the EMU as a member of the Delors-Moreau committee. He has also published many articles in journals for a wider audience and articles in the Greek press, for economic, political, and defense issues. Previous business positions he held include (among others) Directorate General for Research of the European Parliament, Advisor to the government of the National Bank of Greece, Advisor to the Minister of Finance, and Advisor to the Minister of Defense since 1998, and he has contributed as one of the major consultants for the Greek Command, Control, Communications, Computers and Military intelligence (C4I). He is currently a Vice-Chairman of the Quality Assessment Committee of the Legislative Drafting Process of the Hellenic Parliament.

Part IV
Intertemporal Aspects of Democracy Regarding Ancient and Modern Greece and the World

Democracy in Ancient and Modern Times: About the Relevancy of the Ancient Greek Experience for Our Own Societies

Guy Féaux de la Croix

Abstract The paper argues that the Battle of Salamis was a victory for freedom and self-determination which paved the way for democracy to evolve in classical times. It directly addresses the question of its relevancy for our own times. The paper reviews the literature for relevancy studies and builds towards a normative interpretation of Athenian democracy. It raises a series of key intertemporal issues, such as the relationship between freedom and democracy and freedom and equality. It further refers to present-day democratic worries in the light of the ancient experience: Modern democracies show increasing inequality and a degeneration of formal democracy towards de facto oligarchy. Elites seem discredited. In addition to the above, the paper raises a series of further pivotal issues such as (i) the lack of political competence of citizens necessary for participation, (ii) a democracy of populism and of group interests rather than one of democratic values, (iii) the effectiveness of democracy in securing a sustainable future for its people and (iv) quintessential problems that plague modern democracies, such as a lack of cultural education, which could prove to be the Achilles heel of our democracies. The paper concludes that democracy still has value in itself and that more philosophizing is needed, issuing a serious commandment to think clearly and act virtuously. If we prove ready to learn from the classical experience it might help us make the modern world a better place.

Keywords Ancient Greek democracy · Modern democracy · Freedom and equality · Inequality · Populism · Lessons from classical experience · Relevancy of history · Historical relevanced

---

G. Féaux de la Croix (✉)
University of Thessaly, Department of Economics, Volos, Greece

Cologne Chamber of Lawyers, Cologne, Germany

1 Celebrate Battles?

In the twentieth century, we have grown weary of celebrating battles. The Salamis 2500 anniversary, however, is worthy of a retrospective even from a very peace-loving standpoint: The victory of the Greeks was not only a turning point in a defensive war against an imperialist superpower but also had far-reaching consequences for the stabilization and deepening of the then still very young Athenian democracy.

For many anniversary laudators, the matter was obvious, and I have in fact often enough written and spoken about it in similar terms: Salamis was a victory for freedom. It opened the way for democracy to evolve in the classical age. It was a glorious natal hour of the western world.[1] However, not a few have gone beyond this in claiming that, for them, Salamis was the first great proof of Western supremacy.

For my part, I surely would not wish this retrospective to be understood in such a suprematist context. We should rise to the occasion in a rational and critical reflection. Looking back at ancient victories only appears truly legitimate if we consider the consequences they had in history and contemplate what the triumph of the Greeks of 480 BC still means for us today.

2 "Relevancy Studies"

Is it not precisely that what should interest us about history, namely, its relevancy for our own times? Should we not take advantage of the opportunity history represents to learn something from the origins of democracy, which so many now see in serious danger? In fact, "relevancy studies" seems a foreign word to the academic world of "classics", surely in the eyes of our traditional German "Altertumswissenschaften". In any case there is no tradition in Germany that would be anywhere near comparable to the Anglo-Saxon school of "applied classics", as I would phrase it, studies into the relevancy of the ancient experience.

In the twentieth century, a first great step into the direction of relevancy studies was taken when R.W. Livingstone ([1921], 1928) edited his "Legacy of Greece" with its 12 articles ranging from the religion of the ancients to their architecture. Gilbert Murray's introduction "The Value of Greece to the Future of the World" set the tone for the work's ambition to understand Greek antiquity as an obligatory and, moreover, highly useful legacy.

Moses Finley, who studied law in the United States, then emigrated to Great Britain in the course of the McCarthyist persecutions, picked up the thread again in Cambridge, when in 1979 he published a volume of essays entitled "The Legacy of

---

[1] Cf. for such an understanding of the event the title of Barry Strauss' book: *The Battle of Salamis: The Naval Encounter That Saved Greece and Western Civilization*, New York: Simon & Schuster, 2004.

Greece, A New Appraisal" (Finley, 1984). He concluded his own essay with the sentence: "It is in the field of political theory, not of institutions, that one must look for a possible legacy". He was thus moving in the mainstream of classical studies, which have predominantly declared the Athenian democracy to be an *aliud* towards our modern democracy.

In Cambridge, the relay has now been taken over by Paul Cartledge (2016), who recently published a number of earlier works in his volume *Democracy, a Life*. For Cartledge, ancient democracy is of great relevance for our own time, only that in his studies this relevance remains a general postulate stopping well short of relating the ancient experience in concrete terms to our present-day challenges.

Bleicken (1995, p. 682), in his German-language standard work on the Athenian democracy, confirms this deficit that can be ascertained especially in German classical studies in saying: "I would not know of any overall judgement on Athenian democracy from a German historian of the post-war period which deserved the name".[2]

Bleicken (1995, p. 680) traces this aversion much further back into the German intellectual tradition, for example, to Jacob Burckhardt (1819–1897), whose remarks on Athenian democracy testify to an "extreme distance and sharpest criticism". He sees "the deeper cause of the inner rejection by so many in their liberal outlook on the world, in which the main focus was on the right to freedom". Commenting on the works of Robert von Pöhlmann (1852–1914), in his times considered the "Nestor" of the German classical scholars, Bleicken writes:

> He never got tired of inventing new derogatory expressions for the ancient democracy like for example 'mob rule', 'mass majority', 'massism', a 'dilettant form of government, etc.

Canfora (2007, p. 28) characterizes the Hungarian historian Julius Schvarcz as being another bitter critic of the Athenian democracy, which went hand in hand with the latter's belief in the supremacy of the "white human race": "The mission of the white human race (sic) is: To bring the whole surface of the globe under the rule of their culture".[3]

Werner Conze (1979, p. 891f) also made it clear that from the time the German Empire was founded, the discrediting of Athenian democracy was paired with a general rejection of the democratic idea:

> In the sixties and seventies (of the 19th century) when the founding of the empire was prepared, fought for and completed, the 'party' of the democrats (in its various forms and organizations) was defeated and victory fell to those who looked at 'democracy' disdainfully from the traditional viewpoint of the aristocrats or Bourgeois liberalism. Such attitudes marked the prevailing German understanding of 'democracy'.

In the historiography of the nineteenth and early twentieth century, the Athenians and their "democracy" were by no means the glamorous model with which we

---

[2] Bleicken p. 682.
[3] Quoted in Luciano Canfora, Eine kurze Geschichte der Demokratie, 4th ed., Cologne 2007, p. 28, further referring to Julius Schvarcz, Die Demokratie, Leipzig 1876, p. 23.

ourselves grew up. According to Bleicken, the condemnation of Athenian democracy is still echoed by the "incomparable serenity" which he makes out to be the principal attitude of classical scholars: "One could openly praise democracy, but they shy away from it, at least in Germany. The judgments of the past remain all too harsh".

This abstinence will in the present study be contrasted with a different approach, a normative and "subsumptive" approach: In a reversal of the usual and chronological historiography, in the first step, problem areas of our present-day democracy will be identified, in order to only then look to which experiences and institutions of antiquity these phenomena may be related.

Incidentally, this is not the author's first attempt at a normative interpretation of the Athenian democracy: 10 years ago he had the honour of formulating the "Marathon 2500 Declaration – For the Renewal of Democracy – Lessons from the Classical Athenian Experience".[4]

3   Origins and Leitmotifs

3.1   *How Greek Is Our Democratic Identity?*

The concept of identity, like few other terms, comes along with a number of semantic problems. We see it in the current debates about our identity and "identitarian" sectarianism, in the anti-culture of tribalism. Linguists refer to such a term as an "omnibus", which everyone can get into with their suitcase full of ideas and ideologies. If we were to understand identity in the sense of the totality of our properties including our ethnic and cultural origins and if we continue to assume that our origin actually is a property of personal and communal relevancy, then this will lead us to the question of whether we would be who we are without the Salamis victory of the Greeks over the Persians.

We could corroborate the thesis "without Salamis no democracy" by stating that democracy has been an absolute exception against the rule throughout the long history of humankind. In a universe of undemocratic forms of government, Athenian democracy was a lonely blue planet. At least that is how we learnt it. The Renaissance and the Enlightenment, i.e. the rediscovery of the ancient heritage and its philosophical, scientific and ultimately political consequences, indeed speak in favour of the causal and historical context.

---

[4]Guy Féaux de la Croix (2010), "Introduction", in: The Marathon 2500 Declaration – For a Renewal of Democracy: Lessons from the Classical Athenian Experience, Athens 2010. In Greek and English with its 21 articles, published by Psychogios Ed., Athens, p. 18:

> In this declaration we seek to extrapolate, from the experience of the Marathon Battle and the Classical Athenian democracy, a number of suggestions and guide-lines which might be helpful in rethinking and reforming our democracies, not least in the light of certain fallacies of our political systems and of the challenges which democracy faces in the 21st century.

On closer inspection, the ancient democratic polis turns out to be far less of a model of modern democracy than we are generally inclined to assume. In the French Revolution, a short, almost obsessive "flirt" of the Jacobins with the polis of the ancient Athenians[5] soon gave way to an unmasking of the ideal by the Thermidorians and was, a little later, exposed to the fundamental criticism of both liberals and socialists.

Horrified by the chilling experience of the revolutionary "terreur", Immanuel Kant, otherwise an early advocate of parliamentary democracy, decidedly turned against democracy in the classical Greek sense (Mittermaier & Meinhard, 2013, p. 112f). Marx and Engels saw the terror of the French Revolution as the climax of the endeavour to re-instate the "ancient democracy" (Marx-Engels, 1959, p. 129 f). In the historical development, the French Revolution ended in Bonaparte's "Empire", with an orientation predominantly on the Roman res publica, which Bleicken rightly describes as the most successful and longest-lasting oligarchy in world history.

Bleicken explained the undemocratic mainstream of classical studies in the nineteenth century as a traumatic reaction to the excesses of the French Revolution. We already pointed to the works on Greece by Jacob Burckhardt (1819–1897) (Burckhardt, 1982) and Robert von Pöhlmann (1852–1914) (von Pöhlmann, 1911) as being examples of this restaurative, anti-democratic school of thought. In truth, was it not a great misunderstanding of the nineteenth-century bourgeoisie to believe that the French Revolution was a democratic event when in reality it was an oligarchic one?

Set against present-day characterization of the ancient Greek polis as being the mould of modern democracy, more common today, we must not ignore the radical criticism of this claim by a school of thought critical of Euro-centrism. The most prominent protagonist of this line of thinking seems Amartya Sen, the Indian Nobel Prize laureate for economics. Sen asserts that even in antiquity, the Greek polis was by no means the only civilization based on rational and consensual political decision-making (Sen, 1999). Sen argues that the Greek heritage lived on in Asian societies that a Eurocentrist history of democracy ignores egalitarian approaches in other civilizations he reminds us that India, for example, is by far the largest democracy and that altogether intellectual legacies of the great Asian nations are being neglected.

If we take a closer look at the beginning of historiography and the first mentions of the democratic idea, we find in Herodotus himself an indication that democracy as a form of government was invented by the Persians before Cleisthenes.[6] David Asheri and, following him, Lucian Canfora interpret it in such a way that Herodotus

---

[5]Canfora (2007, pp. 69, 354) however points out: "The term 'democracy' rarely appeared in the political vocabulary of the French revolution". The bone of contention was especially the perception that the freedom of the Athenians had been founded on the grounds of their slavery system, which in turn hardly irritated the American founding fathers.

[6]Herodotus ([1910] 1997, III pp. 80–83); cf. also Canfora (2007, p. 353).

considered the Greek belief that democracy was their invention a prejudice (Canfora, 2007, p. 21f). Also Canfora quotes Demosthenes as saying that it was not the Persians but the Macedonians who should be seen as the real enemies of free Athens, in collusion with the anti-democratic partisans inside the city.[7] "According to what we know", writes Paul Nolte (2012, p. 33f):

> classical democracy was not just a Greek special case. In relation to other city-states (the poleis), however, the case of Athens stands out quite clearly. This is not to deny the interweaving of Athens with other factors in the Mediterranean-West Asian cultural context. ... The Greeks, the Athenians invented democracy. But they did not do so as part of the 'West', let alone on a higher mission.

Another counter-thesis to the pivotal model interpretation of ancient Greek democracy would then be that democracy would have come about regardless of the classical mould, albeit possibly more slowly and differently and elsewhere. From this other point of view, democracy would appear to be a historical necessity. In their "historical materialism", Marx and Engels declared capitalism to be an inevitable development, if only as a transitional stage on the way to the equally inevitable stages of socialism and finally communism. Much more obvious, because history has confirmed it as a model of success, as a form of government to which the vast majority of modern states feel committed, at least officially, we could speak of democracy as being a 'historical necessity'. For a modern democracy, there is no alternative to the capitalist market economy, writes Robert Dahl (2006, p. 83). Vice versa? At this point we discover something like a "democratic materialism" of history.

There seems to be a hen-and-egg relationship between the two, democracy and capitalism. If our present-day constitutions result from the evolutionary force of a "democratic materialism", this would suggest that democracy would have taken its course regardless of an ancient Greek ancestry.

If we look at the classical epoch as a whole, it is a testimony to the changeability of collective identity, to its development in many steps, partly revolutionary, but mostly evolutionary. Evolution and revolution reside in the collective will to change a status quo identity, to develop it beyond its status quo and to finally adopt a different identity. In the reactionary case, this may well mean to revert to former identities.

May this suffice to recognize that identity is not confined to static tradition but also to understand it as a dynamic variable, especially in democracy. Identity and the formation of it is a creative, political task. It may help modern societies understand identity as being a voluntaristic concept. We are not fettered to who we are, but free to become who we want to be. In limits.

---

[7] Canfora (2007, p. 22) referring to Demosthenes (*Philippic* 4, 33).

3.2 Democratic Origins: Why in Greece?

Why did democracy flourish in ancient Greece and not in other regions of the world? Why in Greece? A never-ending question, it seems. Why there and not elsewhere? Was the idea of freedom perhaps engrained in the blood of the Hellenic peoples who immigrated from the north? That would be a downright ethnic, if not to say racist answer to the question of "why in Hellas", and an improbable one.

Sometimes it has been considered whether the whole Greek culture of contemplation, reason, knowledge and intellect resulted from the Athenian society of slave-owners, from their "freedom" to devote themselves to the time-consuming business of politics, free from everyday chores (Pfetsch, 2003, p. 44).

Democracy is a result of slavery, what a bleak picture of the beginnings of democracy. It does not, however, seem to me a convincing explanation for the classical and democratic development especially in Hellas:

Firstly recent studies, but also classical sources, for example, Xenophon, confirm that the vast majority of the Athenians were working people, sometimes alongside a trusted slave. They were surely not a leisure class like the Victorian gentry or American landowners in the nineteenth-century democracies. Secondly, slavery was by no means a unique feature of the Greek civilization. In the Mediterranean area and in the Middle East, it was the norm. Since nowhere else slavery resulted in a democratic evolution, we will do well in looking for other factors to explain why democracy took root in Greece and in Greece only.

Rather than looking for its roots in the character of one particular people, it seems the nature of the country which favoured its development. A topographical explanation would, for example, argue that the freedom of the human individual characterizes the culture of island peoples as well as that of mountain dwellers. Whoever can easily escape from tyranny, with the boat on the shore to sail away to the next island, is a free person. Equally one who is able to cross over the mountain passes into the next valley.

Tight border controls are an essential requisite of tyrannies, and more than one has fallen when they could no longer keep their people from running away. Accordingly, we may assume the freedom of the islander or mountain dweller to stand at the beginning of the democratic development in ancient Hellas. With his freedom at the heart of his identity, he would have insisted, once the population agglomerated to the form of urban communities, on investing himself in the polis only under the condition of obtaining a fair and equal share in its decision-making.

3.3 Freedom and Democracy: What Was the Hen, What Was the Egg?[8]

Modern writers have regularly emphasized the freedom of the individual as being the mother soil of democracy. Between the two institutions, freedom and democracy, the hen-and-egg relationship seems to have been resolved: In the beginning there was freedom. How could a society of unfree people have constituted itself as a democracy?

Historical experience seems to confirm this evolutionary sequence: In many cases democracies emerged from acts of liberation, liberations from undemocratic and unfree systems. We see the free human as the result of the revolutionary act, whether the revolution was violent or peaceful, before the liberated then devoted themselves to the task of building a democratic society.

And still, the founding fathers of the American Revolution, were really right when they assumed that "all men by nature are equally free and independent"? The history of humankind seems to stand against it: In truth the unfree individual was the rule. Viewed in this way, freedom appears to be less of a natural human condition rather than a societal construct, an achievement, a destination and a purpose.

So, did the ancient Greeks invent and design freedom, much like James Watt invented and built the steam engine? It is probably more accurate to say that the ancient Greeks *discovered* freedom. Freedom may have resulted from an institutional Darwinism, namely, from the competition of various social models in which the alliance of the free ultimately proved to be the most efficient form of society. It proved its efficiency first and foremost in national defence; see the victories at Marathon and Salamis against the great Persian Empire during the fifth century.

In the light of the achievements of the ancient Greeks, freedom is not so much the origin as rather the purpose and destiny of the individual and one closely tied into the self-determination and well-being of his community. The great achievement of the ancient Greeks was then to recognize the intrinsic ethical quality of freedom and build their institutional system on it, one which in turn strengthened and affirmed the potential of freedom, freedom of thought, speech, the arts, freedom of science and all of this in a free competition of the free that rewarded effectiveness.

It is precisely in this field of dialectics between the self-government of the people and freedom in which we see Plato going astray, in that the great philosopher prince himself did not adequately appreciate the ground on which he stood. In terms of freedom, I consider Pericles to be a no less great philosopher; however fragmentarily the legacy of his political thought handed down to us may be but very clearly formulated in the Funeral Oration, as well as in the intellectual conceptualization of the Parthenon frieze.

---

[8]Cf. Féaux de la Croix (2018, p. 75).

3.4 Freedom and Equality: The Chicken-and-Egg Question No. 2

In the relationship between freedom and equality, too, the question arises: What preceded the other?

Already in the Iliad, in the Trojan War, we see the Danaic (Greek) princes as free equals, not as vassals. Agamemnon performs as primus inter pares only, certainly with privileges, but without the decisive prerogatives of an authoritarian "commander-in-chief". In the historical beginnings of democracy, and how it actually developed in the sixth and fifth centuries, it is not the freedom of the individual but rather the quest for equality that comes to the fore as a leitmotif.

It was not more freedom but greater equality with which Solon, by means of his reforms, sought to avert a revolt of the miserable at the beginning of the sixth century. He did so, for example, by putting an end, in his "Seisachtheia reforms", to the enslavement of debtors (hektemoroi). Adams and Savran (2002, p. 74) add that as a regulator of Athenian society, Solon also formalized its sexual mores. A fragment of the "Brothers" by playwright Philemon the Elder (c. 362–262 BC) suggests that Solon established publicly funded brothels at Athens in order to "democratize" the availability of sexual pleasure.

With or without democratized sex, at the expense however of sexual slaves, Solon's reforms all served the pacification of the poorer classes to save aristocratic privileges. One consequence of greater equality was, of course, a greater degree of freedom. In the elegy of Solon he says: "In equal manner granted I to everyone his equal rights. I made them to be free".[9]

The pacification of underprivileged classes through more and more equality, can also be used to summarize the reforms and then carried out in the classical age with which Athens gradually developed towards a democracy near our present-day understanding.

By comparison, the freedom of the individual had a rather accessory meaning only. Freedom was a fruit of equality rather than equality, in the historical development of democracy, was a fruit of freedom. At the beginning of democracy, the idea of "isonomy" rose to the status of a raison d'état. It is obvious that putting a hitherto underprivileged person on an equal footing with a free citizen also resulted in the liberation of the former. The freedom thus achieved is no contradiction to recognizing that equality was the main driving force of democratic development.

In this primordial role of equality, modern democracy corresponds in its origins, to the ancient model, the reforms first of Solon, then of Cleisthenes, and later also of Ephialtes. Democracy in modern times, possibly with the exception of the American revolution, did not result from popular uprisings, but rather from gradual concessions by the monarchies and oligarchies. In antiquity as in modern times, such acts of democratization were measures with which the privileged sought to prevent further

---

[9] As quoted by Aristoteles, *Der Staat der Athener*, s. Mittermaier and Mair (2013, p. 6f).

revolts among the lower classes. In the German Empire, Otto von Bismarck pursued his social legislation quite openly with the aim of maintaining power: "My idea was to win over the working classes, or should I say to bribe them, to perceive the state as a social institution" (von Bismarck, [1924] 1935, p. 195f).

It is with great scepticism that Robert Dahl looks to the future of political equality. He sees the reasons for decreasing political equality in the unequal distribution of income, which leads to further inequalities, above all a growing discrepancy in political resources. Basically, he sees the mechanisms of the market economy as an explosive device for political equality:

> A market economy inevitably and often causes serious damage to some citizens. Due to the unequal distribution of funds among the citizens associated with it, the capitalist market economy inevitably entails political inequality among the citizens of a democratic country.

Dahl sees further forces of erosion for political equality in the need for non-democratic international organizations, the increase in crises and conflicts that regularly shift power from the elected representatives to the executive. We shall later address the new threats to democracy which the mechanisms of digitalism amount to.

4 Present-Day Democratic Worries: In the Light of the Ancient Experience

But let us now consider even more concretely what the ancient legacy could mean vis-à-vis the challenges which our democracies face in our times. Let us methodically reverse the traditional order of proceeding in opting for a normative-subsumptive method, id est first define our current concerns and then ponder which advice we may deduce from the experience of the ancients. What then worries us in our democracies today?

For example, with no claim to being exhaustive:

- The undermining of democracy by an ever-increasing inequality
- The degeneration of formal democracy into de facto oligarchy
- The widespread revolt against discredited elites
- The lack of political competence of the individual necessary for participation
- The tension between a democracy of interests and a democracy of values
- The threats of populism
- The limits of popular rule
- The defence of democracy
- Digitalism as being a threat rather than an opportunity
- The capacity of democracies to guard the peace
- The effectiveness of democracy in securing people a sustainable future
- The ethical qualities of democracy

4.1 Democracy: An Elitist Construct?

In ancient Greece, democracy was a construct of the elites. At the beginning of the sixth century BC, the aristocrat Solon understood that a popular uprising of the impoverished masses against their oligarchic rulers could only be averted by social reforms and constitutional guarantees for all. However, the reforms did not last long enough to alleviate the anger of the poor against the urban elites. In Peisistratos the "misérables" found a populist leader whom they elevated to become a tyrant. Their revolts resulted in five decades of dictatorship under the Peisistratids.

J. Bazzigher, a Swiss nineteenth-century school master, was not the only one to grant the Peisistratidean tyranny some positive aspects when he wrote:

> Only the noble classes felt the pressure of his rule (Peisistratos'); for the people proper, his government brought about a significant economic advance. The improvement of the routes of transportation, the installation of great aqueducts still in use today. .. let Peisitratos appear to be a kindred spirit of the enlightened despotism of the 18th century. (Bazzigher, 1885, p. 11)

Quite similarly Canfora (2007, p. 18) wrote:

> In the special case of Athens, the rule of Peisistratos was in no way characterized by cruel terror and oppression (which perception corresponds to the 'rhetorical-democratic' image of the tyrant), but rather through the continuous exercise of power in formal line within a constitutional framework, notwithstanding the fact that it was always the same men (namely his relatives) who were at the head of the city.

We may credit school historian Bazzigher from the Grisons for writing it long before Adolf Hitler's autobahn. Peter Funke warns quite rightly:

> While for Solon the redistribution of political power within the citizenry was in the foreground, for the tyrants the integration of each individual citizen into the polis served exclusively to maintain their own power. Any impairment of their political supremacy was to be suppressed from the outset. (Funke, 2003, p. 12)

The ancient Athenians celebrated the murderers Aristogeiton and Harmodius as the "fathers" of democracy. In 514 BC, the couple had killed Hipparchus, the brother of tyrant Hippias, both sons of Peisistratos. In reality, the Peisistratidean rule was not ended by a tyrannicide, nor by a popular uprising, nor a coup d'état, but by an intervention of the Spartans.

It then remained to Cleisthenes, offspring of the princely Alcmaeonid family, to realize that to protect aristocratic rule against further popular uprisings, which would again result in a populist tyranny, could durably only be achieved through a new alliance with the middle and lower classes. The Cleisthenian structural reforms are too complex to describe them here in detail. It must suffice here that their aim and success were to detach the citizens from their previously preponderant group-interests and to reorientate them towards the common wealth of the entire polis.

In any case, the Cleisthenian reforms were the overture to the development of the Athenian republic, which then lasted for a period of almost 250 years, much longer if we add the survival of democratic structures under foreign domination, first Macedonian and then Roman.

In Pericles we then see an inner maturation in this great man from pursuing democratic reforms in the way of a strategic calculation, namely, to save the rule of the aristocrats by restricting their privileges and through greater participation of the people, to an inner personal conviction of the ethical value of democracy. Without such an inner democratic conviction, Pericles would hardly have been able to formulate a commitment to democracy at the end of his life, as Thucydides attributes it to him with the Funeral Oration of 429 BC.

Let us then retain as a leitmotif of Athenian democratization that democracy did not emerge from a popular uprising, but rather from a (successful) effort by the old elites to prevent such a popular uprising.

Finley (1984, p. 15) calls Athenian society a "society of unequals":

> The élite dominated all activities, political, military, athletic and cultural. The acceptance by 'the many' of this perpetual domination by 'the few' is a significant fact in classical Greek history, in Athens even during its most democratic period, from the time of Pericles to the time of Alexander the Great.

What do we make of these elitist origins for our perception of classical democracy? Is it then discredited as an elitist construct? Or are elites an indispensable constituent part of democracy? Robert Michels and with him a whole school of elite theorists in the 1920s and 1930s of the last century considered it an "iron law" that democracy inevitably leads to oligarchy[10] (Michels, 1915, p. 18).

Is that true, according to our own perception as citizens of a democracy? Do we still have elites? And what should they be like? And what are we to do if they prove themselves unworthy of their position and tasks? What could take their place? These are questions from the classical experience that lead straight to our current concerns about the destabilization of Western democracies.

4.2 Participation and Civic Competence

The tension between political participation and the competence of the citizen required to exercise his participatory rights has always been a fundamental question of the legitimacy, practicability and efficiency of the democratic form of government. The topos stands at the beginning of political science, namely, with Plato's conviction that since the normal citizen lacked the skills necessary for an efficient self-government, their fate would better be entrusted to benevolent trustees, ideally the philosophers. As the second best solution, Plato admits that if the philosophers could not become kings in his ideal state, then at least the kings should develop into being philosophers.

---

[10]Michels at first was a supporter of the German social democracy movement, until ultimately he turned to Mussolini's ideology, s. Finley (1986, p. 15).

We could, theoretically, bring Plato's philosopher state into harmony with our democracy by only electing philosophers or at least representatives with a philosophical inclination, talent and knowledge. Only that Plato denies the people the competence for such a selection and the ability to distinguish pseudo-philosophers from true philosophers. The trouble seems that for choosing the philosopher-leaders the citizen would have to be a philosopher himself or at least a philosophically inclined person.

The Athenians of antiquity regarded it as a moral duty to take part in the political life of the polis. Anyone who abstained from his civic duties, who would not commit himself to the polis, was apostrophized as an "idiot", a private person who placed himself outside the community (Simon, 1961).

Public idleness at assembly times was a punishable misdemeanor.

Admittedly, not all citizens could afford to stay away from their workplaces in order to hold state offices or to attend the estimated annually 40 days of the people's assembly sessions. They were therefore paid daily diets that roughly corresponded to the income of an average family. In any case, democratic practice in ancient Athens was a time-consuming business – and it is certainly no less today. For this reason, it is sometimes suggested in literature, as mentioned before, that the service of slaves at home or in the field was a prerequisite for a more or less equal participation in the polis' decision-making.

Philosopher Bertrand Russell interpreted the system of ancient Athens as an oligarchy and relativized the importance of the right to vote (Russell, 1978, p. 81). His criticism includes the reference to one of the most problematic circumstances of the Greek polis, which was even more apparent in the Spartan system: The polis had only thrived on the grounds that most of the life-sustaining work was foisted off on enslaved ethnic groups.

From political theory, but also from democratic practice in ancient Athens, we can record at least three qualifications for participation in governance as an interim result, namely, knowledge, virtue and, last but not least, available time. The modern answer to the "time quagmire" is the professionalization of politics, with the result of a professional political class that can hardly avoid to grow into a kind of political oligarchy.

In our modern times, more political education is regularly propagated to be the right vaccine against the emergence of anti-democratic movements. And more state funds are called for first and foremost by those who see in more political education an important professional task for themselves.

There were no institutions of political education in ancient Athens, certainly not in our categories. The teachings of the sophists (much reviled by Plato and others) served more as a rhetorical training for the next generation of politicians. From the point of view of the critics, the sophists were coaching the few to seduce the many, by the means of demagoguery. If so, they were coaches for those who could afford their high fees.

Others assume the key to the political education of the Athenians lay in their being part of a highly cultivated society. Finley (1984, p. 18) writes:

> Growing up and living in such a society was a form of education in itself. Much of what we would consider elite culture or high culture was public and therefore popular, probably not so much science and philosophy, but literature and visual arts.

Ancient Athens was a cultural democracy. The educational institution of the broad people was the theatre. The attendance of the whole electorate in the performances of both tragedies and comedies was considered essential for the community. It seemed so important that theatre-goers were eventually paid a fee for attending it. "Theorika" was the name given to these daily allowances to fulfil the "civic duty of attending the theatre".

How closely politics and theatre were interwoven in ancient Athens is also shown by the fact that every year a political leader was commissioned to organize the theatre festival and to direct individual plays. So it was for Pericles when in 472 BC, and at the age of 18 years only, he was asked to lead the choir in the premiere of "The Persians" by Aeschylus. "Liturgy" was the name given to such an honour, a civic honour implying very high expenses which in turn only the most affluent of the polis could afford. Just imagine our present-day political leaders were expected to direct a theatrical performance or conduct the choir!

The ancients recognized a broad and broadly educated middle class to be an indispensable building block of the democratic foundation. Are we not experiencing the exact opposite in that in our time it is often the language, manners and tastes of culturally disadvantaged social classes which influence the general climate and aesthetics? To only point here to the widespread practice of tattooing or the very common use of four-letter words, earlier generations would simply not have tolerated. Altogether the general denigration of good manners.

In our time, the term "educated middle class" (in German "Bildungsbürgertum", a bourgeoisie qualified by its education and culture) has sunk into being an invective. If we recognize the need for a broad cultural citizenry as being a precondition for a functioning democracy, would not this call for political mandate to include as many citizens as possible in this societal body of culture? Where do we stand in this regard? How could it work?

Let us retain from this study of ancient democracy that democratic competence would be too narrowly understood if it was limited to political education in the sense of the school curricular subject. The challenge is about a culture of democracy on a much broader basis, which includes, for example, historical knowledge and knowledge of other cultures. And beyond knowledge, a minimum of ethical convictions.

Offering solutions for this borders on squaring the circle. It seems less difficult to name developments that run counter to the ideal of a democratic cultural citizenry: the elimination of general education from school curricula, the decline of the public media and the newspapers. It all seems to undermine the foundations of our democracies.

And one more thing can be retained from ancient experience that the most valuable thing a citizen owes his community is his time.

4.3 Democracy of Values vs. Democracy of Interests

Values seem to be the vogue. Which political party would not claim to stand up for ethical values? At a closer look, the reality exposes a sore point of our democracies. In truth it seems to be taken for granted that it is the task of politicians to represent interests.

We often see an ominous confusion of particular interests on the one hand and ideal goals on the other. Mandataries with particular interests will regularly assert that what is of benefit to their clientele also serves the welfare of the whole. For this reason, when it comes to political initiatives that appeal to ethical values, one will have to look carefully to see whether the "values" really mean something more virtuous rather than their sharcholder values or the real estate values of their high-end electorate.

Such an understanding of democracy as an interplay of interests should not be taken for granted. Certainly not in the sense of the classical origins.

In ancient Athens, too, power was linked to economic interests, usually closely related to the political ambition of the patrician families. The military constitution was an example of the struggle between class interests: The upper classes favoured a territorial defence on land, in which they played a pivotal role as hoplites (heavily armed infantrymen) and the most distinguished on horseback. On the merit of their military service rendered to the polis, they could claim and justify their prominent role in politics and society.

The lower classes, on the other hand, gained recognition and influence as ship crews, especially rowers. The Sea Battle of Salamis was the first great example for it. Later, the establishment and defence of the maritime empire required the recruitment of broad strata of the people for the navy, which in turn resulted in their increased participation in political decisions.

All in all, the Athenian democratic reforms from Cleisthenes onward were designed to at least relativize the particular interests of the citizens in their political behaviour and to orient them more towards the common good. Such a refocusing on the overriding interests of the state was already the guiding principle of the Cleisthenian reforms and then returns once again as the state ideology brilliantly reflected in the philosophy of the Periclean Parthenon frieze. The classic ideal of man was that of a citizen who was actively committed to the common good and, in this sense, virtuous.

Politics serve the shaping of the future. A good democracy is one in which the competing parties are not or not predominantly guided by particular interests but by an ethical responsibility. By values. They all claim to do so. And still:

> 'Those who are wealthy thanks to their talents, their hard work or their origins should not claim that what is useful to them is also good for the whole people', so we said it in our Marathon 2500 declaration a decade ago.

Interest politics may be legitimate as long as personal advantage does not exhaust the ambition. Declaring one's own interests or the interests of one's own clientele as serving the common good is however not legitimate. To distinguish the one from the other requires an alert and problem-conscious citizen, including critical media that unveil dubious political motivations and programmes as such. In ancient Athens it was a criminal offense for an orator to deceive the people.

4.4 Popular Rule and Populism

"Democracy" is usually translated into the word "the rule of the people". The world "ruler" may, in our times, give us the creeps. In principle, we no longer want "rulers". At most the people should rule with the help of the elected. But we will not allow rulers to dominate us. And still, when the people ruled, in history, it did not per se mean something good for the world.

The people can be good or bad, virtuous or malicious. At times it seems that the benevolent individual, once he or she joins with others to form a mass, suddenly mutates into an evil-minded character. Such an evil people will then crave their executor, their populist. If the demagogue deems the people not evil enough, he will drive it further into evil.

In this way, populism can be distinguished from those democratic politicians who pay attention to the will of the people but also strive to educate them to be virtuous. The populist, on the other hand, seems to be someone who knows how to exploit the lower instincts of the people.

Attic democracy was not immune to demagogues and populists. Already in the epoch between Solon and Cleisthenes, the Peisistratids had put themselves at the head of a populist tyranny. With the help of the impoverished masses from the countryside, they had been able to establish a tyranny of the ones over the others. Understood in this way, the entire democratic effort of the Cleisthenian reforms is to be read as a safeguard against a relapse into a populist, not to say fascist tyranny, not dissimilar to the German Basic Law of 1949.

Attic democracy, a century later, experienced its greatest populist catastrophe in the so-called Sicilian Expedition of 415–413 BC. The second Peloponnesian War had lasted for more than 10 years and had led to a stalemate between Athens and its allies on the one hand and Sparta and its allies on the other. In 421 BC the deadlock resulted in an agreed armistice. Then, however, the multi-talented demagogue Alcibiades whipped the people into a naval expedition to Sicily, promising the masses that it would be the turning point to the final victory, there in the distance. For the Athenians, the Sicilian catastrophe rang the final bell to their total defeat, as it later tolled for Napoleon in distant Moscow and for Hitler in distant Stalingrad.

Already the first known populist tyranny in world history, that of the Peisistratids, had made the resentment of an impoverished rural population their stepping stone. For the two great and terrible derailments of German history, the Wilhelmine Empire and then the Nazi regime, it was, far beyond real injustice, a sense of suffering injustice which paved the way. As ever so often, out of the feeling of injustice arises a hatred of the supposed authors and finally the will to destroy them. If the injustice actually suffered seems not enough, then another one is sought and constructed.

Scapegoats are then viciously branded against whom the people may discharge their hatred, which takes us straight into our worrying and so often hateful actualities.

All in all, populism has led the peoples addicted to it often enough to their ruin. But what can we do against such a degeneration of the popular rule? In our search for the antidotes, we will do well to understand how populism and fascism work. What makes people angry? What makes them vulnerable to evil? If not some wrong done to them, it often seems the mere feeling of being treated unjustly, rightly or wrongly.

Julian Nida-Rümelin (2006, p. 130) points to the deep offense that unequal treatment tends to enflame in people, especially in societies that are based on the idea of equality. In the direction of such traumatizations, too, we should probably look for the deeper reasons for the populist seductiveness of voters who feel they have been treated unfairly. Nida-Rümelin writes: "The postulate of equality harbours an explosive device".

Understanding the reasons for a specific populism requires listening to what people perceive as an unfair treatment. Where it appears to be nonsensical, it will have to be explained. However, the pain caused by a sick organ often occurs elsewhere in the human body. Likewise, specific societal complaints may well hide that in truth they are articulations of wounds suffered in a totally different domain, for example, in the broadening imbalance between democratic freedom and democratic equality.

Let us retain the lesson: A happy democratic community and a cultural bloom do not require an empire. But its happiness may not last long if it is not accompanied by a willingness to resolutely defend democracy and its culture.

4.5 *Popular Rule and the Defence of Democracy*

The Athenian people's assembly (ekklesia) had an overall authority. There was no separation of powers. The courts, composed from the ranks of the citizens, were institutions of the people's assembly in a different guise, possibly with the exception of the Areopagus, which originated from oligarchic preclassical times and was increasingly weakened in the course of democratic reforms.

Socrates was sentenced to death by the people's assembly, which had constituted itself as a people's court, in a second vote with 361 of 501 votes.

A limitation of this universal parliamentary competence would have been alien to the ancient Athenians. Basically, on closer inspection, we do see restrictions on the omnipotence of the ancient Athenian assembly. Procedurally, the plenary assembly on Pnyx Hill was bound by the agenda set by the Council of 500 (boulé) and the draft resolutions (probuleuma) prepared by it. With a paranomy lawsuit (graphê paranómôn), every citizen could object, on the grounds of violating a pre-existing law, to any legislative resolution or even to a bill, be it for formal reasons, e.g. due to a lack of preparation by the council, be in terms of content. The immediate suspension of the law or draft was the result.

The constitutional order of ancient Athens and ours concur in that even an overwhelming parliamentary majority is not authorized to abolish the fundamental principles of democracy. In the Attic democracy, paranomy was just one of the many instruments available for the protection of the constitution, a popular complaint that corresponded to its character of a direct citizen democracy.

Sunday speakers often invoke the strength of our defensive democracy. What we are experiencing today, however, is a fairly defenceless democracy. In the young Attic democracy, it was clear that they had to reckon with internal enemies at any time, especially from the side of the oligarchist revisionists. It prepared itself against potential coup plotters according to the precautionary principle: Politicians who were believed to represent a threat to the democratic order or who simply caused discomfort with their prominent behaviour were banned from the city for 10 years by an ostracism. Such ostracism did not require a verdict of proven guilt. It only required a majority of votes, initially in the council and later in the popular assembly.

Many of the ostracisms decided by the Attic ecclesia may seem deeply unjust to us today. Statesmen with great merits were banned and not infrequently in order to exclude them as domestic rivals. Physical assaults on public officials were capital crimes. Even the greatest of the philosophers, and only because he had asked some uncomfortable questions in the agora, which the prosecutors believed might undermine the state morality of the Athenian youth, was sentenced to the hemlock cup. Individual justice or guilt weighed little against the security of the state.

Paranomy and nomosthenia lawsuits were practised as means of a precautionary protection of the constitution. With both instruments, every individual citizen could assert that bills did not comply with the fundamental legal order or the rules of procedure. Bleicken (1995, p. 385f) offers us an overview of the various instruments employed to protect the constitution in ancient Athenian times. In addition to those already mentioned, he points to the comprehensive "eisangelia" complaint, which for the Oxford reference platform is a form of impeachment. However, unlike the paranomy, the eisangelia procedure not only served to defend rights against acts or drafts of legislation but rather generally addressed any possible offence against the public interest. These included, for example, subversive plans, treason and high treason, deceiving the people but also other offences of all kinds. Those found guilty had to face the death penalty.

The most effective protection of the constitution in ancient days was the obligation of every single citizen to resist assaults on the state and its legal order, on which every citizen had to swear an oath according to the law of Demophantos (Shear, 2008).

By contrast, our Western democracies seem quite unconcerned about the constitutional loyalty of the citizens.

Are not our democracies already in a state of emergency? Do we want to live in democracies which have so little means to defend themselves against their enemies, which take risks? Where is the red line beyond which the democratic emergency begins and resistance is called for?

Karl Popper (2011, p. 581) addressed Plato's paradox of tolerance in his book *The Open Society and Its Enemies* in 1945 by explaining:

In the name of tolerance we should actually demand the right not to tolerate intolerance. We should be determined to put any movement preaching intolerance outside the law, and prosecute incitement to intolerance as criminal in the same way as incitement to murder, kidnapping or the reintroduction of the slave trade.

4.6 Digitalism: Opportunity or Threat?

Some see digital communication as a participatory opportunity, a way to more political equality, a solution to the representative dilemma and for the "time problem", id est the time required for the time-consuming chore of political participation. For others, digital communication is an explosive device for democracy.

In our brave new digital world, anti-democratic and often criminal forces seem to have a systemic advantage over the defenders of democracy. Does digitalism promote the evil in the world? Or may we look forward to paradisial conditions?

As things stand today, it can be determined empirically: The opportunities are still hypothetical, but the risks are not. From the presidency of Donald Trump to Brexit, digital communication has proven to derail an honest and transparent process of democratic politics. Digitalism has already done a serious damage to democracy and to the rule of law.

Plato had calculated the population of his ideal state with precisely 5040 citizens. He judged this to be the right number of real estate possessing men to ensure an effective national defence. For Aristotle, the area of a polis should not extend further than the horizon that could be seen from the highest mountain.

Does digital network communication solve the "oversize" problem of our democracies? The face-to-face communication that was once guaranteed in the Athenian people's assembly can it be reinstalled in chats, blogs or tweets?

The socio-political handling of digitalization is characterized by a downright shocking naivete. An undifferentiated political enthusiasm seems to go hand in hand with a total ignorance concerning the fundamental democratic questions of digitalization. A mechanistic view of the digital challenges is the general tenor of the politico-digital debate.

Let us once again fall back on the foundations of democracy, freedom and equality, with which we at the beginning looked at the origins of democracy. Let us, for a moment, consider unfreedom and inequality as being antonyms.

Since time immemorial, one typical form of people's unfreedom has been a state of dependence. Digitalization leads to particularly extreme forms of dependency. A whole sub-discipline of psychotherapy is now devoted to psychological dependence on the Internet.

The question cui bono, on to whose profit we depend on the net, immediately leads to the problem of inequality. If the market economy and capitalism did not lead us into an even greater state of inequality and unfreedom, then it is because for a long time their intrinsic thirst for power could be opposed and balanced out by forces of containment, without which the end of democracy would long have come. By contrast, there are no democratic means of containment in sight against the expansion of digital capitalism. Setting bounds to a monopolisation of digital market power have proven to be a hopeless endeavour and not much less the struggle against criminal abuses of the net. At the aggregate level of distribution of wealth and power, the concentration of capital in the hands of a very few seems irreversible.

Here we risk to lose what was the holiest of holies to the ancient Athenians, even more sacred than democratic equality and especially individual freedom, namely, our collective self-determination. Without self-determination, however, there is no true government of the people by the people.

4.7 Democratic Peace?

Peace is often considered to be a beneficial effect of democracy (Geis, 2001, p. 282). A whole sub-science has devoted itself to the pacific character of democracy. The democratisation and pacification of a society seem to go hand in hand. There are, however, also sceptical voices against the democratic peace thesis who see it empirically refuted, the opposite as being true. And indeed not a few wars have been waged by democracies (Daase, 2004).

When it comes to peace and peaceful attitudes in the international arena, there seems little to learn from ancient Athens. The Attic polis was a war machine from the beginning, proving its efficiency already in its first years in the defence against the Persian Empire. Not to forget that the defence of Greece against the Persian aggressor was preceded by a Greek incursion into the Persian Empire when the Athenians, for whatever "good" democratic or anti-imperialist reasons, had invaded the Asian coasts in support of the rebellious Ionian colonies.

The Athenians waged war every other year. Their wars were shaped by democracy, their democracy by their wars and finally by an empire held together by military force. To argue that ancient Athens had at least temporarily shown itself to be peaceable in her external relations would require more detailed argumentation. One would, for example, have to investigate the peace agreements Athens concluded with other powers. Inside and the sharp political struggles, and coup attempts should not mislead us in this respect, the democratic form of government ensured the Athenians a peaceful existence over long periods of the classical age.

Another feature to think about when we look at the history of war and peace in ancient Greece is the practice of "oblivion". Especially after internal fratricidal wars, there was a tradition of including a "clause of forgetting" in peace treaties, according to which the reasons for the conflict should no longer be mentioned (Mitthof & Harter-Uibopuu 2003). Offences against the oblivion were severely punished. A "peace-promoting forgetting" of war causes, a taboo on the "war guilt", was to secure peace in ancient Greek times.

In modern times, similar clauses can be found, for example, in the Peace of Westphalia, the Peace of Utrecht (1713) and the Parisian Treaty of 1783. The fact that the Versailles Treaty of 1919 did not contain such an obligation is often held against its allied authors and explained as a principal reason for its failure: In a letter to the *Frankfurter Allgemeine Zeitung* in 16 July 2014, the author of the present study (Féaux de la Croix, 2019, p. 7) countered that the Allies had in fact abstained from condemning the German Reich in the preamble of the Versailles Treaty (on intervention of the British and American delegations). The Versailles peace contains more oblivion than is generally thought.

Returning to the ancient Greeks, we have reasons to doubt the effectiveness of their oblivion rule. The repeated Peloponnesian wars between Athens and Sparta stand against it. Similarly the "Persian wars" that by no means ended with the Greek victories at Salamis, Plataea and Mycale represent an overall picture of hereditary enmities. Leaving this open, it should not prevent us from pondering the validity of the oblivion for our own times. Just to think of the situations we encounter in the peoples of the former Yugoslavia, in the Near East and now in Afghanistan, or in fact the Ukraine.

As for the horror of the Holocaust, our German approach to the past is different. To this day remembrance of the Holocaust is considered an unquestionable raison d'état of the German post-war democracy. What will one day better serve the peace between Israelis and Palestinians, a reconciliation between the Syrians civil war factions, in Myanmar between Rohinyas and the Buddhist majority, Ukrainians and Russians remembrance or oblivion? We cannot ignore the conflict between the two principles. It is an issue which deserves to be deepened.

4.8 On the "Future Competence" of Democracy

Plato and Aristotle already expressed doubts as to whether democracy is a suitable form of government for solving important problems. For both the primordial measure for the effectiveness of government was its capacity to ensure justice. Today systemic doubts are being voiced about the capacity of democracy to meet the great challenges of our time. Will democracies have the far-sightedness and the perseverance needed to effectively counteract climate change or global pandemics? If we consider this to be a responsibility to future generations, then that too is indeed a question of justice, intergenerational justice.

The Attic democracy developed as a sustainable model of success for the duration of 2 ½ centuries, building up an enormous economic growth that surpassed all competitor states, initially thanks to the maritime empire, later in the fourth century as a prosperous society even without hegemony. It experienced golden times, not least thanks to the economic forces released in a democratic society. Finley summarizes the history of the Athenian democracy as follows:

> Through this government system ... Athens succeeded for almost two hundred years to become the most prosperous, powerful, most stable, internally peaceful and culturally by far richest state in the whole of Greece.

And finally, there is an entirely different measure of the success of a society, namely, that of cultural growth. If, after covering the basic material needs of the people, we understand culture and the participation of a large number of people in cultural life as the meaning and purpose of a community, then we can confidently name Attic democracy as one of the most successful states in world history. And after all, the cultural future of Attic democracy, viewed ex tunc, extends well into our own time. Without its cultural success, we would not be here to talk about its present-day relevancy.

In our modern democracy, we encounter a dual problem, the one of its short-term nature, namely, not being able to react timely to emergencies due to protracted political processes, but on the other hand not being able to provide long-term strategies because elected officials have no interest to look beyond the date set for their re-election, which seems particularly true in a "democracy of interests".

Climate change and now the Covid-19 pandemic are currently the most prominent topics for such a critical debate about the short-term nature of democratic interest politics. Another example of the inadequate long-term nature of democratic politics is the massive trade dependencies Western countries have built up in their trade with China or Russia. For decades, short-term business interests made governments enter into trade arrangements, whether at a national or on an international level, which resulted in very unequal market opportunities. The present dilemmata must be blamed on the politics of short-term gains in the face of an adversary who has always kept his strategic long-term objectives in mind.

By contrast and as we have seen, the effectiveness of a government to ensure long-term strategies was very much an issue of classical political philosophy. China's success in its industrial and technological development, in rigidly regulating the growth of its enormous population and in these times the remarkable containment of the Covid-19 pandemic, should be heard as a wake-up call, as a challenge to review the strategic capacity of our democracy and to consider political programmes and an institutional framework readjusted to bring forth long-term strategies.

4.9 More Philosophy: For Democracy!

With our question about the strategic capability of democracy, we return once more to the doubts about its efficiency, which had been formulated already by Plato and his pupil Aristotle. They are commonly portrayed as opponents or at least sceptics of democracy. Finley (1973) comments on this as a major misunderstanding insofar as the Platonic-Aristotelian criticism of democracy did not refer to the form of the state as such, but to the influence, which in their perception, completely unqualified masses had gained on the political decision-making.

For Aristotle, in his comprehensive study of the constitutions of antiquity, it is by no means a foregone conclusion that democracy produces morally better results than an oligarchy. It is also worth considering that in his analysis democracy and oligarchy are not absolute opposites, but that oligarchic dimensions are inherent in any democracy. At one end of its scale, there are oligarchies in a democratic guise, and at the other end, there are forms of direct democracy with an unrestricted popular assembly.

All democracies, according to Aristotle, contain oligarchic elements, some more, others less. Aristotle regarded the politeia (republic) as the best possible constitution under normal circumstances (*Politeia*, 1295 b 34, cf. 1295 a 25ff.):

> He defines it as a mixture of oligarchy and democracy, more precisely democracy as the form of this mixture tending towards the rule of the people (the other would be the rule of the aristocracy). The mix has to be so good that one can regard it as both a democracy and an oligarchy, or even neither of the two. (Meier, 1979, p. 831)

Where would our democracies rank on the Aristotelian oligarchy scale? What would an international ranking based on the oligarchic dimension look like? Where would we stand there, Germany, the USA, Great Britain, or Greece in its present state of politics? And what about the European Union?[11]

From the state philosophy and state practice of classical antiquity, we could very well come up with the idea that democracy is a concrete utopia. Is it not an objective which in its pure form can never be achieved, but which is nonetheless an ethical imperative to pursue? The practical application of such an insight is that we would not disqualify democracy simply on the grounds that obviously it cannot translate equal political rights into real political equality. Because this imperfection is in the nature of democracy.

We can and should strive for equality as a constitutional goal. But we will do well not to expect democracy to actually deliver more than it is able to. Excessive demands on de facto equality harbour the risk of disqualifying democracy as a highly inconsistent form of government because of its participatory deficits.

For our political use, we could learn from the Platonic call for a philosopher's state to demand a higher degree of philosophical thinking from democratic politics than is present in the current state of affairs. More philosophy!

Philosophy is many things. For our present relevancy study, I only want to point out two of its dimensions, namely, firstly the commandment of clear and intelligent thinking—and is intelligence not tantamount to far-sightedness? And secondly, the human obligation to act virtuously, which begins with wanting to act virtuously. We are only able to recognize the good if we make an effort to do so.

4.10 Emotional Democracy?

For Plato and Aristotle, it was the highest mission of politics to strive for a virtuous and just society, with their well-known scepticism if democracy was a suitable framework. As for the virtuous and ethical balance of achievements, one would

---

[11] First answers are suggested in the Economists "Democracy Index", https://infographics.economist.com/2020/democracy-index-2019/index.html: Among the 'full democracies', Norway ranks 1st, Germany 13th, Britain 14th, France 20th, the USA 25th, Greece 39th, etc.

assumably need a highly systematic, philosophically founded measure of judgement. Following Rousseau, Kant was particularly strict about it:

> Everyone must admit that a law, if it is to be considered moral, must be absolutely necessary, that the reason must not be sought in human nature, but a priori only in terms of pure reason. (Kant, 1911, pp. 389–398)

To support his thesis that the emotional dimension of politics should not be neglected in a democracy, Robert Dahl points to a kind of anthropological behavioural experiment: Capuchin monkeys are overjoyed and grateful when you hand them a slice of cucumber (Dahl, 2006, p. 46 f., 51 ff.). But the monkey's happiness lasts a short moment only when monkey B is offered a grape in the neighbouring cage, which offends monkey A deeply. The latter now no longer accepts slices of cucumber and prefers to starve, in his feeling of being unjustly treated rages against his fellow monkeys and possibly even more against himself.

It is one experiment to show that unreasonable attitudes of the people cannot be dealt with rational arguments alone. In the case of deep frustrations, in particular of the sense of injustice, every attempt to convince such a citizen that he is in fact doing well is bound to fail. Such a citizen who feels that he is being neglected will often fall victim of political demagogues satisfying his emotional needs no matter how their political agenda may actually improve the situation of their followers. Such emotional needs are most likely satisfied by punishing the elites and other "guilty parties".

From the long heydays of Athenian democracy, we can infer that its constitution and practice certainly satisfied the emotional needs of the citizens. How that happened in detail at that time and how it could happen again today would be another broad field to study.

Seen in this way, more philosophy seems a necessary but not yet sufficient condition for a successful and virtuous democracy. More emotion would have to be added. Only how to do this may well seem tantamount to squaring the circle.

5 Final Considerations: Athenian Democracy Is Not an Aliud!

> Pondering the challenges to liberal-democratic states and how they might be mastered, the history of ideas teaches us not only to look for institutional solutions, but also to consider and review the ways of thinking in a society.

So Maria Kreiner (2013, p. 349) concludes her helpful collection of material on the history of ideas of democracy.

The urgency of deepening the democratic idea is also perceived in political science. Utilization for our democratic practice seems to be just at a beginning. I would add to Maria Kreiner's plea my firm belief that studying the democratic practice in ancient Athens could open up new perspectives.

The relevance of ancient Athens in the Athens of our times is an open question, surely a research desideratum especially for the Greeks themselves. But more generally, it should be instructive to investigate the attitudes, varying attitudes I suspect, of societies towards the classical democratic legacy. From it we might learn at least as much about ancient times as about ourselves.

Ultimately, much in a democracy is about the weighting of the freedom and equality of its citizens. In the classical balance, the reform steps in the direction of ever more equality have regularly brought forth greater freedom. In terms of democratic theory, this poses the question of how an ever greater degree of freedom could also promote equality. As long as there is no answer to this, we must suspect that the latter may be the source of former but that the former may not be the source of the latter. Because "Wherever the freedom of the market creates inequalities, it finds ways to consolidate these socially" (Nida-Rümelin, 2006, p. 137).

To this end, we would have to look at our constitutions and constitutional case law. Constitutional law has drawn up the walls protecting freedom higher and higher but has nothing comparable to show for in the promotion of equality.

Freedom and equality reside in different dynamics: Equality harbours the germ of freedom, freedom of the ones, on the other hand, the germ of the unfreedom of others. Basically. Whether these dynamics materialize in one sense or another is of course a question of historical or political circumstances. Historically, liberations have generally brought about more equality, for example, the American Revolution and the French Revolution when it liberated the citoyens from the Ancien Régime, only very briefly though.

The struggles of liberation from colonialism leave us to this day an uncomfortable doubt if the people there are materially better off now than they were before or could be. From Salamis to the Greek struggle of independence, begun now 2500 years ago, the historic lesson is however that national self-determination outweighs economic expediency and the urge for collective freedom regrettably often the freedom rights of the individual.

Evidence is lacking that in a functioning democracy an ever greater degree of freedom produces an ever greater degree of equality.

Obviously, this is of fundamental relevance to democracy at all times. The problems of antiquity are always close enough to ours to accept them as a stimulus to rethink freedom and equality. There seems, however, little to hope for from ideological viewpoints passed over by history rather than from new concepts of balancing the two maxims.

There is surely a much greater potential of relevance in the ancient experience than I could possibly address in this study. Admittedly I have not said much to address the manifest weaknesses of the Attic polis, like the political exclusion of women and of the many foreigners, the ancient practices of slavery and the Athenian militarism and imperialism.

Another obvious deficit of this study is certainly the connection between democracy and the rule of law. It can only be added here that in archaic times the rule of law, as we can see it in the Draconian reforms, preceded the beginnings of the Attic democracy by at least 200 years. Historically we should therefore have placed the rule of law at the top of the prerequisites for democracy. The relevance is obvious in the light of the rule of law deficits of a number of our partner states in the European Union.

Finally, I have to admit yet another deficit in relation to the strict control exercised in ancient Athens over the righteous conduct of its officials. At the end of their tenure, they had to give an account, namely, to prove that they had not abused their office for personal gain. The principle was the "transparent mandate holder" and in such a radical way that our current representatives would denounce it as a deep interference with their personal rights.

With our study on relevance, we relate two worlds, namely, ancient history to our modern democracy. Both fill entire libraries. This essay could only offer the first glimpse of what a much broader debate should unfold. Basically, only a retrospective codification of Attic democracy, a summary of all traditions in a constitution-like overall document and a "commentary on Attic democracy" linked to this could provide an overview. A great task indeed.

Some trains of thought may have convinced the reader, and others may have appeared less plausible. I hope to have shown that even where the reference might seem prima facie far-fetched, such as to the digitalist threat, the "classic perspective" can in the end open up a new view of our current affairs.

6 Attic Democracy Was Not an Aliud to Ours

I conclude with great respect for the democratic and cultural achievements of the ancient Greeks. Without them the world would be a different one, a much poorer one. If we looked at least at some of the lessons to be learnt from the classical experience more seriously, it might help a little to make our world a better place.

And after all, that is what makes the effort of democracy worthwhile, to make the world an even better place.

References

Adams, R., & Savran, D. (Eds.). (2002). *The masculinity studies reader*. Wiley-Blackwell.
Bazzigher, J. (1884/1885). *Die Athenische Demokratie, Beilage zum Kantonalschulprogram*. Chur 1885. Druck von Conzett & Ebner.
Bleicken, J. (1995). *Die athenische Demokratie. 4. Völlig überarbeitete und wesentlich erweiterte Auflage*. Paderborn, München & Wien. Ferdinand Schöningh.
Burckhardt, J. (1982). *Griechische Kulturgeschichte*, 4 volumes (1889-1902), new ed., Deutscher Taschenbuchverlag = dtv Verlagsgesellschaft mbH & Co KG, München.
Canfora, L. (2007). *Eine kurze Geschichte der Demokratie* (4th ed.). PapyRossa.
Cartledge, C. (2016). *Democracy, a life*. Oxford University Press.
Conze, W. (1979). Zurückdrängung des Demokratiebegriffs. In O. Brunner, W. Conze, & R. Koselleck (hrsg), *Demokratie, Geschichtliche Grundbegriffe, Historisches Lexikon zur politisch-sozialen Sprache in Deutschland*, Band 1, Stuttgart.

Daase, C. (2004). Demokratischer Frieden – Demokratischer Krieg. Drei Gründe für die Unfriedlichkeit der Demokratien. In C. Schweitzer, B. Aust, & P. Schlotter (hrsg) *Demokratien im Krieg* (pp. 53–71). Baden-Baden: Nomos Verlag.

Dahl, R. A. (2006). *On political equality*. New Haven, London: Yale Unversity Press, German translation: *Politische Gleichheit, ein Ideal?*.

Féaux de la Croix, G. (2010). Introduction. In *The Marathon 2500 Declaration – For a renewal of democracy: Lessons from the Classical Athenian Experience*. Psychogios Editions.

Féaux de la Croix, G. (2018). Freedom and friendship, some thoughts on the renewal of our democracy. In S. Vliamos & M. S. Zouboulakis (Eds.), *Institutionalist perspectives on development*, Palgrave Studies in Democracy (pp. 75–87).

Féaux de la Croix, G. (2019). So schlecht war der Vertrag nicht. *Frankfurter Allgemeine Zeitung*, 16-07-2014.

Finley. (1986). *Antike und moderne Demokratie*. Reclam, Philipp, jun. GmbH, Verlag.

Finley, M. I. (1973). *Democracy ancient and modern*. New Brunswick: Rutgers University Press (German edition, published by Reclam, Stuttgart 1980, p. 27).

Finley, M. I. (Ed.). (1984). *The legacy of Greece. A new appraisal*. Oxford University Press.

Funke, P. (2003). *Athen in klassischer Zeit*, 2. München: C. H. Beck.

Geis, A. (2001). Diagnose: Doppelbefund – Ursache ungeklärt? Die Kontroverse um den "demokratischen Frieden". *Politische Vierteljahreszeitschrift, 42*(2), 282–298.

Herodotus ([1910] 1997). *The Histories*, transl. George Rawlinson, New York 1910, reedited 1997.

Kant, I. (1911). Grundlegung zur Metaphysik der Sitten. In *Kants Gesammelte Schriften* (hrsg). Berlin: Königlich Preußische Akademie der Wissenschaften.

Kreiner, M. (2013). *Demokratie als Idee. Eine Einführung*. UTB 2013 See also (= *UTB*. Band 3883). UVK/UTB, Konstanz/ München, ISBN 978-3-8252-3883-4 (Lehrbuch, das die Idee der Demokratie von der Philosophie der Antike bis zur Moderne anschaulich und anhand von Originaltexten zwölf exponierter Denker der Ideengeschichte aufbereitet.).

Livingstone, R. (Ed.). ([1921] 1928). *The legacy of Greece*. Oxford: Clarendon Press.

Marx-Engels. (1959). *Werke*, Bd. 2. Berlin: Dietz Verlag.

Meier, C. (1979). Demokratie, Antike Grundlagen. In *Geschichtliche Grundbegriffe, Historisches Lexikon zur Politisch-sozialen Sprache in Deutschland*, Band 1, Stuttgart.

Michels, R. (1911). *Zur Soziologie des Parteiwesens in der modernen Demokratie*. Leipzig: Klinkhardt (Engl. translation: *Political Parties*, London 1915).

Mittermaier, K., & Mair, M. (2013). *Demokratie. Die Geschichte einer politischen Idee von Platon bis heute*. Wissenschaftliche Buchgesellschaft / WBG.

Mitthof, F., & Harter-Uibopuu, K. (2003). Vergeben und Vergessen? Amnestie in der Antike, Wiener Kolloquien zur antiken Geschichte, Holzhausen-Verlag.

Nida-Rümelin, J. (2006). *Demokratie und Wahrheit*. C. H. Beck.

Nolte, P. (2012). *Was ist Demokratie? Geschichte und Gegenwart*. Beck Verlag.

Pfetsch, F. R. (2003). Theoretiker der Politik, von Platon bis Habermas, p. 44.

Popper, K. (2011). *The open society and its enemies*. Routledge.

Russell, B. (1978). *Philosophie des Abendlandes*. Europa Verlag AG Zürich.

Schvarcz, J. (1876). *Die Demokratie*. E. Avenarius.

Sen, A. (1999). Democracy as a universal value. *Journal of Democracy, 10*(3), 3–17.

Shear, J. L. (2008). The oath of Demophantos and the politics of Athenian identity. In A. Sommerstein & J. Fletcher (Eds.), *Horkos, The Oath in Greek Society*. Liverpool University Press.

Simon, M. (1961). Idiot von ἰδιώτης. In E. C. Welskopf (Ed.), *Das Fortleben Altgriechischer Sozialer Typenbegriffe in der Deutschen Sprache*. Berlin

Strauss, B. (2004). *The Battle of Salamis, The naval encounter that saved Greece – and western civilization*. Simon & Schuster.

von Bismarck, O. (1924/1935). *Gesammelte Werke. Friedrichsruher Ausgabe* (Vol. 9).

von Pöhlmann, R. (1911). *Aus Altertum und Gegenwart: Gesammelte Abhandlungen*. C. H. Beck.

Guy Féaux de la Croix is a retired German diplomat, now lawyer, writer and artist living and working in Bad Münstereifel near Bonn, Germany.

Born in Berlin in 1948, he owes his name to a French family which in March 1793 emigrated from France to Germany.

After his studies at the universities of Bonn and Geneva, he joined the German Foreign Service in 1978. In his last postings, he served as Minister Plénipotentiary of the German Embassy in Athens (2005–2012) and ultimately as Minister Plénipotentiary of the German Embassy at the Holy See.

In Greece he became the founder of the Marathon Friends International Association and the original author of the Marathon 2500 Declaration – For a Renewal of Democracy: Lessons from the Classical Athenian Experience (Psychogios 2010) and of other publications (i.a. Istoria Sept. 2010). His writings on Greek topics furthermore include a novel on "Plato's True Love", published together with Nicholas Kyriazis in the Okeanos Editions 2014 and translated in several other languages, an essay on "Freedom and Friendship: Some Thoughts on the Renewal of Our Democracies" (Palgrave Studies on Democracy, Springer 2018) and on "Freedom for the Greeks, freedom for Europe – observations on the bicentenary of the Greek revolution" (Duesseldorf 2021).

As an artist, Guy Féaux de la Croix has initiated and curated a number of art events in Greece and elsewhere. He has shown his own paintings and sculptures at exhibitions, i.a. in Paris (Images Nocturnes 1991), Munich ("Greek Team 2005") and Athens (EcoArt 2007–2012, ArtCargo Kifissia 2010–2011).

In June 2014 the University of Thessaly (Volos) conferred on him the title of a "doctor honoris causa".

Guy Féaux de la Croix is married, has three children and five grandchildren and comes to Greece whenever possible to sail between the islands of the Aegean Sea.

Europe in Modern Greece: The Constant Navarino

Kevin Featherstone

Abstract Greece has defined 'Europe' in many and diverse ways. But Europe—in the form of the Great Powers and/or the European Union (EU)—has also structured so much of Greece's developmental path. Historically, the Great Powers—Britain, France and Russia—were drawn in to determine the fate of the emergent modern nation, but their intervention drew back from supportive actions that would enable the country to prosper. Their motivation was, primarily, one of the strategic interests, rather than the normative pull of Philhellenism. Latterly, the country's quest for a 'catch-up' with Europe has been something of a psycho-drama: with a modernising elite never quite reaching its 'Ithaca'. Today, it is a moot point whether member states like Greece can achieve sufficient domestic reform without the EU developing new mechanisms for intervention and support. And, with a more heterogeneous EU, Greece today defines Europe's incompleteness—the limits on the EU's capacity to act. This may prove consequential for both the EU and Greece in the future.

Keywords Navarino · Great Powers · Europeanization · External intervention · Catch-up

---

This chapter is based on his public lecture for the Athens University of Economics and Business; 17 May 2021.

K. Featherstone (✉)
Eleftherios Venizelos Professor of Contemporary Greek Studies and Professor of European Politics, London School of Economics and Political Science (LSE), London, UK

Hellenic Observatory, LSE, London, UK
e-mail: k.featherstone@lse.ac.uk

© The Author(s), under exclusive license to Springer Nature Switzerland AG 2022
E. M. L. Economou et al. (eds.), *Democracy in Times of Crises*,
https://doi.org/10.1007/978-3-030-97295-0_10

1 Introduction

That 'Europe' has been an *important* factor in the development of the modern Greek nation is indisputable (Featherstone, 2014). We might also immediately add, of course, that Greece has defined Europe in many diverse and crucial ways.

Roddy Beaton (2019) has recently pointed out that the English philosopher, John Stuart Mill, argued that the Battle of Marathon was of greater consequence to British history than was the Battle of Hastings in 1066. This is a major claim. Together with Thermopylae and Salamis, the battles against the Persians defined a fault line. The way in which Herodotus wrote of them is akin to what we would now call a 'clash of civilisations'. The Greeks, across their city states, were fighting for Hellenism: The Persians understood slavery, but they did not understand 'freedom'. And these civilisational values were adopted by Europe later.

What I want to do here is to examine Greece's relationship with Europe, in the modern period—to see what Europe has given Greece. I want to consider Europe as an external 'other', structuring so much of the country's development path. I do so in the context of Greece celebrating the bicentenary of its revolution and later emergence as an independent state from the Ottoman Empire. So let me draw on some of the crucial events of the 1820s onwards to place some important contemporary issues in that historical context.

For there is a constancy, I will suggest, in some of the structures linking modern Greece with Europe that date back to the Battle of Navarino in 1827.

This constancy involves the Great Powers of the day being regularly drawn to help determine Greece's fate but drawing back from an intervention that would allow her to thrive and prosper. The motivation was a strategic interest far more than a normative pull to philhellenism.

For the new Greek nation, however, it was almost the reverse situation: a normative desire to emulate a modernity defined by the European powers was stymied by a strategic incapacity to fully do so.

Domestically, the quest for 'catch-up' with Europe has been something of a *psycho-drama*. A modernising elite has never quite reached its 'Ithaca', and the journey has often been one of self-torture—with liberal elites embarrassed at the failings of their compatriots but also limited by their domestic resources.

Some years ago, in another context, with a co-author, I referred to Italy's ties to the European Union as showing the strategic utilisation of a *vincolo esterno* (Dyson & Featherstone, 1999). In Italian, literally 'an external link'. But I saw it as having much more meaning than that. The *vincolo esterno* empowered domestic leaders to unblock the path to reform at home on the basis of securing gains from Europe. An Italian technocrat, Guido Carli, had argued that Italy's economic progress since 1949 had rested on this *vincolo esterno* with Europe. Today, the *vincolo esterno* does not seem to be working too well in Italy: It is a source of domestic conflict.

I want to finish with some reflections on why a new kind of *vincolo esterno* with Europe is needed for Greece today. It is a moot point whether member states like Greece can achieve sufficient reform without the EU developing new mechanisms for intervention and support. Those new EU mechanisms need to go beyond the format of the Troika in the recent debt crisis, of course. Whether the new 'European Recovery and Resilience Facility' is a game-changer in this regard is unclear.

2 Modern Greece in European History

As philhellenes through time have rightly declared, Greece defined Europe. But, we might add that today Greece defines Europe's incompleteness—the limits on the EU's capacity to act—and this may prove consequential in significant ways.

Let me first say a little more on what I draw from the experience of the Battle of Navarino in 1827. I will use themes from the battle as a heuristic device in order to develop my argument. The 1827 battle was, of course, a critical stage for Greece but also a formative moment for Europe. The new nation became part of a new wave of liberal nationalism spreading across the continent—one of the first 'new nations' of the C19th.

The Great Powers stumbled into Greek affairs, almost by accident: Navarino epitomised their stumble. In general, the Great Powers could *not* have been less supportive. Their intention was to isolate a 'problem' and avoid it de-stabilising the established international order. Tellingly, most Greeks at the time were probably unaware of the Great Power intervention. As Mark Mazower (2021) argues in his new book, the revolutionaries and the emergent nation lacked a strong central direction, the new state would have a fragile fiscal base, and the society was impoverished. Yet, the Great Powers did little to provide Greece with the capacity to thrive thereafter.

Navarino reflected an important dimension of an earlier European narrative on Greece—that it was a fallen great, whose contemporary reality would always disappoint. In the words of Byron, some years before the revolution:

> Fair Greece! sad relic of departed worth!
> Immortal, though no more; though fallen great!
> [Lord Byron, Childe Harold's Pilgrimage, Canto II (1812), Stanza 73]

A book from 1954 by Spencer takes these words as its title to show how European conceptions of Greece, prior to the revolution, were moulded by the emotions and opinions of generations of writers that had travelled to Greece when it was under Ottoman occupation.

Yes, the revolution could not have succeeded without the spread of philhellenism internationally, but beyond individual artists and a few others, the reality is that the Great Powers acted *not* out of emotion, but *realpolitik*, and how they acted was limited, bequeathing a Greece that was small and economically unviable and they hoped would cause no more trouble.

The Greek state's fiscal weakness meant that it was placed on life support via emergency international loans. Some might argue that this external support reflected a philhellene sentiment. Stathis Kalyvas (2015) talks of the 'glass being half full' in terms of a benign external help to Greece. Perhaps, I am not a historian of the nineteenth century, but it seems to me that we might consider the empty half of the glass as well.

The international loans to Greece in its first decades were less than benign. The 1824 and 1825 loans raised in London were from private speculators. And Greece only received part of the 1825 loan because a part was withheld to cover interest expenses, brokerage and the repayment of previous loans. In the following year, Greece had to default. A further loan in 1832, underwritten by the Great Powers, involved service payments thereafter that practically crippled the new Greek state. Greece had to ask for additional loans *each* year simply to meet the repayments.

By 1843, tough austerity measures had to be imposed by King Otto. And he was forced to accept humiliating new terms—giving up part of the state's tax revenues each year to the agents of the creditors. A decade later, the terms of the 1832 loan were used as a pretext by Britain and France to force Otto into further humiliation. With the threat of sequestration of Greece's state revenues, London and Paris obliged him to withdraw all Greek fighters (irregulars) from Ottoman territory, to help keep the 'sick' Ottoman Empire alive.

Later, the loans to Greece, after it had to declare bankruptcy in 1932, were somewhat different but also more prescient. Having tied itself to the pound sterling and to the gold standard, the Greek state—in effect—declared bankruptcy. The international loans were again prompted by a systemic interest: endeavouring to limit the international fallout from Greece's default.

That strategic interest had been evident at Navarino, of course. It was also clear in 1843, when the House of Commons debated Greece not honouring the interest payments on her loans. Some illustrative quotes give us a sense of the recurring images and perceptions of Greece. As the British Prime Minister (Robert Peel) said in the House of Commons in 1843:

> I think it is impossible for any inhabitant of a country in which civilization has made progress to profess indifference for the fate of Greece—a country to which we owe all civilization and attainments which are not connected with the Christian dispensation. Independently, however, of those considerations, Greece must always be an object of interest. From her geographical position, the internal tranquillity of Greece must necessarily exercise an important influence on the general tranquillity of Europe. [15 August 1843]

In the same debate in August 1843, one Member of Parliamemt (MP) warned the Prime Minister (PM) that, despite Britain's past interventions, Greece now threatened to undermine her international standing:

> Do not tell me that Greece interest you not—that her fate can little affect you. She did interest you in 1827, when you signed the Treaty of London—she did interest you in 1832, when you sent a Bavarian prince to sway her destinies—she did interest you when you sent your fleets to Navarino, and your protocols to Constantinople. And, although it be admitted that her happiness and welfare cannot affect your power, yet will you, by permitting a continued violation of these treaties, suffer the greatest of all injuries—a loss of your character for consistency and integrity among nations? (Mr. Cochrane, MP [Pontefract], 15 August 1843)

He went on to bemoan the domestic situation in Greece:

> It [has] also been discussed in the French Chambers in 1841... M. [François] Guizot [then French Foreign Minister] said that— The state of Greece demanded the most serious

consideration of his Majesty's government; it appeared to us essentially bad; the interior condition of the country was endangered alike by the weakness of the public administration and the conflict of national prejudices. At home, vices of a different description occasioned great alarm; the administration appeared powerless—destitute of energy—incapable not only of ameliorating the social condition of the people, but even of exercising power. (Mr. Cochrane, MP [Pontefract], 15 August 1843)

This potted history has raised some relevant themes: of the strategic self-interest of the Great Powers, of the early loans retarding Greece's economic development and of little being done to foster her domestic capacity. We might ask: which of these themes do *not* resonate today? As such, the 'Navarino' syndrome speaks to us in the present in terms of recurring images and perceptions.

2.1   *Greece and the European Union*

If we fast-forward to more recent times—the biggest transformation for Greece's relations with the rest of Europe was her accession to the, then, European Community (EC)—the 40th anniversary of which we celebrate this year also. The EC was a club that traded material support for market access: a very different kind of *quid pro quo* from the past.

And, in the first two decades of Greece's EC membership, Europe was the focus for a light-touch modernisation process. The funding flowed into Greece—with the Integrated Mediterranean Programmes, the Cohesion Funds, etc. European money constituted most of Greece's infrastructure investment. We think of the roads, the electrification of the railways, airports, etc. Europe did not ask too many questions as the EC did not see itself as that kind of intrusive club (Featherstone & Papadimitriou, 2008, 2020).

But with the Greek crisis in 2010, it was Europe that made a transformational shift in this respect—with hard constraints imposed on Greece. Tough conditionality came with a Troika and a severe austerity.

Just as at Navarino, Europe wanted to isolate the 'Greek problem'. It rejected the narrative of George Papandreou that 'Greece has a problem, but it is not *the* problem'. Europe's discursive resistance was underscored by the economics of 'ordo-liberalism' from Germany. A nation had to put its own house in order. It should not be allowed to disturb the prevailing European system.

The problem—just as in 1843—was that the conditions placed upon Greece greatly inhibited her growth and recovery. For domestic leaders, to put the 'house in order' was made hugely problematic.

Consider the speech in Parliament of the former British PM, Lord Palmerston, in August 1843: Palmerston was criticising the failure of Greece to keep up with its payments under the 1832 Treaty:

> The Greek government was at that time oppressed with expenses of a temporary nature and it always held out the expectation, that those would, in a short time, be diminished... Budgets were proposed, but we doubted them. They were not prospective, but retrospective..... We were always assured, that these budgets had been reviewed by the council of state, and, that reliance might be placed on their accuracy....
>
> There is no disguising the fact that there has been an undue expenditure of money in Greece. This may be owing to the want of ... control....

Palmerston's words sound like those of Wolfgang Schauble or Poul Thomsen more recently. The Greek government lacked credibility—It didn't keep its promises. All this rhetoric neglected the domestic costs of keeping up with the loan repayments, the capacity to do so.

In the recent crisis, the question was posed: '*Who* wants reform in Greece?' To answer that question, we might note several relevant conditions from political economy:

- *That a reform agenda defined by principles of economic liberalism is relatively alien to the Greek tradition.* Just think of the negative connotations associated with neoliberalism in Greece today, as elsewhere.
- *That such an agenda is an imported good with little domestic demand.* The domestic constituency for reform inspired by open, flexible markets is relatively small. Historically, the political voice for economic liberalism has been weak. There is a structural explanation that helps explain this weakness: The economy has very few large firms but innumerable small and micro-enterprises. Those in an oligarchic position have no structural interest in liberal economics at home.
- *We might also add that clientelism and rousfetti (favours) political practices constrain the scope for economic liberalism, by increasing the political cost.*
- *And, that state institutions are weak in the face of this clientelism, nepotism, etc.* This isn't because of a simplistic imposition of such practices on the electorate by a corrupt elite. Instead, as Bo Rothstein's frame on the 'quality of government' internationally would have it, there is a cultural symbiosis between those running the institutions and key parts of the electorate. In other words, state institutions are caught in a 'social trap': those in charge create and serve the expectations of key groups of voters. Aristides Hatzis has also adopted this theme in his writings on Greece.

When we reflect on these conditions, we can note their long and deep historical roots. The consequences of a lack of trust in institutions, the lack of strong middle-sized enterprises, and a popular base that feels vulnerable and seeks rentier politics have deep historical roots. There is a 'late-modernizer' syndrome here, as Kalyvas has argued.

Even before the recent crisis, there were serious warning signs of Greece slipping behind the EU's mainstream—that its convergence with the EU was declining. Indeed, in the state's regulation of the economy, the effectiveness of state institutions, the 'ease of doing business', etc., Greece was showing a convergence not so much with the EU's core, but rather with its immediate neighbours. Greece was actually looking more 'Balkan' or central European. We can note that this was not a

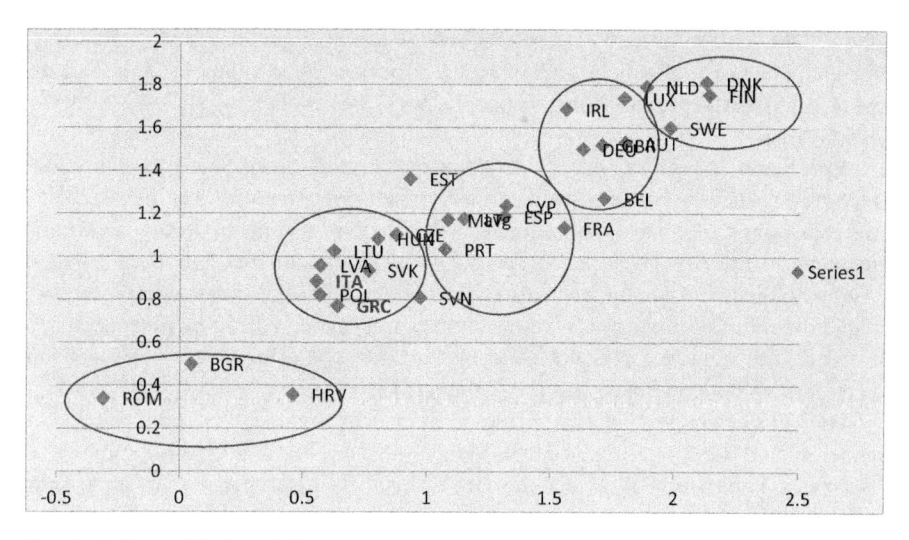

Fig. 1 Different 'Worlds of Governance'? Regulatory quality (X) by government effectiveness (Y): 1996–2013. Source: WGI, World Bank

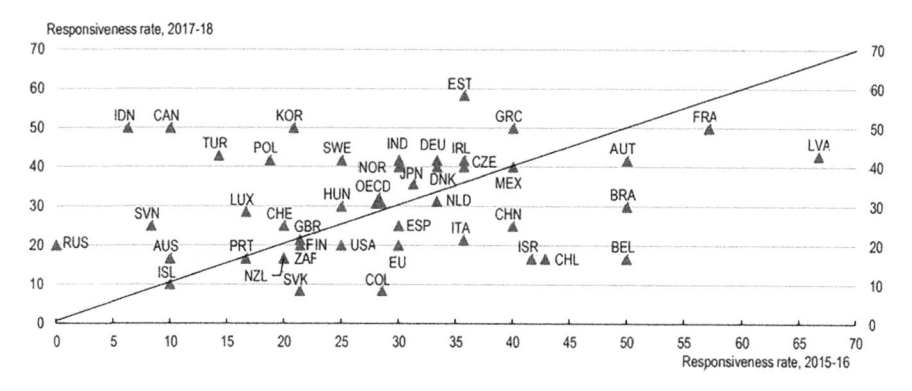

Fig. 2 Responsiveness to Going for Growth recommendations

trend shared by Spain or Portugal, both of which showed greater convergence with France and Germany in this period.

Figure 1 illustrates some of this point: It combines scores on regulatory quality with those on government effectiveness to demarcate different groups in terms of quality of governance. Greece is located alongside Italy, but each of the other EU member states in their group is Balkan or Central European. Greece is highlighted in the red font. The two indicators are from the World Bank's 'Worldwide Governance Indicators'. But we could repeat the same picture if we used other data on government quality, impartiality, or corruption developed by the University of Gothenburg and others.

Of course, the level of Greece's reform activity shot up during the years of the recent bailouts. The external constraint was very strong and directive. Figure 2 shows OECD data for the last years of Greece's third bailout. The OECD charts how far member governments are adopting its reform recommendations. It shows that what it terms Greece's 'reform responsiveness' was higher in 2017–2018 than in 2015–2016.

But there is now a list of independent reports from international bodies recognising that the bailout conditions were often misconceived, that they deepened the recession more than was needed, and that they missed the opportunity for more meaningful reform. These are points made in reports for the European Court of Auditors, the IMF and more recently the European Stability Mechanism. In short, the conditionalities of the bailouts were a clumsy, misconceived and ineffectual *vincolo esterno*. The evidence was not clear that the EU could manage a heterogeneous economy, in which Greece was a key outlier.

And this, I suggest, is one of the most critical issues facing both the EU, in general, and Greece, in particular, today—that is, in a deepening process of European integration, *how* can the EU manage its heterogeneity by intervening effectively and legitimately into member states in need, in order to better promote convergence and cohesion amongst the EU as a whole? This issue is a critical strategic challenge for the EU in the coming years. If it repeats the mistakes of the Greek bailouts, the EU will likely face deeper existential challenges—confronting the EU's values and purposes. And, as we saw from the graph on the World Bank data, *there are* major divergences between EU member states in terms of the quality of domestic governance—the ability to deliver public goods and the ability *indeed* to deliver *EU* policies. There is a structural problem here for some member states and a strategic problem for the EU.

In the new phase for the EU, it will need a *vincolo esterno* mechanism of a different order. The mechanism will need to have much more capacity and legitimacy than the recent Troikas. For member states like Greece, the *vincolo esterno* will only be made effective if three key conditions are satisfied:

1. The political will exists to reform and converge.
2. The content of the reform agenda is attractive and accepted.
3. There is a domestic institutional capacity to deliver the reforms.

These are tough conditions for Greece to meet. The reform 'buy-in' often doesn't extend across parties or governments, even between ministers. Much of the international reform paradigm seems alien. And, there is a widespread criticism of the failings of public administration to deliver.

The bailouts for Greece were problematic because they were defined by an agenda that was narrowed by one national tradition, *ordoliberalism*. The bailouts redefined Europe's values, and they were separate from many national policy models.

Today, internationally, we're seeing a seismic shift in economic thinking. The USA and the EU are exhibiting a return to Keynesian principles of 'pump-priming' the economy. In principle, the European Recovery and Resilience Fund looks like a game-changer. And, even Wolfgang Schauble supports its basic thrust.

But who can be confident that all member states will use the new funds effectively, in accordance with future priorities for economic success? Did anyone really think that the Greek crisis could have been solved on a long-term basis simply by throwing more money at the problem? Money is one thing; structural issues are another. Structurally, we would note the endemic problems of governance, the weaknesses of institutions and the lure of clientelism and talk of the risks of 'new wine in old bottles' once again.

3 Conclusion

So, we are back to the 'Navarino' legacy. There are too many risks today in Europe remaining distant from member states struggling to converge. Managing the European club requires much greater reciprocity: Europe needs to intervene more effectively, and member states like Greece need to legitimise that intervention more strongly. The Navarino stance did not really help Greece Europeanise then, and it would not today. Europe at Navarino settled for a macro-strategic interest, while Greece developed its normative narrative of emulation. That kind of asymmetry serves neither party well today.

While Greece defined Europe in the past, today, it defines Europe's incompleteness. It's time for Greece and Europe to move on.

References

Beaton, R. (2019). *Greece: Biography of a modern nation*. Allen Lane.
Dyson, K., & Featherstone, K. (1999). *The road to Maastricht: Negotiating Economic and Monetary Union*. Oxford University Press.
Featherstone, K. (Ed.). (2014). *Europe in modern Greek history*. Hurst & Co.
Featherstone, K., & Papadimitriou, D. (2008). *The limits of Europeanization: Reform capacity and policy conflict in Greece*. Palgrave Macmillan.
Featherstone, K., & Papadimitriou, D. (2020). The politics of Europeanization. In K. Featherstone & D. A. Sotiropoulos (Eds.), *The Oxford handbook of modern Greek politics*. Oxford University Press.
Kalyvas, S. (2015). *Modern Greece: What everyone needs to know*. Oxford University Press.
Mazower, M. (2021). *The Greek Revolution: 1821 and the making of modern Europe*. Allen Lane.
Spencer, T. J. B. (1954). *Fair Greece, sad relic: Literary philhellenism from Shakespeare to Byron*. Weidenfeld and Nicolson.

Kevin Featherstone is Eleftherios Venizelos Professor in contemporary Greek studies and Professor in European politics in the European Institute at LSE, where he is also the Director of the Hellenic Observatory. He has held visiting positions at the University of Minnesota, New York University, Harvard University and the European University Institute (Firenze). He was the first foreign member of the National Council for Research and Technology (ESET) in Greece, serving from 2010 to 2013. In 2013 he was made 'Commander, Order of the Phoenix' by the President of the Hellenic Republic and in 2021 had bestowed the award of 'Grand Commander, Order of the Phoenix' of the Hellenic Republic. He has written extensively on European and Greek politics. In 2014, the European Parliament selected one of his books (co-authored with Kenneth Dyson) as one of its '100 Books on Europe to Remember'. He has contributed regularly to international media on European and Greek politics.

Part V
Modern Aspects of Law in Relation to the Present-Day Democratic Institutions

Democracy and Social Rights

Joaquim de Sousa Ribeiro

Abstract It is argued that deprivation of basic goods not only obstructs the full exercise of liberties and the free development of personality, but it also distances people from the public sphere and the deliberative processes that take place there. Democracy presupposes equal opportunity for all to participate in the political affairs. To have that possibility, people need to enjoy a minimum of material conditions for a dignified life. By providing citizens in need with the goods and services necessary to satisfy that interest, social rights contribute to a successful approach to the democratic ideal.

Keywords Political equality · Civic rights · Social rights · Negative and positive freedom · Constitution · Personal autonomy · Capabilities · Human dignity · Participatory democracy

1. Linking democracy and social rights puts together two fields of the constitutional order normally seen as separate and mutually unconnected. Speaking of democracy evokes more directly free elections, multiparty system and separation of powers, in short, institutional forms of organization of the political power. Social rights, in turn, as a category of human and fundamental rights, apparently point to a different direction, since their references are the persons, their status and their living conditions.

The question I propose to address is whether, challenging the usual distance between the two concepts, social rights may be granted some role in the full realization of democracy or, in other terms, if a successful approach to the democratic ideal presupposes that those rights be guaranteed.

J. de Sousa Ribeiro (✉)
Law Faculty, University of Coimbra, Coimbra, Portugal

2. Democracy and political equality necessarily go hand in hand. The one does not exist without the other.[1] Political equality requires as a necessary condition the guarantee of universal suffrage. But this is only the first level of political equality.

In order to truly embody this value, democracy cannot be restricted to the polling stations. As a basic principle of the democratic order, political equality demands material and legal conditions and institutional and social practices that should be structurally present on all moments of the collective life and not just during election times.

It presupposes, from the outset, recognition and respect for civil and political freedoms and rights, the exercise of which is instrumental for an open public debate, in which the various trends of opinion may make themselves heard. One of the lessons to be drawn from Athenian democracy is precisely that involving the citizens in public decisions that concern them, enhancing their sense of identity and responsibility for the destiny of the *polis*, is essential for the functioning of the democratic system in perfect harmony with its underlying principle of popular sovereignty.

This requires the ownership of constitutionally protected positions and, first and foremost, *freedom of expression* and *freedom of the press and the media*. The ancient Athenians were already perfectly aware that *vote* and *voice* are interconnected as conditions of democracy.[2] In fact, freedom of expression does not have simply an individual dimension, as a possibility of revealing one's own personality to others. It is also a democratic public good, "the lifeblood of democracy", as someone has said.

But, equally, the freedom of assembly and demonstration, the freedom of association and, in the end, all civil and political rights and freedoms contribute, to a greater or lesser degree, individually or through parties and other organizations of collective interests, to give the citizens the opportunity for free, autonomous and informed participation in the building up and controlling of political power. A general framework of rights is essential to ensure democratic deliberative processes.

Under this perspective, democracy, connected to the values of freedom and political equality, is not fulfilled simply by a given system of government, even less by a given system of government choice. It does not depend solely on a certain structure of political power. The concept makes procedural and substantial demands on how to govern, subjecting the actions of the majority to "indicators of legitimacy" that will make it possible to assess their degree of compatibility with the democratic ideal. Unjustified measures or measures disproportionately restrictive of personal and collective rights, opening the door to the exercise of oppressive power over minorities, do not simply bring about an erosion of the rule of law. They represent true "democratic regressions", even if electoral procedures themselves remain formally untouched.

---

[1] According to Beetham (1999, p. 91), the "basic democratic principles" are "control *by* citizens over their collective affairs and equality *between* citizens in the exercise of that control".

[2] See Ash (2017, pp. 95–96).

It can therefore be concluded, beyond any possible doubt, that civic and political rights are *intrinsic* and *constitutive* elements of democracy. Whenever they are threatened or insufficiently protected, it is democracy itself that is in danger.

3. The same cannot be said of economic and social rights, which do not present the same degree of necessary connection with the democratic order. Their relationship to democracy is far less immediate, which gives rise to quite different ideological and legal-political positions in this regard.

Putting aside extreme libertarian orientations, such as Hayek's one, the coexistence of liberal democracies and market economies with forms of social protection is accepted by practically everybody. The radical opposition to the idea that the democratic state should also assume the goal of promoting decent existential conditions for all citizens does not enjoy political viability today, at least with regard to a social minimum. The hegemonic market reason is, therefore, forced into compromises, more or less extensive, with the state reason, which takes responsibility for ensuring minimum levels of well-being.

Within this broad spectrum, the most diversified political and doctrinal positions line up. This even has a clear constitutional impact, on whether or not social protection is incorporated in the constitution and, if it is, as in general is, on the heterogeneity of the forms and degrees of guardianship that constitutions dispense to the interests protected by social rights. Some constitutions, including the Portuguese one, enshrine explicit guarantees, with the status of true fundamental rights; in others, the tutelage is inferred, through interpretation, from constitutional principles or from the recognition of certain civil and political rights; in others still, it is implicit in the setting up of goals that should command the exercise of state powers.

Even in the constitutional systems that set up fundamental economic, social and cultural rights, such rights and civil and political rights are usually placed in separate normative universes and distinct spheres of value. The latter are seen as *rights of freedom*; the former, as *rights of equality*.

This counterposition reflects well what is at stake here, which is the understanding of the values of freedom and equality and the way in which both are mutually articulated. And as always happens when ultimate foundational values are at stake, we are faced in this domain with an almost inexhaustible multiplicity of positions.

4. For a solidly established current of thought, democracy has only to do with the political sphere, separated from the economic and social ones. Demands for equality are only acceptable within that sphere. Social rights are left outside the conceptual and political field of democracy. Even when admitted, they are not related to the values that give meaning to the democratic principle but, rather, to the realization of an autonomous principle of justice.

Under the light of such an understanding, the relationship between freedom and equality is one of tension and confrontation, as some kind of zero-sum game: a little more equality, due to state intervention, is always a little less freedom.

Such an idea is based, at least implicitly, on two interconnected premises. On the one hand, that freedom is defined in purely negative and minimalist terms as the absence of coercion and of obstructing interference. On the other hand, that political equality is immune to all forms of inequality in the other spheres of social life.

Both premises are contestable.

5. Against the first one, it is emphasized that freedom cannot be assessed irrespective of the value it represents for the person who holds it and therefore of the scope and nature of the choices and possibilities of action it allows. Freedom, linked to the normative idea of dignity, is performed through the exercise of personal autonomy and the free development of the personality. For this, the absence of unjustified compulsions is a first and necessary condition. But this is not enough. The concept of the person as a subject of choices and of meaningful action through the exercise of freedom presupposes and involves access to goods and opportunities, possession of capacities and availability of resources for the satisfaction of vital interests.

In the life world, however, there are multiple existential situations that expose the individual to deprivations and risks that divest him from the real possibility of autonomy. Social rights are, quite correctly, seen as having the emancipatory function of removing obstacles and promoting satisfactory conditions for the holder to take advantage of the sphere of freedom granted to him. An adequate level of access to education, health, social security and jobs provides concrete possibilities of action otherwise non-existent. All the social rights are, in this sense, *empowerment rights*, as the United Nations Committee on Economic, Social and Cultural Rights has said about the right of education.

Without the support of this category of rights, protection of traditional civil rights is insufficient in its own field of application. President Franklin Roosevelt had an acute perception of this when he, in his speech address to the congress about the state of the union on January 11, 1944, proposed a *Second Bill of Rights* covering economic and social rights. His words are still striking today by their lucidity and frontality:

> We have come to a clear realization - he said - of the fact that true individual freedom cannot exist without economic security and independence. Necessitous men are not free men.

Roosevelt's proposal remained unfulfilled. But the idea that the guarantee of certain rights upon material goods is instrumental to freedom has made it easier to overcome the difficulty of formulating in the language of the rights the claim for access to goods by public benefits. It found an echo in the Universal Declaration of Human Rights, which specifically states some economic and social rights, together with a general clause (Article 22), in the terms of which:

> [e]veryone (...) is entitled to realization (...) of the economic, social and cultural rights indispensable for his dignity and the free development of his personality.

That idea is also the basis for the increasing opposition to the representation of the classic civil rights and the economic and social rights as two separate normative blocks, closed unto themselves. There is a growing awareness of the complementarity and interpenetration of the two categories of rights, both in the field of the international law of human rights and in the field of fundamental rights. The right to life itself—the most elementary right of the individual, because it is condition of all the others—is today understood by many, including in constitutional courts decisions, as the right to a dignified life, incorporating demands for quality of life. Just as human personality and dignity are one and indivisible, so the rights that protect and promote them form a unitary system, within which the social rights are as fundamental as the civil and political rights. The dignity of the human person is as deeply affected by arbitrary arrests and the degrading treatment of detainees as by living conditions of extreme poverty and deprivation of the most basic goods.

Democracy needs freedom. But freedom, in turn, needs material conditions of exercise. Bonding the state to social rights is the most solid legal-constitutional way of ensuring them.[3]

6. But also the idea that democracy is satisfied with the equality of political rights and that it is indifferent to the economic and social condition of the citizens does not withstand criticism.

In fact, political equality presupposes equal opportunities for intervention in the political process, in order to influence decisions concerning the course society should take. It presupposes, in short, democratic practices and democratic participation. This is a key idea in all streams of *deliberative democracy*.

Any form of inferiorization, marginalization or social exclusion of individuals or groups that do not correspond to the dominant identity contradicts and weakens that possibility. Discrimination of certain categories of citizens, on racial, ethnic, gender or other grounds, undermines the equal dignity of those affected. But it is also a factor of underrepresentation in government institutions, blocking equal opportunities for access to public office and participation in the public sphere. A democracy that does not pursue a model of social organization that promotes equality runs the risk of remaining very far from fulfilling the democratic ideal, even at the level of political equality.

The democratic ideal is not materialized simply by a certain model of political organization but also by a certain model of society, inclusive and open to the potential equal participation of all citizens in collective decision-making processes. The imperative of non-discrimination and treatment of people with equal consideration and respect is, therefore, the first requirement concerning the shaping of a social order favourable to the realization of the democratic ideal.

And what about severe economic inequality? Does it have a negative impact on a substantive notion of political equality, which goes beyond the participation in periodic elections and implies the capacity for broader involvement in the political process?

It is clear that, beyond a certain measure, inequalities in the civil society affect *social cohesion*. The general increase in inequality we are witnessing today, despite growth according to macroeconomic indicators, causes tensions and resentments that the institutional system is unable to absorb. This is one of the problems of our time, as has been seen in recent inorganic street protests, sometimes very violent, with the transversal participation of various classes of citizens.

---

[3] Social rights are *material preconditions of autonomy*, wrote Möller (2012, p. 82).

Deprivation of basic goods, beyond a certain degree, not only obstructs the development of personality and the possibility of leading an autonomous life, but it also distances people irrevocably from the public sphere and the deliberative processes taking place there. For acting as citizens, people should enjoy the independence that the minimum protection of social rights grants. Ensuring a minimally decent life, social rights also ensure, at the same time, the minimum requirements for active citizenship.[4] They are tools that remove structural barriers to full and equal participation in society, enabling the functioning of participatory democracy.

In our contemporary democratic societies, where mechanical solidarity has been diluted and pluralism of values prevails, fair decision-making processes presuppose parity of participation and real capacity of active engagement of citizens at various levels and through a range of institutions that exercise power over people's lives. However, this ideal model of participatory democracy has, as an inhibitory factor, the social exclusion or the subordination of groups of people, as they are deprived of the goods necessary for a dignified life. Combating and reducing the impact of this factor is a task of social rights, not only enshrined in proclamatory texts but also truly implemented, as *law in action* in socio-political practice.

7. In this approach, socio-economic rights are valued not only as mere commodities but also because of what they enable human beings to be and to do. Deprived of the goods that they provide, humans are prevented from developing their capabilities, in order to fulfil their life plans and participate effectively in political, economic and social life. On the other hand, in that way, society is being deprived of the contributions of all its members, which impoverishes the quality of social life.

Beyond the redistribution of goods, it is this effect of recognition and inclusion that we must ascribe to the social rights.[5] By compensating and removing the situations of need that violate human dignity, they give their holders the feeling that they count as persons and that they have value to others as persons. This sense of "constitutive belonging" undoubtedly makes it possible or, at least, easier for them to be willing to act jointly with others in social and political life, since this is understood as something that also concerns them, as something deserving their active involvement.

Let me say with emphasis: social exclusion leads too easily to political exclusion. And that being so, the participation of individuals in the political sphere of democratic states presupposes their integration into social processes. And contrary to what

---

[4] See Olsen (1998, pp. 215 s., 220):

> Public autonomy most clearly requires the kinds of positive enablements that we would call "social rights" in addition to political and civil ones (...).

[5] As Frankenberg (1995, pp. 1365 s., 1369), wrote:

> Therefore the quest for social security has to be understood not only as a struggle for decent living conditions and for adequate protection against the risks of life (...) but also for the creation of a polity/political community that grants its members the recognition, social appreciation, and political participation necessary for self-realization within the cultural horizon of a society.

some fear, this integrating effect by state action does not make social rights an instrument of social homogenization. Quite the opposite, by giving material support to the free development of one's unique personality, they promote pluralism and diversity, as values that are politically salutary to democracy and culturally enriching.

8. Social rights are, definitely, a matter of human dignity, both at the individual and social levels. A democracy concerned with this value must not only respect individual identities but also foster the material conditions in which they can flourish and shape autonomous choices.

Social rights are powerful weapons to exercise this fundamental commitment. They contribute to tell us how the society conceives itself and what it means to be a person and a citizen in a modern democracy.

Being able to count, in case of need, on public benefits derived from social rights is a guarantee that contributes to the self-perception of the self as a member of a community united by ties of solidarity.[6] It is also through the eyes of the others and through their recognition and consideration that a sense of self-worth is gained and strengthened.

9. In its troubled journey across history, democracy, since its Athenian cradle, has shown to be a dynamic, non-linear process, vulnerable to factors of limitation, degradation and perversion but also open to ways of consolidation, enhancement and "re-signification". Beyond its institutional dimensions, it is an ideal, a value and a principle. Democracy, in this dimension, "is not a once-and-for-all achievement, but an ongoing struggle to realize the conditions in which citizens can exercise control over their collective affairs in a context of political equality".[7]

The recognition and implementation of economic, social and cultural rights give an invaluable contribution for promoting and securing these conditions.

References

Aschall, C. E. (2012). Is the problem of European citizenship a problem of social citizenship? Social policy, federalism, and democracy in the EU and United States. *Sociological Inquiry, 82*(1), 123–144.
Ash, T. G. (2017). *Liberdade de expressão. Dez princípios para um mundo interligado* (portuguese translation from *Free Speech – Ten Principles for a Connected World*). Lisboa: Temas e Debates.
Beetham, D. (1997). Linking democracy and human rights. *Peace Review, 9*(3), 351–356.
Beetham, D. (1999). *Democracy and human rights*. Polity Press.
Frankenberg, G. (1995). Why care – The trouble with social rights. *Cardozo Law Review, 17*, 1365.
Möller, K. (2012). *The global model of constitutional rights*. Oxford University Press.
Olsen, K. (1998). Democratic inequalities: The problem of equal citizenship in Habermas's democratic theory. *Constellations: An International Journal of Critical & Democratic Theory*,

---

[6]Aschall (2012, pp. 123 s., 132–133).
[7]Beetham (1997, pp. 351 s., 356).

5(2). Available at: https://www.deepdyve.com/lp/wiley/democratic-inequalities-the-problem-of-equal-citizenship-in-habermas-s-Ds236YL7wx

Joaquim de Sousa Ribeiro is an emeritus professor at the School of Law of the University of Coimbra. He was prorector of this university, a judge of the Portuguese Constitutional Court and, from 2012 to 2016, the president of this Court. His most recent publication on the topic of fundamental rights is *Direitos Sociais e Vinculação do Legislador* (*Social Rights and the Bonds of the Legislator*) (2021).

Public Confidence and the Judiciary in a Democratic Society

Michail N. Pikramenos

Abstract The judiciary guarantees the fundamental principle of the rule of law and ensures the legal protection of every person by the courts which are responsible for the proper application of the law in an impartial, just, fair and efficient manner. Judicial independence and impartiality are essential prerequisites for the operation of justice. Courts are accepted by the public as being the proper forum for the ascertainment of legal rights and obligations and the settlement of disputes. The ECHR has declared the prominent place among state organs that the judiciary occupies in a democratic society. The court has emphasised the special role in society of the judiciary, which, as the guarantor of justice, a fundamental value in a law-governed state, must enjoy public confidence if it is to be successful in carrying out its duties, and in this framework, judges have more duties and responsibilities than the ordinary civil servants.

Keywords Accountability · Public confidence · Rule of law · Integrity · Criticism · Legitimacy of justice · Media · Society · Judicial independence · Democracy

1 Judicial Independence in the International and European Framework

1.1. In modern, Western democracies, a fundamental principle of the system of government, and foundation on which the state is organised, is the separation of powers, which is enshrined in the democratic-liberal constitutions. That principle asserts that state powers should be divided into three separate branches: the legislative branch which enacts the laws; the executive, which implements the laws and generally speaking takes policy decisions about how the state should be governed; and the judiciary, whose mission is to resolve disputes arising from the

---

M. N. Pikramenos (✉)
Supreme Administrative Court (Council of State), Athens, Greece

Law School of Aristotle University of Thessaloniki, Thessaloniki, Greece

© The Author(s), under exclusive license to Springer Nature Switzerland AG 2022
E. M. L. Economou et al. (eds.), *Democracy in Times of Crises*,
https://doi.org/10.1007/978-3-030-97295-0_12

implementation of the laws, whether those disputes are between citizens or between them and the state.

The judiciary guarantees the fundamental principle of the rule of law and ensures the legal protection of every person by the courts which are responsible for the proper application of the law in an impartial, just, fair and efficient manner. State power is therefore distributed between several bodies that act independently of each other, ensuring a balanced system of government, avoiding the concentration of power in any single body and offering the opportunity for the acts of government and parliament to be reviewed by the judiciary.[1]

Judicial independence and impartiality are essential prerequisites for the operation of justice. The basic principles on the independence of the judiciary adopted by the 7th United Nations Congress on the prevention of crime at Milan (26 August–6 September 1985) to assist member states in their task of securing and promoting the independence of the judiciary. The principles have been formulated principally with professional judges in mind, but they apply equally to lay judges where they exist. According to the *Magna Carta of Judges*,[2] judicial independence must be statutory, functional and financial and shall be guaranteed with regard to the other powers of the state and to those seeking justice, other judges and society in general, by means of national rules at the highest level. The state and each judge are responsible for promoting and protecting judicial independence.

1.2. In Vienna in April 2000 on the invitation of the United Nations, the Judicial Group on Strengthening Judicial Integrity recognised the need for a code against which the conduct of judges may be measured. The result of this initiative is the Bangalore Principles of Judicial Conduct which establishes standards for ethical conduct of judges, and they are designed to provide guidance to judges and to afford the judiciary a framework for regulating judicial conduct. They also assist members of the executive and the legislature, the lawyers and the public to better understand the judiciary. Among the principles are impartiality, integrity and propriety which are fundamental components of the judiciary. Impartiality is essential to the proper discharge of the judicial office and applies not only the decision itself but also to the process by which the decision is made (Value 2). A judge shall perform his or her judicial duties without favour, bias or prejudice (2.1) and shall ensure that his or her conduct, both in and out of court, maintains and enhances the confidence of the public, the legal profession and litigants in the impartiality of the judge and of the judiciary (2.2).

Judges have an absolute duty to safeguard the fundamental principle of the equality of citizens in the eyes of law and to ensure that public confidence in justice is maintained. Impartiality requires the absence of prejudices. This has a subjective

---

[1] Michail Pikramenos, *The Court System: Organisation - Functions - New Directions*. Judiciary in Greece. Proposals for a modern judicial system, 2019, publications diaNEOsis, Athens, p. 19. Available at: https://www.dianeosis.org/2019/02/dikaiosyni-stin-ellada/.

[2] Consultative Council of European Judges, Magna Carta of Judges (Fundamental Principles), adopted during its 11th plenary meeting (Strasburg 17-19.11.2010). Available at: https://rm.coe.int/16807482c6.

element, meaning judges must explore and identify their own personal beliefs in a specific case (subjective impartiality which can be presumed until the contrary is proven) and an objective element, where there are facts which could raise doubts about a judge's impartiality and whether he or she will try the matter correctly. The case law of the ECtHR and all the documents already cited above persistently refer to how a judge's stance *appears* to others. Judges, in this regard, should avoid any out-of-court activities which could prevent them from being able to try a case, because others might reasonably believe that judges are predisposed one way or the other or because such activity could give rise to conflicts of interest. What is at risk here is the confidence that courts should inspire in the public within a democratic society.[3] Integrity is essential to the proper discharge of the judicial office (Value 3).

A judge shall ensure that his or her conduct is above reproach in the view of a reasonable observer (3.1). The behaviour and conduct of a judge must reaffirm the people's faith to integrity of the judiciary. Justice must not merely be done but must also be seen to be done (3.2). Propriety and the appearance of propriety are essential to the performance of all of the activities of a judge (Value 4). A judge shall avoid impropriety and the appearance of impropriety in all of the judge's activities (4.1). As a subject of constant public scrutiny, a judge must accept personal restrictions that might be viewed as a burdensome by the ordinary citizen and should do so freely and willingly (4.2) and shall, in his or her personal relations with individual members of the legal profession who practise regularly in the judge's court, avoid situations which might reasonably give rise to the suspicion or appearance of favouritism or partiality (4.3).

Through their public and private conduct, judges help reinforce citizens' confidence in the integrity of the justice system. They must accept limitations greater in number than those on ordinary citizens and do so freely and of their own choice. The office of judge entails restrictions on one's public and private behaviour, but it is in the joint interest of all judges for members of that profession to participate in public life, insofar as their position permits. Forms of behaviour which would be deemed simply infelicitous for other citizens are unacceptable for judges because their office is there to judge the conduct of others. Judges demonstrate the importance they attach to the image of justice through their own propriety, honour, self-restraint, caution and discretion. Just like other citizens, judges are entitled to express themselves, to hold personal political and religious views and to join associations. However, they must exercise those rights in a way that maintains the dignity of their office and the independence and impartiality of justice.[4]

1.3. The Consultative Council of European Judges (CCJE) has published the Opinion No 7 (2005) with the title "Justice and Society". In this Opinion CCJE notes

---

[3] Katerina N. Sakellaropoulou, *Introduction: The Constitution, Justice and Judges*, Judiciary in Greece. Proposals for a modern judicial system, 2019, publications diaNEOsis, Athens, p. 53. Available at: https://www.dianeosis.org/2019/02/dikaiosyni-stin-ellada/.

[4] Katerina N. Sakellaropoulou, Introduction: *The Constitution, Justice and Judges*, Judiciary in Greece. Proposals for a modern judicial system 2019, publications diaNEOsis, Athens, p. 54. Available at: https://www.dianeosis.org/2019/02/dikaiosyni-stin-ellada/.

that the development of democracy in Europe states means that the citizens should receive appropriate information on the organisation of public authorities and furthermore it is important for citizens to know how judicial institutions function. Courts are accepted by the public as being the proper forum for the ascertainment of legal rights and obligations and the settlement of disputes. Adequate information about the functions of the judiciary and its role, in full independence from the other state powers, can effectively contribute toward an increased understanding of the courts as the cornerstone of democratic constitutional systems. The CCJE notes that the first way to make judicial institutions more accessible is to introduce general measures to inform the public about courts' activities, such as periodic reports, printed citizen's guides, Internet facilities, information offices, visits for schoolchildren and students or any other group with interest in judicial activities. The CCJE considers that such programmes go beyond the scope of general information to the public and the aim is a correct perception of the judge's role in society. In fact such programmes have the goal of improving the understanding and confidence of society with regard to its system of justice and generally of strengthening judicial independence.

1.4. The Council of Europe has published a Plan of Action on Strengthening Judicial Independence and Impartiality which was adopted by the Committee of Ministers on 13 April 2016. Its aim is to identify the ways to which the Council of Europe will guide and support its member states in the implementation of concrete measures needed to strengthen judicial independence and impartiality. According to the Plan of Action, the member states must achieve concrete results. Among these results is to build public trust in the judiciary and broader recognition of the value of its independence and impartiality, by ensuring transparency in the workings of the judiciary and in its relations with the executive and legislature and by the judiciary or courts adopting a proactive approach toward the media and to the dissemination of general information, which must be respectful of the rights of the defence and of the dignity of victims.

One of the Actions (1.4) is to ensure that public criticism of the judiciary by the executive and legislature respects the authority of the judiciary. In this framework public criticism of particular judicial decisions should be avoided in general or of individual judges. Codes of ethical behaviour for the executive and legislature should be in place to restrain interventions and protect the integrity of the judicial decision process from undue political pressure and attacks. Measures should be in place to prevent inappropriate use of the media by the executive and legislature aimed at discrediting the judiciary as well as to protect the reputation and rights of the judges and to maintain the authority and impartiality of the judiciary. The Council of Europe proposes also that a proactive approach to the media and more generally with the public should be adopted by the judiciary with a view to increasing the public confidence in the judiciary.

2 Accountability and Legitimacy of Judiciary

2.1. The one side of the coin is independence and the other side is accountability. The general importance of accountability is accepted across all public services. The legitimacy of most kinds of public power now depends on satisfactory accountability mechanisms (Le Sueur, 2013, p. 201). Professor Stephen Colbran notes the importance of judicial accountability:

> Firstly, it relates to traditional forms of judicial accountability including the principle of "open justice", parliamentary accountability and appellate review. Secondly, it relates to analysis of judicial attributes such as legal ability, impartiality, independence, integrity, temperament, communication skills, management skills and settlement skills, based on the opinions of those directly involved with the legal system. Thirdly, it relates to court and administrative performance measurement—with its focus on time and motion of judicial activity. This is an approach often linked with case management initiatives. While all three approaches to judicial performance evaluation strengthen judicial accountability, the traditional approaches and analysis of judicial attributes focus on the work of individual judges, while court and administrative performance measurement focuses on the aggregate work of the court.

It is obvious that several parameters and functions of the judiciary play a significant role in the building of public confidence.

According to Professor Stephen Burbank (2007, p. 912):

> Judicial accountability should run to the public, including litigants whose disputes courts resolve, and who therefore have a legitimate interest in court proceedings that are open to the public and in judicial decisions that are accessible. Judicial accountability should also run to the people's representatives, who appropriate the funds for the judiciary and whose laws the courts interpret and apply, and who therefore have a legitimate interest in ensuring that the judiciary has been responsible in spending the allotted funds and that, as interpreted and applied by the courts, public laws are functioning as intended. Finally, judicial accountability should run to courts and the judiciary as an institution, both because individual judicial independence exists primarily for the benefit of institutional independence and because appropriate intrabranch accountability is essential if potentially inappropriate inter- branch accountability is to be avoided. In each instance, proper regard for the other side of the coin—that is, for judicial independence—requires that accountability not entail influence that is deemed to be undue.

Professor Stefan Voigt (2005) makes a very interesting remark:

> But judges who are independent from most other decision-makers can also constitute a danger: they could render decisions only with hefty delays, render decisions that neglect much of the available evidence, render decisions that rely on irrelevant legislation, or render decisions that are patently false. Independent judges are not only a necessary condition for the rule of law, they also constitute a threat to the rule of law: if there is a rule of judges, the rule of law will not be realized.

M. Mogoeng, Chief Justice of the Republic of South Africa, in his speech at the constitutional court in November 2018, notes:

> The confidence of the public in an independent Judiciary is of paramount importance for a vibrant and functional democracy. Lack of public confidence in the Judiciary has the potential of eroding the moral authority of the judiciary. We neither control the army, the

police nor the public purse. Our orders are obeyed because of our public confidence generating moral authority. If we lose it then we are finished. Accountability is therefore important because it is a foundational value of our democracy which is applicable to all, including the Judiciary.

Public confidence of judiciary does not mean that judges should be accountable to the people and to the populace that they serve. This system exists in the USA where judges are elected by popular vote; it allows the voters to remove a judge who has lost their confidence. The problem of this system is that it makes the judiciary accountable to majoritarian politics and effectively undermines the ability of the judiciary to perform its constitutional role: "to protect the minority from the tyranny of the majority". Courts need to be able to give constitutional protection to unpopular parties and should not be subject to the shifting winds of politics (Pimentel, 2016, p. 166).

2.2. The National Center for State Courts in the USA has conducted a number of state and national public opinion surveys to identify the factors that most directly affect public confidence in the courts (Warren, 2005). The survey findings consistently identify the direction in which courts must proceed to build greater public trust. First, the extent of public confidence in the courts depends substantially more on the respondents' perceptions of the extent of judicial fairness than on any other aspect of court performance. Whereas attorneys' (and judges') views of court performance depend more on their perceptions of the fairness of court outcomes (in contrast to the fairness of court procedure), the views of litigants and members of the public are influenced almost twice as much by their views of the fairness of court procedure than by their views of the fairness of court outcomes. What do we mean by the fairness of court procedure? The survey used four procedural characteristics to define the concept of procedural fairness: whether the courts (1) are unbiased, (2) treat people with respect, (3) listen carefully to what people have to say and (4) are trustworthy, i.e. care about the people before them and take their individual needs into account. The single factor that most greatly influences respondents' perceptions of the extent of procedural fairness is their perception of whether judges are honest and fair. Second, although those with prior jury service experience hold more favourable views than others of the fairness of court processes, those with direct prior experience as litigants holds favourable views of the courts' procedural fairness. The types of cases in which respondents are most critical of procedural fairness are the high-volume cases in which ordinary citizens and unrepresented litigants most frequently appear: traffic, family and small-claims cases.

3 Judiciary and Public Confidence in the Case Law of European Court of Human Rights

3.1. The ECHR has declared the prominent place among state organs that the judiciary occupies in a democratic society. The court has emphasised the special role in society of the judiciary, which, as the guarantor of justice, a fundamental value in a law-governed state, must enjoy public confidence if it is to be successful in carrying out its duties, and in this framework, judges have more duties and responsibilities than the ordinary civil servants.[5] Judges have also restrictions in their fundamental rights which ensure that they exercise their duties with respect to the principles of neutrality and impartiality.[6] It is for this reason that judicial authorities, insofar as concerns the exercise of their adjudicatory function, are required to exercise maximum discretion with regard to the cases with which they deal in order to preserve their image as impartial judges.[7] Under these circumstances the state can impose on judges, on account of their status, a duty of discretion, and the ECHR examines in every case if a fair balance has been struck between the fundamental right and the legitimate interest of a democratic state in ensuring that its judiciary properly furthers the purposes enumerated in a certain article of the Convention. In a number of cases, the ECHR has examined the fair balance between the fundamental right of the individual to freedom of expression (Article 10 of the Convention) and the legitimate interest of a democratic state. The court accepted that whenever a civil servant's right to freedom of expression is in issue the "duties and responsibilities" referred to in Article 10 § 2 assume a special significance, which justifies leaving to the national authorities a certain margin of appreciation in determining whether the impugned interference is proportionate to the above aim.[8]

Given the prominent place among state organs that the judiciary occupies in a democratic society, the court reiterates that this approach also applies in the event of restrictions on the freedom of expression of a judge in connection with the performance of his or her functions, albeit the judiciary is not part of the ordinary civil service.[9] At the same time, the court has also stressed that having regard in particular to the growing importance attached to the separation of powers and the importance of safeguarding the independence of the judiciary, any interference with the freedom of expression of a judge in a position such as the applicant's calls for close scrutiny on the part of the court.[10] Furthermore, questions concerning the functioning of the

---

[5] Baka v. Hungary par. 164; Kudeshkina v. Russia, par. 86, *Prager and Oberschlick v. Austria,* § 34), *Morice v. France,* par. 128.

[6] *Wille v. Liechtenstein, par.* 64; *Kayasu v. Turkey, par.* 92; *Kudeshkina,* cited above, § 86; *Di Giovanni v. Italy* par. 71.

[7] *Olujić v. Croatia* par. 59.

[8] V*ogt v. Germany ,par.* 53; *Albayrak v.Turkey,* par. 41.

[9] *Albayrak,* cited above, par. 42; *Pitkevich v.Russia.*

[10] *Harabin v. Slovakia* ; see also *Wille,* cited above, § 64).

justice system fall within the public interest, the debate of which generally enjoys a high degree of protection under Article 10.[11]

Issues relating to the separation of powers can involve very important matters in a democratic society which the public has a legitimate interest in being informed about and fall within the scope of political debate.[12] In the context of Article 10 of the Convention, the court must take account of the circumstances and overall background against which the statements in question were made.[13] It must look at the impugned interference in the light of the case as a whole[14], attaching particular importance to the office held by the applicant, his statements and the context in which they were made. The court reiterates that issues concerning the functioning of the justice system constitute questions of public interest, the debate on which enjoys the protection of Article 10. However, the court has on many occasions emphasised the special role in society of the judiciary, which, as the guarantor of justice, a fundamental value in a law-governed state, must enjoy public confidence if it is to be successful in carrying out its duties. It may therefore prove necessary to protect that confidence against destructive attacks which are essentially unfounded, especially in view of the fact that judges who have been criticised are subject to a duty of discretion that precludes them from replying.[15] The phrase "authority of the judiciary" includes, in particular, the notion that the courts are, and are accepted by the public at large as being, the proper forum for the settlement of legal disputes and for the determination of a person's guilt or innocence on a criminal charge.[16] What is at stake as regards protection of the judiciary's authority is the confidence which the courts in a democratic society must inspire in the accused, as far as criminal proceedings are concerned, and also in the public at large.[17]

3.2. The court reiterates that the press plays a pre-eminent role in a state governed by the rule of law. Although it must not overstep certain bounds set, inter alia, for the protection of the reputation of others, it is nevertheless incumbent on it to impart—in a way consistent with its duties and responsibilities—information and ideas on political questions and on other matters of public interest.[18] This undoubtedly includes questions concerning the functioning of the system of justice, an institution that is essential for any democratic society. The press is one of the means by which politicians and public opinion can verify that judges are discharging their heavy responsibilities in a manner that is in conformity with the aim which is the basis of the task entrusted to them.[19] Regard must, however, be had to the special role of the

---

[11] *Kudeshkina*, cited above, par. 86; *Morice*, cited above, par. 128.

[12] *Guja v. Moldova*, par. 88.

[13] *Morice*, cited above, par. 162.

[14] *Wille*, cited above, par 63; *Albayrak*, cited above, par. 40.

[15] *Prager and Oberschlick v. Austria*, par. 34.

[16] *Worm v. Austria*, par. 40.

[17] *Fey v. Austria*.

[18] Castells v. Spain, par. 43.

[19] *Prager and Oberschlick v. Austria*, par. 34.

judiciary in society. As the guarantor of justice, a fundamental value in a law-governed state, it must enjoy public confidence if it is to be successful in carrying out its duties. It may therefore prove necessary to protect such confidence against destructive attacks that are essentially unfounded, especially in view of the fact that judges who have been criticised are subject to a duty of discretion that precludes them from replying. The assessment of these factors falls in the first place to the national authorities, which enjoy a certain margin of appreciation in determining the existence and extent of the necessity of an interference with the freedom of expression. That assessment is, however, subject to a European supervision embracing both the legislation and the decisions applying it, even those given by an independent court.[20]

4 Judiciary-Media-Society

The Lord Chief Justice told the House of Lords Select Committee on the Constitution on 15 December 2010:

> The relationship between the judiciary and the media is very interesting...Judges have to face the fact that they live in a very fast moving information world and that what judges do is a matter of public interest and sometimes concern. Judges have to realize that where is a concern, it needs to be thought about....[21]

Media have an overwhelming interest in high-profile cases, and they have a significant influence in the society. Public confidence depends on the relations with media and society. The European Network of Councils for the Judiciary (ENCJ) in the Report 2011–2012 "Justice, Society and the Media" gives recommendations which will improve the relations of judiciary with the media and the society: (a) all countries should develop a system of judicial spokesman who should have a deep knowledge about the judicial system, how to inform the public in an understandable language and who has social and media skills; (b) social media could be useful for the courts in their communication, and for that reason they must develop a strategy, including target groups and goals for the use of each social media; and (c) there is a need for regulation on the relation between the judiciary and the media. Introducing a set of press guidelines, whether they are implemented by law or as a morally binding protocol is recommended. The press guidelines should be part of a national strategy plan with a planning and reporting cycle on the communication with the media and the society. Press guidelines should clarify the different goals and interests of both the judiciary and the media. It should state what media may expect of the staff of the courts and how the courts should deal with the needs of the media before, during and after court proceedings, (d) all countries are

---

[20] Barfod v. Denmark, par. 28.

[21] Media Guidance for the Judiciary, Approved by the Judicial Executive Board, February 2012, p. 1.

encouraged to develop a proactive media approach. This approach should be focused on individual court cases as well as the entire judicial system.

5 Conclusions

The European Network of Councils for the Judiciary in the Report 2017–2018 "Public Confidence and the Image of Justice" notes that public confidence is vital for the independence of a nation's judiciary. According to the Report (https://www.encj.eu/):

> Public trust in the European judiciaries varies significantly from country to country. However, the level of trust cannot be viewed as distinct from the general differences between high trust societies, mainly in the north-west of Europe, and low trust societies, mainly in the south and east. Historical, social and economic reasons account for these differences.... Trust is the bedrock of any successful operation whether it be private or State. The Judiciary is not in competition with other branches of power but it is fundamental that trust is established and there is a recognition of its independence in the way it functions. Trust cannot be demanded, it must be earned in the way the Judiciary functions together with all other participants in the process including prosecutors and court officials. The objective and subjective independence of the Judiciary is closely related to public confidence as can be seen from the results of the ENCJ Project on Independence and Accountability. It is vital that it is fully understood that Independence of the Judiciary is not for the benefit of the Judiciary but is fundamental for the protection of the general public. It is an indispensable condition to ensure access to justice for all as is enshrined in the core message of the ENCJ. It is recognised that increasing and improving trust in the Judiciary is not fully possible in isolation but must be accompanied by building trust in institutions.

References

Le Sueur, A. (2013). Parliamentary accountability and the judicial system. In N. Bamforth & P. Leyland (Eds.), *Accountability in the Contemporary Constitution*. Oxford University Press. Available at SSRN: https://ssrn.com/abstract=2347479

Pimentel, D. (2016). Balancing judicial indepedence and accountability in a transisional state: The case of Thailand. *UCLA Pacific Basin Law Journal, 33*(2), 155–186.

Voigt, S. (2005). The economic effects of judicial accountability. Some preliminary insights. International Centre for Economic Research. Working Papers Series. Working Paper No. 19/2005. Available at: https://papers.ssrn.com/sol3/papers.cfm?abstract_id=732723

Warren, R. K. (2005). Judicial accountability, fairness, and independence, court review. *The Journal of the American Judges Association, 42*(1), 3–7.

Michail N. Pikramenos is the Vice President at the Supreme Administrative Court (Council of State), an Associate Professor of the Administrative Law at the Law School of Aristotle University of Thessaloniki and the General Director at the National School of Judges (2013–2016). He is also the President of the Special Court for the Liability of Judges (Art. 99 of the Constitution), the President of the Inspection Board of Judges at the Council of State, the President of the Working Group for the new judicial map of administrative courts and the President of the Working Group for the Drafting of the Code of Conduct for the Judges of Administrative Courts. He has participated in several European organisations (European Committee for the Efficiency of Justice, European Training Network, Venice Commission, EU Justice Scoreboard, Focal Point of the Council of State with the European Court of Human Rights). He has written monographs and articles in the fields of constitutional and administrative law.

Index

A
Accountability, 10, 79, 82, 100, 142, 217–218, 222
Aeschylus, 3, 178
Agamemnon, 173
Akerlof, G.A., 147, 150, 156, 157
American, 3, 4, 6, 22, 24–30, 32–34, 36, 50, 171–173, 185, 189
Ancient, 2–5, 9–11, 26, 33, 74, 83, 111, 113, 118, 120, 122, 123, 138–140, 142, 143, 150, 156, 157, 166–190, 206
Anti-democracy, 7, 71
Anti-EU, 54, 57
Anti-immigrant, 23, 25, 46, 54, 57, 63
Areopagus, 181
Aristotle, 5, 26, 83, 106, 138, 183, 185–187
Arrow, K.J., 75, 99, 149, 150
Assembly, 7, 9, 28, 53, 74, 76, 79, 82, 83, 105, 109, 118–133, 139, 151, 177, 181, 182, 187, 206
Assembly of citizens, 2, 9, 107–110, 112, 123, 125, 129, 133, 148
Asymmetry of information, 104, 110
Athenian, 2–4, 7–11, 83, 94–96, 101, 104–112, 120, 123, 138, 148, 151–153, 156–158, 166–171, 173, 175–177, 179–185, 188–190, 206, 211
Athens, 2–4, 11–13, 74, 83, 94, 99, 105, 109, 111, 118, 120, 122, 123, 138, 151, 152, 155, 156, 158, 170, 173, 175–180, 182, 184, 185, 188–190
Augsburg, 4
Australian, 120
Authoritarianism, 22, 62
Authoritarians, 6, 43, 53, 54, 56–60, 64, 87, 173

B
Battle of Hastings, 194
Battle of Navarino, 12, 194, 195
Battle of Salamis, 1, 2, 5, 7, 94–96, 105, 111, 166, 179
Bavaria, 4, 157
Bazzigher, J., 175
Belgium, 45, 48, 49, 121
Bleicken, 167–169, 182
Borda Rule, 153
Boulé, 181
Bounded rationality, 151
Brennan, J., 76
Bretton Woods, 97
Brexit, 5, 22, 23, 31, 35, 36, 41, 48, 76, 79, 108, 109, 147, 183
British, 4, 12, 22, 23, 25, 27, 30, 33, 36, 37, 101, 108, 185, 194, 196, 197
British Columbia, 120, 133
Buchanan, J., 149, 156
Buchanan, J.M., 97, 99
Burckhardt, J., 167, 169
Burke, E., 75, 100

C
California, 24, 29
Canada, 79, 139, 157
Capitalism, 170, 183, 184
Capitalist, 84, 170, 174
Capture, 5, 102, 104, 125, 127
Catholics, 23, 79
Checks and balances, 6, 26, 36, 53, 57, 60, 62, 63, 73, 76, 109
China, 7, 35, 36, 95, 104, 111, 186

Chinese, 35, 36
Citizens, 2, 3, 5–14, 22, 28, 29, 42, 43, 48–51, 59, 63, 64, 71, 72, 74, 75, 77–83, 87, 94, 95, 98–103, 105, 107–113, 118–133, 138–140, 142, 143, 148, 151–157, 173–183, 188, 189, 206, 207, 209–211, 214–216, 218
Citizenship, 13, 31, 32, 42, 87, 156, 210
Civic culture, 7, 87
Civil, 58, 59, 75, 76, 103, 106, 120, 157, 185, 206–209, 219
Classical, 3, 9, 11–13, 26, 27, 83, 99, 105–107, 109, 111, 151, 155, 166–171, 173, 176, 179, 184, 186, 187, 189, 190
Classical period, 1, 3
Cleisthenes, 94, 107, 156, 169, 173, 175, 179, 180
Cleisthenian, 175, 179, 180
Clientelist, 102
Climate change, 79, 80, 185, 186
Common good, 10, 32, 77, 81, 95, 102–104, 110, 111, 148–154, 179
Communications, 12, 112, 118, 183, 217, 221
Communist, 52, 95, 111
Competition, 8, 84, 85, 87, 88, 97, 98, 102, 110, 172, 222
Condorcet rule, 154
Conduct, 13, 14, 79, 106, 108, 142, 178, 190, 214, 215
Confidence, 5, 13, 14, 41, 49, 52, 95, 213–222
Confucianism, 95
Conservatism, 56, 80
Constitutional, 4, 5, 7, 9, 13, 23, 24, 26, 27, 29–31, 36, 50, 57, 74, 80, 87, 88, 101, 118, 120, 121, 123, 139, 141, 175, 182, 187, 189, 205, 207, 208, 216, 218
Constitutions, 4, 9, 26, 27, 29, 31, 33, 53, 54, 98, 101, 106, 112, 121, 123, 139, 141, 143, 157, 170, 179, 182, 186–189, 207, 215, 221
Consultative Council of European Judges (CCJE), 214–216
Cooperatives, 84, 85
Corruption, 28, 59, 64, 88, 107, 139, 199
Council of 500, 105, 181
Council of Europe, 14, 216
Courts, 6, 14, 35, 50, 51, 57, 58, 60, 75, 105, 106, 120, 138, 181, 200, 208, 214–222
Covid-19, 5, 186
Crisis of democracy, 5, 6, 22–37, 42–44, 50, 51, 58, 64
Cultural, 3, 11, 105, 151, 168, 170, 176, 178, 181, 185, 186, 190, 198, 207, 208, 210, 211
Czechia, 45, 49, 59

D
Dahl, R.A., 170, 174, 188
Darwinism, 172
Deliberation, 9, 28, 33, 75, 77–79, 82, 88, 110, 118, 121, 122, 126, 138, 156
Deliberative, 7, 28, 74, 77–80, 82, 83, 85, 88, 110, 118, 120–122, 140, 149, 154, 157, 206, 209, 210
Demagoguery, 25–27, 33, 177
Demagogues, 24, 25, 33, 180, 188
Democracy, 1–14, 22, 24–28, 30, 33–36, 41–64, 71–88, 94–112, 118, 120–123, 137–143, 147–158, 166–190, 205–211, 213, 216–218
Democracy in deficit, 97, 98
Democratic, 2, 4–14, 22, 24, 28–30, 32, 33, 35–37, 41–64, 72–74, 81, 83–88, 96, 98, 118, 122, 138, 140, 143, 155, 156, 167, 169–174, 176–190, 205–207, 209, 210, 213–222
Democratic regimes, 1, 3, 149
Democrats, 4, 24, 25, 34, 51, 52, 71, 77, 167
Demosthenes, 105, 152, 170
de Tocqueville, A., 72, 81
Dewey, J., 33, 72, 73, 77, 80, 87
Dictatorship, 7, 51, 60, 72, 87, 88, 175
Digital, 12, 101, 183, 184
Digital direct, 8, 108, 112
Digitalization, 183
Dikastiria, 105
Direct, 2, 5, 7, 10, 11, 30, 34, 35, 63, 71, 72, 74, 80, 82, 83, 88, 99, 109, 120, 123, 148–151, 153–158, 178, 182, 187, 218
Dokimasia, 142
Dollar, 3, 96, 97
Downs, A., 75
Drachmae, 3, 152
Draconian, 189
Dutch Republic, 4

E
Ecclesia of Demos, 95, 105, 111, 112
ECHR, 219
Economic institutions, 3
Economy, 3, 23, 54, 57, 58, 61, 62, 72, 73, 94, 97, 102–104, 119, 123, 148, 170, 174, 183, 198, 200, 207
Education, 11, 12, 14, 33, 61, 62, 80, 88, 108, 113, 153, 177, 178, 208
Ekklesia, 83, 181
Elected, 8–10, 22, 25, 27, 33, 34, 51, 71, 72, 75, 79, 82, 84, 99–101, 104, 118–133, 138–143, 151, 153, 157, 174, 180, 186, 218

Elections, 5, 8, 9, 13, 22–25, 27, 29, 41, 50, 52–62, 74, 76, 86–88, 98, 99, 110, 111, 119, 122–125, 127–133, 138, 141, 143, 153, 157, 205, 206, 209
Electoral, 9, 22, 25, 43, 51–54, 59, 60, 63, 76, 79, 86–88, 98, 100–102, 108, 119, 120, 123, 125, 131, 133, 138–140, 151, 206
Elites, 6–8, 11, 26, 28, 30, 31, 36, 42, 43, 57, 60, 63, 88, 112, 118, 122, 156, 174–176, 178, 188, 194, 198
Empire, 2, 94, 95, 167, 169, 172, 174, 179–181, 184, 185, 194, 196
Engels, F., 169, 170
England, 4, 120
Ephialtes, 152, 173
Equality, 9, 11, 13, 73, 121, 122, 138, 140, 156, 173, 174, 181, 183, 184, 187, 189, 206, 207, 209, 211, 214
Equity, 118, 123
Europe, 3–6, 12, 22, 30–32, 41–64, 73, 194–201, 216, 222
European, 4, 6, 12, 30, 42–53, 58, 59, 63, 194, 195, 197–201, 213–216, 219–222
European Community, 197
European integration, 6, 42–44, 47, 48, 55, 58, 63, 200
European Network of Councils for the Judiciary (ENCJ), 221, 222
European Stability Mechanism, 200
European Union (EU), 5, 6, 12–14, 22, 23, 25, 30, 42, 47, 48, 50, 55, 59, 61, 63, 64, 79, 108, 187, 190, 194, 195, 198–200
Exclusion, 189, 209, 210
Executive, 72, 105, 174, 213, 214, 216, 221
Extremism, 5, 6, 64

F
Factionalism, 8, 109
Federal, 4, 27, 31, 97, 112, 154, 155
Federalist, 27, 36
Finances, 2, 73, 80, 83, 96, 140
Financial, 7, 12, 42, 64, 97, 120, 124, 138, 155, 214
Finland, 45, 48, 49
Florence, 4, 120
Florida, 86
France, 4, 12, 30, 45, 49–51, 59, 121, 133, 196, 199
Franklin, B., 102
Free agency, 100
Freedom, 6, 11, 13, 33, 51, 72, 79, 141, 149, 156, 166, 167, 171–174, 181, 183, 189, 194, 206–209
Freedom of expression, 14, 206, 219, 221

French Revolution, 4, 26, 33, 169, 189
Functional, 74, 80, 81, 214, 217
Funeral, 4, 158, 172, 176

G
German, 35, 154, 166, 167, 174, 178, 180, 185
Germany, 4, 12, 45, 46, 48–51, 157, 166, 168, 187, 197, 199
Gold standard, 196
Governance, 3–6, 8, 13, 26, 99, 103, 105–108, 110, 111, 141, 177, 199–201
Government, 2, 4–8, 10, 22, 23, 25–27, 29, 31–37, 41, 42, 49, 50, 52, 53, 56–63, 72, 75, 76, 79–83, 85, 86, 88, 96–98, 100, 102–104, 108, 112, 118, 120, 121, 123, 147, 148, 150, 151, 155, 167–170, 175, 176, 184–187, 197–200, 206, 209, 213, 214
Graphê paranómôn, 109, 181
Great Britain, 45, 48, 49, 166, 187
Great Powers, 12, 194–197
Greece, 2–5, 11, 12, 45, 49, 51, 73, 94, 138, 140, 142, 143, 152, 153, 158, 166, 169, 171, 175, 184, 185, 187, 194–201
Greek, 1–5, 9, 11–13, 26, 94, 111, 113, 138, 139, 141, 156, 166, 168–190, 194–198, 200, 201
Greek victory, 2
Green, and far-left, 123

H
Hayek, F.A., 96, 97, 207
Hektemoroi, 173
Hellenic, 1, 2, 171
Herodotus, 138, 169, 194
Hippias, 175
History, 2–4, 6, 11, 22, 25, 32, 55, 63, 83, 100, 105, 109, 138, 157, 158, 166, 168–170, 172, 176, 180, 184–186, 188–190, 194, 197, 211
Ho boulomenos, 151
Hoplites, 179
House of Commons, 27, 196
House of Lords, 27, 139, 221
Human rights, 5, 7, 24, 54, 85, 87, 208, 219–221
Hungarians, 51–54, 61, 62, 167
Hungary, 6, 22, 43, 45, 46, 49–64

I
IMF, 61, 200

Immigration, 6, 23, 24, 27, 42–47, 55, 58, 63, 121, 153
Impartiality, 14, 199, 214–217, 219
Imperialism, 189
Impossibility of representation, 104
Individual, 5, 11, 13, 32, 49, 73, 75–85, 88, 120, 149, 150, 153, 154, 156, 157, 171–175, 178, 180, 182, 189, 195, 206, 208–211, 215–219, 222
Individual freedoms, 104, 111, 184, 208
Inequality, 11, 13, 23, 97, 128, 129, 174, 183, 189, 207, 209
Informational asymmetry, 8, 100, 110
Initiatives, 2, 6, 11, 28, 29, 31, 32, 34, 35, 56, 97, 148, 154, 155, 157, 179, 214, 217
Institutions, 4, 5, 7, 12, 13, 31, 36, 44, 46–51, 53, 59, 73, 74, 81, 85, 98, 101, 105–107, 112, 119, 123, 124, 149, 151, 167, 168, 172, 174, 177, 178, 181, 198, 201, 209, 210, 216, 217, 220, 222
Interests, 7, 8, 10–13, 27, 29, 31, 35, 71, 75–77, 88, 97, 98, 100–103, 107, 111, 112, 118, 122, 123, 132, 143, 151, 156, 166, 174, 179, 182, 186, 194, 196, 198, 201, 206–208, 215–217, 219–221
Ireland, 9, 30, 45, 48–50, 121, 133, 139
Italy, 4, 30, 45, 49, 138, 194, 199

J
Judge, 13, 14, 34, 58, 64, 106, 122, 138, 152, 214–221
Judiciary, 13, 14, 24, 57, 88, 213–222

K
Kaczynski, J., 6, 52, 56, 57, 60, 62
Kant, I., 158, 169, 188
Keynesian, 96, 98, 200
Keynes, J.M., 96
King Otto, 196
Knight, 156
Knowledge, 5, 10, 12, 72–74, 78, 80, 85, 99, 101, 105, 110, 138, 148, 150, 156, 171, 177, 178, 221

L
Labour Party, 30, 73, 86
Latvia, 157
Laurion, 2, 94, 111, 152
Law and Justice, 43, 50, 55–59, 61, 62
Left-wing, 30, 60, 123

Legal, 35, 53, 75, 86, 102, 106, 120, 140, 182, 206, 214–217, 220
Legislative, 9, 10, 29, 31, 36, 53, 76, 98, 103, 105, 108, 139, 140, 143, 157, 181, 213
Legislators, 29, 35, 118, 122, 133, 139, 143
Legislature, 29, 31, 32, 122, 137–143, 214, 216
Lenin, V.I., 72
Liberal, 28, 35, 52, 59, 74, 76, 83, 167, 169, 194, 195, 198, 207
Liberalism, 80, 167, 198
Liberty, 4, 76, 102, 104, 111, 149
Lincoln, A., 4, 42
Lippmann, W., 63, 73
Lithuania, 45, 49
Liturgy, 178

M
Maastricht Treaty, 30
Macedonian, 170, 176
Madison, J., 36, 71, 101
Majority, 2, 6, 10, 25, 27, 28, 36, 53, 56, 57, 59, 60, 71, 72, 74, 82–84, 87, 99, 101, 108, 110, 118, 123, 143, 149, 150, 153, 154, 157, 167, 170, 171, 182, 185, 206, 218
Management, 8, 84, 101–103, 105, 107, 112, 217
Marathon, 2, 94, 152, 168, 172, 179, 194
Market, 3, 84, 85, 97, 102, 103, 106, 110, 147, 148, 170, 174, 183, 184, 186, 189, 197, 198, 207
Marx, K., 169, 170
Merkel, A., 46
Michels, R., 74, 102, 176
Mill, J.S., 72, 75–77, 80, 87, 194
Mises, 103
Mixed, 5, 6, 25–27, 33–37, 58, 78, 79
Montesquieu, 27, 36

N
Napoleon, 180
National, 4, 8, 22, 29–34, 42, 51, 53, 57, 61, 62, 64, 74, 82, 83, 88, 97, 103, 141, 148, 155–157, 172, 183, 186, 189, 197, 200, 214, 218, 219, 221
National Center for State Courts, 14, 218
Nationalist, 53, 87
Neoliberal, 23, 60
Netherlands, 45, 49–51, 79, 133
Network, 3, 78, 85, 183
Nicophon, 110, 151, 154
Nomothetai, 109

Non-partisanship, 123
Normative, 11–13, 42, 122, 168, 194, 201, 207, 208
Northern Ireland, 23, 25
Norway, 45, 49, 50

O

Old Swiss Confederacy, 4
Oligarchy, 11, 143, 169, 173, 174, 176, 177, 186, 187
Oligopoly, 102
Ontario, 120, 133
Oration, 4, 158, 172, 176
Orbán, V., 6, 46, 51–55, 57–62
Ordo-liberalism, 197, 200
Ottoman, 2, 12, 194–196

P

Pareto, 75
Parliament, 4, 6, 9, 23, 30, 32, 34, 41, 42, 44, 49, 50, 53–55, 57–59, 61–63, 75, 82, 108, 120–123, 138–143, 197, 214
Parliamentary, 23, 30, 52, 53, 57, 58, 72, 75, 76, 82, 86, 87, 123, 138, 141, 143, 169, 181, 217
Parliamentary system, 140, 143
Participation, 7, 8, 11, 12, 32, 46, 49, 59, 63, 72–74, 78, 84, 85, 88, 98, 110, 118, 156, 174, 176–179, 183, 186, 206, 209, 210
Participatory, 2, 5, 33, 35, 71–74, 85, 88, 110, 157, 176, 183, 187, 210
Party, 2, 6, 8–10, 22–25, 27–34, 36, 41, 43, 44, 46, 49–63, 74, 75, 86–88, 96, 98–104, 108, 109, 111, 112, 118, 119, 122–124, 126, 140–143, 151, 153, 167, 179, 188, 200, 201, 206, 218
Peace of Westphalia, 184
Peisistratos, 175
Peloponnesian, 4, 109, 138, 180, 185
Pericles, 4, 151, 152, 158, 172, 176, 178
Persians, 2, 3, 94, 111, 152, 156, 168–170, 172, 178, 184, 185, 194
Peru, 157
Philhellenes, 195
Philippines, 22, 157
Plataea, 94, 185
Plato, 26, 83, 138, 172, 176, 177, 182, 183, 185–187
Plato's Republic, 149
Plebiscitarianism, 23, 34, 36

Poland, 6, 22, 43, 45, 46, 48–64
Poles, 36, 50, 52, 56–58, 62
Polish, 52, 55, 58
Political, 2–13, 22–24, 26–28, 30, 31, 33–36, 42–44, 46–55, 57–61, 63, 64, 72, 74–88, 98, 100–105, 108, 112, 118, 119, 122, 126, 131, 137–143, 148, 151, 153, 156, 157, 167–170, 172, 174–180, 183, 184, 186–189, 198, 200, 205–207, 209–211, 215, 216, 220
Political system, 2, 10, 26, 42, 50, 82, 100, 102, 139, 143
Politicians, 6–9, 25, 28, 29, 32, 36, 41, 42, 44, 49–51, 54, 55, 57–59, 61, 62, 73–75, 79, 87, 97–101, 118–133, 152, 177, 179, 180, 220
Polybius, 5, 26
Popper, K., 182
Popular, 5–9, 13, 22–24, 26, 27, 29, 30, 32–36, 43, 50, 52–54, 56–58, 60, 72, 75–77, 82, 86, 106, 108, 112, 118, 122, 141, 148, 154, 157, 173–176, 178, 180–183, 187, 198, 206, 218
Populism, 5, 6, 10, 11, 25, 36, 42, 43, 51, 52, 141, 147, 174, 180, 181
Portugal, 13, 45, 48–50, 199
Possibility theorem, 148–150, 158
Power, 2, 5–7, 9, 12, 26, 28, 33–36, 43, 47, 52, 53, 55, 56, 58–61, 63, 72, 74, 75, 79, 83, 85–87, 95, 98, 99, 102, 104–107, 111, 118, 119, 123, 124, 128, 131, 133, 138, 141–143, 152, 174, 175, 179, 183, 184, 194, 196, 197, 205–207, 210, 213, 214, 216, 217, 222
Presidential, 22, 24, 25, 30, 33–35, 37, 58, 76, 82, 86, 120
Principal-agent problem, 8, 100, 101, 158
Principle, 4, 5, 13, 14, 23, 24, 36, 83, 88, 99, 101, 107, 140, 151, 179, 180, 182, 185, 190, 198, 200, 206, 207, 211, 213, 214, 217, 219
Progressive, 27–30, 34, 77, 137, 139
Protestants, 23
Proudhon, P.-J., 72
Prytany/prytaneis, 105, 106, 151
Public, 5, 6, 8, 10, 13, 14, 27, 30, 35, 41–64, 71, 73, 75, 76, 79–83, 86–88, 94, 96–98, 100, 101, 104–106, 109, 111, 112, 118–120, 122–126, 130, 133, 138–143, 151, 153, 156–158, 177, 178, 182, 197, 200, 206, 208–211, 213–222

R

Randomly selected, 8, 9, 79, 118–133, 137, 139, 142, 143
Randomness, 9
Rational, 28, 78, 99, 111, 119, 122, 123, 133, 141, 149, 156, 166, 169, 188
Rawls, J., 77, 80
Recall, 11, 28, 148, 157
Referendum, 2, 6, 11, 22, 23, 28–32, 34–36, 48, 76, 79, 108, 121, 139, 147, 148, 155, 157
Reforms, 7–9, 13, 25, 28, 35, 79, 87, 88, 96, 98, 104, 107, 111, 112, 120, 121, 124, 133, 173, 175, 176, 179–181, 189, 194, 198–200
Reich, 185
Rent-seeking, 102, 104, 123
Republic, 2, 24, 26, 121, 138, 175, 187, 217
Republican, 22, 24, 25, 27, 34
Revolutions, 2, 4, 12, 53, 60, 72, 170, 172, 173, 189, 194
Rights, 4, 13, 32, 51, 59, 60, 71–74, 76, 81, 82, 84, 86–88, 102, 105, 109, 113, 123, 124, 129, 131, 141, 149, 151, 152, 155, 167, 172, 173, 176, 177, 182, 183, 187, 189, 190, 205–211, 215, 216, 219
Right-wing, 32, 41, 44, 52, 53, 55, 63
Roman, 4, 6, 26, 169, 176
Rousseau, J.-J., 72, 188
Russell, B., 95, 104, 177
Russia, 51
Russian, 4, 12

S

Salamis, 1, 2, 5, 7, 10, 11, 94–113, 153, 166, 168, 172, 179, 185, 189, 194
Schumpeter, J.A., 75
Self-interested, 29, 31, 36, 133
Separation of powers, 6, 26, 33, 36, 181, 205, 213, 219, 220
Slovenia, 45, 49, 50, 59
Smith, A., 107
Social, 2, 3, 6, 12–14, 25, 44–47, 53, 54, 58–61, 63, 72–74, 79, 80, 83, 85–87, 95, 103, 111, 112, 120, 121, 123, 137, 139, 148–150, 153, 157, 172, 174, 175, 178, 197, 198, 205–211, 221, 222
  choices, 10, 75, 147–158
  cohesion, 13, 86, 94, 98, 102, 209

welfare, 10, 122, 150, 153, 154
Socialists, 52, 60, 72, 73, 75, 88, 123, 169
Solon, 173, 175, 180
Sortition, 9, 109, 118–120, 122, 123, 132, 133, 137–140, 142
Sortition parliaments, 9, 10, 137, 139–143
Spain, 45, 50, 51, 84, 199
Sparta, 26, 158, 180, 185
Spartans, 94, 175, 177
Status, 59, 123, 130, 156, 170, 173, 205, 207, 219
Strategoi, 105, 106
Strict agency, 100
Suffrage, 4, 31, 76, 206
Supreme Court, 23, 35, 36, 106, 121
Sweden, 45, 46, 48, 49, 51, 59
Swiss, 31, 32, 120, 155, 156, 175
Switzerland, 2, 4, 31, 32, 35, 45, 48–50, 138, 154, 155, 157, 158
Symmetrical, 151, 152

T

Taiwan, 30, 157
Taxation, 153
Themistocles, 2, 3, 7, 10, 94, 95, 111, 151–154, 156
Theorika, 178
Thermopylae, 94, 194
Thucydides, 2, 3, 5, 26, 109, 158, 176
Treasuries, 105
Treaty, 30, 184, 185, 196, 197
Trireme, 2, 94, 95, 111, 152
Trojan War, 173
Trump, D., 5, 22–25, 30, 35, 41, 74, 76, 86, 183
Trust, 6, 10, 13, 14, 42–44, 49, 50, 55, 58, 59, 61, 62, 64, 82, 98, 152, 156, 198, 216, 218, 222
Turkey, 22, 32, 51, 59

U

Ukraine, 157
United Kingdom (UK), 7, 22, 41, 72, 73, 75, 79, 86–88, 121, 133, 139
United Nations (UN), 139, 208, 214
United Provinces, 4
United States (US), 3, 6, 7, 22, 23, 73, 76, 86, 95, 97, 101, 103, 139, 140, 154, 166
Uruguay, 154, 157

Utility, 9, 73, 75, 80, 124–127, 131–133, 153, 154

V
Varoufakis, Y., 47, 73
Venezuela, 22, 59
Venice, 120, 138
von Bismarck, O., 174
von Pöhlmann, R., 167, 169
Voting, 3, 8, 10, 23, 43, 52, 53, 60, 74–76, 80, 81, 84, 86, 100, 105, 108, 118, 122, 150, 152, 154

W
Weber, M., 86, 101, 102
Welfare state, 42, 102
Western, 3, 5, 8, 29, 35, 36, 51, 58, 105, 112, 153, 166, 176, 182, 186, 213
World Bank, 61, 199, 200

X
Xenophon, 142, 171

Printed in Great Britain
by Amazon